The Caribbean and the
Second World War

The Caribbean and the Second World War

Colin Douglas

Lawrence Wishart
London 2024

Lawrence and Wishart Limited
Central Books Building
Freshwater Road
Chadwell Heath
RM8 1RX

Typesetting: e-type
Cover design: River Design
Printing: Imprint Digital

Cover image: Flight Sergeant Colin Joseph from Trinidad (right) and Pilot
Officer Arthur O'Brien Weeks from Barbados (left). Spitfire pilots in Britain
in 1944 © Imperial War Museum, CH 11976.

First published 2024
© Colin Douglas 2024

British Library Cataloguing in Publication Data.
A catalogue record for this book is available from the British Library

ISBN 9781913546793
E-ISBN 9781913546816

Contents

Preface

During the Second World War's darkest hours, Winston Churchill spoke of the great struggles of history that involved 'wresting victory in the teeth of odds or upon the narrowest of margins'.[1] Securing such narrow margins would require the full support of the British Empire. Yet, these vital contributions continue to be underestimated, few more so than that of the Caribbean. The region provided three essential elements in Britain's struggle for survival: vital mineral resources for the war machine; geopolitical leverage to draw a reluctant US into the Allied war effort well before the Pearl Harbor attack; and desperately needed wartime personnel.

The stories of West Indians who served in the war, many of whom settled in Britain, Canada, the US and Europe afterwards, have been told over recent decades in biographies and histories. These have added much welcomed balance to the history of the period. Alongside these have been a growing body of research from West Indian historians that have described the military, political, economic and social impact that the war had in the region, and how the region contributed to the Allied victory. This book seeks to pull together these and other sources to paint a broad picture of the Caribbean's contribution and its complex relationship with European and North American powers. Although focusing mainly on the British West Indies, the following pages will touch on the entire Caribbean – the independent states and those under the control of the colonial powers of Britain, France, the Netherlands and the US. This is essential since the role of any of the Caribbean sub-groups cannot be fully appreciated without placing them in the context of the whole.

As I researched and wrote this book, my thoughts would regularly stray to my Jamaican parents (Kendrick and Adassa Douglas) who experienced this period first-hand. They are no longer with us. They would have felt the shortages and rationing of the early 1940s in Jamaica. My father was among the migrant workers driven to find employment overseas because of the lack of opportunities at home (described in Chapter One). After the war, they were part of the Windrush generation, who came to Britain in the mid 1950s. They are a constant reminder to me that history is personal. It is the aggregate of many individual stories, actions and experiences.

This is my second book on the West Indies and the Second World War. Over thirty years ago, my great friend Ben Bousquet and I wrote *West Indian Women at War*, published by Lawrence Wishart in 1991. We had regularly discussed co-authoring another book but never got around to it before his sad and untimely death in 2006. I would like to think that the following pages represent the book we would have written together.

I am grateful to Lawrence Wishart for publishing this book and their continued commitment to Black history; and I am thankful for the incredibly helpful editing suggestions made by Jumanah Younis. Mostly, I am grateful to my darling wife Petrina for her love, support, encouragement and patience throughout the research and writing of this book. It is dedicated to her.

NOTE

1 Winston Churchill, *The Second World War (Volume 3): The Grand Alliance*, Cassell & Co Ltd: London, 1950, p134.

I

Prelude: The Making of a Fighting Force

MAP OF THE CARIBBEAN AND CENTRAL AMERICA
COURTESY OF UNIVERSITY OF TEXAS LIBRARIES

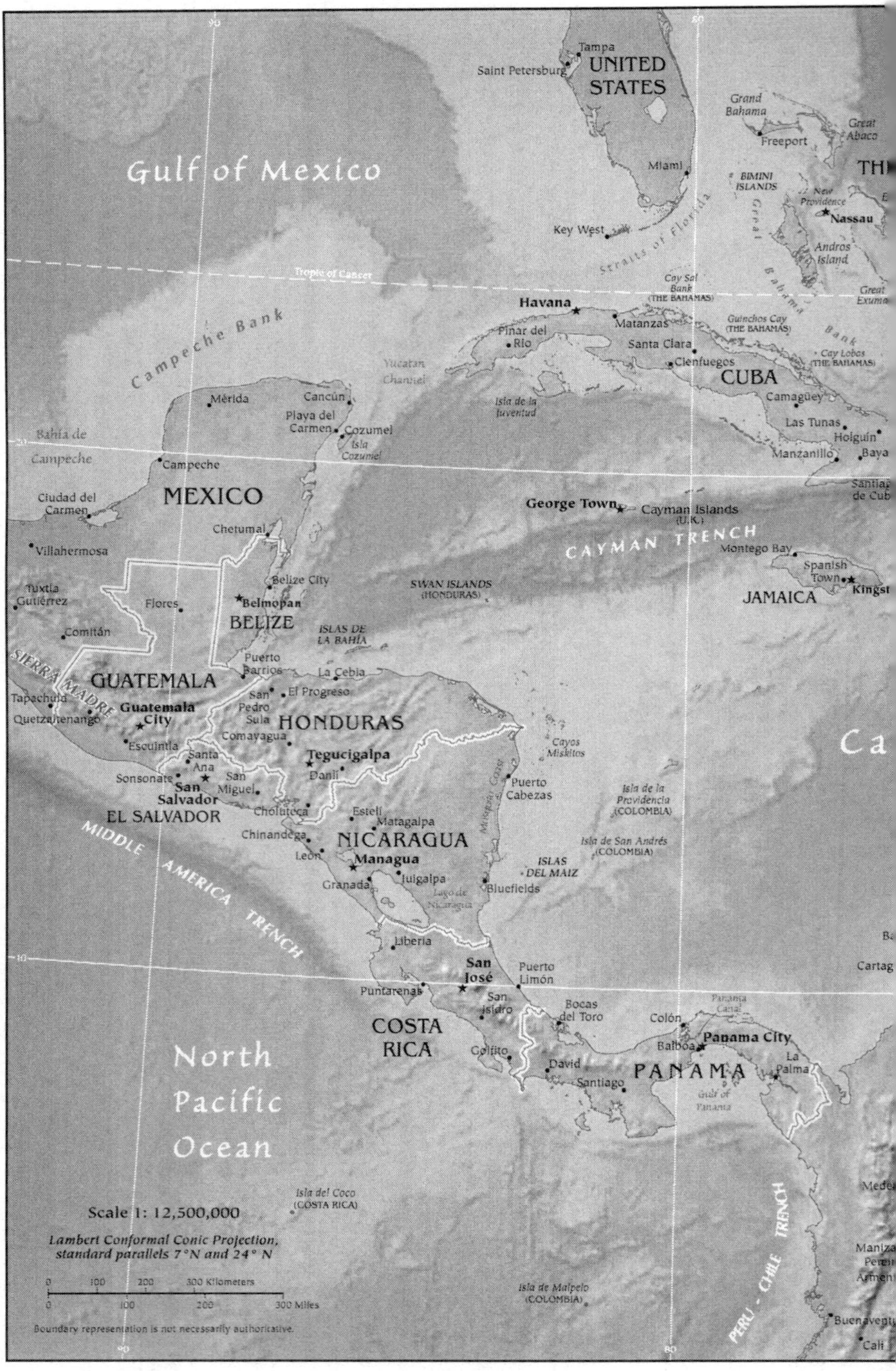

North
Atlantic
Ocean

AS

n Salvador
ay
nd
Samana Cay
Crooked Island
Acklins
Island
Mayaguana
nagua

Turks and
Calcos Islands
(U.K.)
★Grand
Turk

Tropic of Cancer

20

Milwaukee Deep
(deepest point of the
Atlantic Ocean, -8605 m)

PUERTO RICO TRENCH

Cap Haïtien
Santiago
Gonaïves

HAITI
rt-au-Prince
Les Cayes

DOMINICAN
REPUBLIC

Santo
Domingo

Mona
Passage

Isla
Mona

San Juan

Puerto Rico
(U.S.)

St. Croix

British
Virgin Is.
(U.K.)

Charlotte
Amalie
Virgin Is.
(U.S.)

Road Town

Anguilla
The Valley Anguilla (U.K.)
Marigot
Saint-Martin Philipsburg Sint Maarten(NETH.)
(FRANCE)
Gustavia Saint Barthélemy (FRANCE)
Saba and
Sint Eustatius(NETH.)

ANTIGUA AND BARBUDA
Saint John's

Basseterre
SAINT KITTS AND NEVIS

Plymouth
Montserrat (U.K.)

Guadeloupe
(FRANCE)

Isla de Aves
(VENEZUELA)

Basse-Terre
Marie-Galante

DOMINICA
Roseau

ean Sea

Aruba
(NETH.)
Oranjestad

Curacao
(NETH.)

Bonaire
(NETH.)

Willemstad

Punto
Fijo

Golfo de
Venezuela

Lago de
Maracaibo

alledupar

Maracaibo

Barquisimeto

Valencia

La Guaira

Maracay

Caracas

Isla
La Tortuga

Isla de
Margarita

Cumaná
Barcelona

Fort-de-
France

SAINT
LUCIA

Kingstown

Martinique
(FRANCE)

Castries

BARBADOS
Bridgetown

SAINT VINCENT AND
THE GRENADINES

Saint
George's

GRENADA

Tobago

Port-of-
Spain

Trinidad

TRINIDAD AND
TOBAGO

Gulf of
Paria

Maturín

Mérida

Barinas

San Fernando

Cúcuta
San Cristóbal

icaramanga

Ciudad
Bolívar

Ciudad Guayana

VENEZUELA

Georgetown

Linden

GUYANA

D

OLOMBIA

otá
Villavicencio

Puerto
Ayacucho

Embalse
de Guri

GUIANA HIGHLANDS

BRAZIL

Boa Vista

1

Fighting against the empire: Poverty and unrest during the interwar years

The Caribbean of the 1930s faced major social unrest and political turmoil caused by grinding poverty and racial injustice. As a decade, it was very much in keeping with the history of the region. The modern Caribbean was built on slavery and, because of this dehumanising experience, rebellion had been an integral part of its history. When, in 1502, Nicolás de Ovando arrived as the new Spanish governor of Hispaniola (the West Indian island that comprises modern Haiti and the Dominican Republic), his group of settlers included enslaved Africans. One enslaved person escaped immediately, fleeing to the interior to become the first recorded 'African maroon' in the Americas.[1] For the next 460 years, the colonising powers had to address the questions of how to keep the enslaved on plantations and then how to control Black populations that grew to outnumber Europeans in the region.

This chapter describes how, in the years leading up to the Second World War, the Caribbean's long history of rebellions caught up with its colonial rulers.

THE STRUGGLE FOR LIBERTY (1600s TO THE LATE 1800s)

Records show that slave revolts were common across the Caribbean from the seventeenth century until the abolition of slavery.[2] In the British West Indies alone, the historian Michael Craton lists seventy-five slave rebellions between 1638 and 1837 (an average of one every two and a half years). Of the fourteen territories covered in Craton's list, almost a third of all rebellions came from just one island – Jamaica.[3] These rebellions sometimes included acts of self-liberation, with enslaved people running away to create maroon communities. Such 'marronage' was particularly powerful in Jamaica where the Maroon Wars of the 1700s forced Britain to sign treaties giving the Maroons semi-independent status within their mountain regions. This status still exists for several communities to this day. Among Jamaica's most famous Maroon generals was Nanny of the Windward Maroons, who developed a reputation as both a brilliant military leader and a powerful spiritual leader (or Obeah). Utilising guerrilla tactics to confuse British forces, the Windward Maroons eventually signed a peace treaty with Britain in 1740.

Jamaican Maroons were not alone in winning concessions from Britain, and similar treaties were secured in British Guiana allowing freed slaves to live autonomously within their jungle territories.[4] Maroon communities were established in other territories including Suriname, French Guiana, Cuba, Puerto Rico, Haiti and the Dominican Republic.

Although Maroon societies often existed as detached communities, there were many examples of them collaborating and trading with colonial societies. They were often democratic, with many accounts of their leaders being elected. Because the very nature of Maroons was that they were 'outsiders' to colonial societies, it was natural for them to form connections with another group of outsiders – the pirates, or buccaneers, of the Caribbean. Some estimates suggest that a quarter of all the pirates operating in the Caribbean in the seventeenth and eighteenth centuries were Black or mixed-heritage. Indeed, men of colour (such as Francisco Fernando of Jamaica) were often elected to lead pirate crews.[5]

Of all the rebellions, the most significant and famous was the audacious overthrowing of French colonial rule by the slaves of Saint-Domingue. They were led by a series of charismatic leaders and impressive military strategists including Boukman, Biassou, Jean-Jacques Dessalines, Henri Christophe and Toussaint Louverture. Over the course of thirteen years, they curtailed the power of the French plantocracy before declaring a new independent state of Haiti in 1804. Twenty-eight years earlier, the United States of America had won its independence from Britain, making Haiti only the second independent nation in the Americas. The Haitian Revolution inspired enslaved people across the region and had a seismic impact on the colonial powers, who recognised the threat to their grip on the Caribbean. After the British Parliament voted to abolish the slave trade in 1807 (but not slavery, which would continue for several more decades), impatience for freedom grew. In 1816 Barbados faced a well-planned revolt involving many hundreds led by Bussa, an African-born enslaved man. Among his many collaborators were several literate enslaved people including Nanny Grigg who, long before the rebellion, would read the local newspapers and inform her fellow enslaved people of developments in Haiti and the wider world. Although the Bussa rebellion was brutally quashed within days, it was another test of colonial authority.[6]

As slavery ended during the 1800s, freedom did not follow. The hated apprenticeship systems (introduced in the British, Dutch and Spanish West Indies) forced the formerly enslaved to remain on their plantations working unpaid for up to forty-five hours a week. Formerly enslaved people resisted this form of servitude, with apprentices in St Kitts, Trinidad and Jamaica refusing to work for free. The apprenticeship was supposed to last for six years in the British West Indies but had to end early in response to popular resistance. But even after the system ended, the Caribbean ruling classes sought novel ways to tie the formerly enslaved to their plantations. In Jamaica, the governor noted numerous examples of the formerly enslaved being paid five shillings a week but being charged eight shillings in rent for their smallholdings on the planters' estate, thus tying them to their employer through debt. And in the French islands of Martinique and Guadeloupe, exorbitant urban taxes forced labour to remain in rural areas to survive.[7] Despite these methods, around 20 per cent of ex-slaves left the plantations within five to seven years of emancipation in Jamaica and the French Caribbean. The exodus was even greater for women, with one Jamaican plantation recording its female labour force shrinking from 137 before emancipation to a mere nineteen after. Women workers on plantations received worse pay than men, and they could achieve greater flexibility in farming for themselves whilst bringing up their children.[8]

RACE CONSCIOUSNESS AND THE FIGHT AGAINST POVERTY (LATE 1800s TO 1929)

Weighed down by poverty, rebellion remained the only form of expression that was available to the Black population. One such rebellion started in the Jamaican town of Morant Bay. Along with his associates, Paul Bogle (a Baptist deacon) called on Black Jamaicans to take up their guns and cutlasses and fight against their white rulers. On 11 October 1865, Bogle led several hundred people on a march into Morant Bay, where they stormed the police station and the courthouse. The rebels killed eighteen people, wounded thirty-one and suffered seven fatalities themselves. The uprising quickly spread across the island. The governor swiftly assembled a force which included white militia, Maroons and the West India Regiment (WIR), made up of Black soldiers led by white officers, and proceeded to crush the rebellion. After a month of martial law, the rebellion was put down with 400 people killed.

By the end of the nineteenth century, the plantation economy of the British West Indies was a shadow of its former self. Although sugar remained an essential part of European life (accounting for one fifth of the calories in the English diet), the dominance of British Caribbean producers had come to an end.[9] The industry was being changed by competition from sugar beet producers and the re-emergence of Spanish Caribbean plantations that were benefiting from the injection of American capital. This imbalance in regional economies caused mass migration from poorer British West Indian territories to richer British and Spanish-speaking parts of the region during the early twentieth century.

These Black migrant workers were radicalised by their experience of overt racism, particularly in Cuba, Costa Rica and Panama, pulling them closer together as they developed a greater racial awareness.[10] The radicals that this produced were important proponents of racial consciousness across the globe, and they included Jamaica's Marcus Garvey and his Universal Negro Improvement Association (UNIA). Such was the power and contagion of West Indian radicalism that the movement founded by Garvey (who had spent time as a migrant worker on the plantations of Costa Rica) grew a global network of up to two million people. The UNIA operated through more than 1000 local branches spread across every continent, with much of its activities concentrated in the US. It has been described as the largest mass movement in the history of the US by the time Garvey was deported in 1927.[11]

This increasing sense of race consciousness was the backdrop to the Caribbean's entry into the Great War of 1914-18. The experiences of West Indian servicemen in the First World War would further radicalise them as they faced racism in military camps in Europe (see Chapter Two). Whilst West Indian servicemen had a poor experience of British racism during the war, their compatriots in postwar Britain would fare no better. The global trading links that resulted from the empire brought merchant mariners from all corners of the world to British shores. Large numbers of these sailors were people of colour.

Two months after Armistice Day, communities of colour came under attack from white rioters in nine towns and cities across the UK (Glasgow, South Shields, London, Salford, Hull, Newport, Barry, Cardiff and Liverpool). The main causes of this social unrest were unemployment and poor living conditions faced by ex-soldiers returning from the war. People of colour living in their communities were easy scapegoats. It started on 23 January 1919 in Glasgow when a group of white sailors, looking for work on merchant ships, shouted abuse at Black sailors who were seeking the same work. Fighting broke out between the two groups and the white sailors were joined by locals in attacking the Black mariners. Eventually, thirty Black sailors were taken into protective custody by the police. In Liverpool, on 5 June, Charles Wootton (a twenty-four-year-old Black, Bermudan sailor) was chased through the streets to Queen's Dock by a mob of several hundred people. As the mob swelled to around 2000, Wootton was forced into the water and drowned. In the disturbances that followed, 700 Black people had to take shelter in the Liverpool Bridewell. The secretary of state for colonies, Lord Milner, expressed his concerns about the impact of these riots in the colonies, writing on 23 June: 'I have every reason to fear that when these men get back to their own colonies they might be tempted to revenge themselves on the white minorities there, unless we can do something to show that His Majesty's Government is not insensible to their complaints'.[12]

At the beginning of the 1920s, many thousands of young men were returning to the Caribbean bruised and embittered by their treatment in the war and in the cities of the UK. These men would swell the ranks of movements that were demanding change. When the Great Depression struck in 1929, the already weakened economies of the Caribbean took a further battering. Over the next decade, unemployment and underemployment would soar – people who were just about scraping by and desperate for change, were now not even scraping by.

THE TURMOIL OF THE GREAT DEPRESSION (1929 TO 1940)

The Caribbean of the 1930s was constitutionally, politically and demographically diverse. Towards the end of that decade, estimates put its population (depending on how the region is defined) at over 12 million people (see Table 1). Around 2.4 million people lived in the British West Indies. The most populous territories were Spanish speaking, followed by French, English and Dutch speaking areas. The British West Indies was made up predominantly of people of African descent (80 per cent), with those of South Asian descent accounting for 12 per cent and mainly living in British Guiana and Trinidad and Tobago. The white population, although dominant in terms of economic and political power, accounted for just 3 per cent of inhabitants. The demography of the rest of the region, particularly the Spanish speaking Caribbean, was more mixed. A fall in the death rate across the Caribbean, along with differing patterns of migration, had resulted in a significant population growth during the first forty years of the twentieth century. This included major flows of Spanish immigrants into Cuba from the end of the 1890s through the 1920s, with the clear intent to drive down wages and 'whiten' the population.[13] The increasing population placed great pressure on governments to create jobs and expand public services and infrastructure, but the financial strictures imposed by the Great Depression pushed most of the region in the opposite direction.

Table 1 – Population of the Caribbean in 1930s

British West Indies (1937 population in brackets):

Bahamas (67,000)
Barbados (173,000)
British Guiana (335,000)
British Honduras (57,000)
Jamaica (1,123,000)
Leeward Islands
    Antigua (33,000)
    Montserrat (15,000)
    St Kitts, Nevis and Anguilla (42,000)
    British Virgin Islands (6,000)
Trinidad and Tobago (452,000)
Windward Islands
    Dominica (49,000)
    Grenada (75,000)
    St Lucia (67,000)
    St Vincent (56,000)

Cuba (1937 population = 4,126,000)

Dominican Republic (1937 population = 1,586,000)

Dutch West Indies (1937 population in brackets):

Aruba (23,000)
Curaçao (60,000)
Bonaire, Saba, St Eustatius, St Martin (10,000)
Suriname (150,000)

French West Indies (1937 population in brackets):

French Guiana (37,000)
Guadeloupe (307,000)
Martinique (248,000)

Haiti (1919 population = 1,631,250)

USA (1937 population in brackets):

Puerto Rico (1,777,000)
US Virgin Islands (24,000)

Haiti, the Dominican Republic and Cuba were the only independent Caribbean states, and all three had been subjected to significant US military intervention and direct rule during the early decades of the century. Puerto Rico was to all intents and purposes a colony of the United States, despite America's efforts to construct convoluted constitutional arrangements to pretend otherwise. The 1917 Jones Act had given US citizenship to Puerto Ricans, and eligibility for conscription into the First World War, but not the right to vote in US elections.[14] The four territories that were most heavily under US control (Puerto Rico, Cuba, Haiti and the Dominican Republic) had a combined population of approximately 9 million in 1937, accounting for three quarters of the Caribbean's people. In reality, whether living in independent states or colonies, the people of the Caribbean had little control over their political and economic destinies. Their future was largely shaped by decisions and actions taken in Europe and the United States.

The population of the French West Indies (around 600,000 in 1937) had been granted the right to vote since the abolition of slavery. Throughout the 1930s, the Dutch West Indies (a population of around 240,000) imposed severe restrictions on voting rights. There were only two British West Indian colonies (the Bahamas and Trinidad and Tobago) where more than 6 per cent of the population had the right to vote.[15] In three of Britain's Caribbean colonies, women were not allowed to be elected to legislative councils, and in the other territories the property and income qualifications that acted as a bar to elected office for most Black people were an even greater restriction for Black women.[16] The most powerful political force in each British West Indian territory was the governor, and the shape and power of the overwhelmingly white legislative councils varied across the territories. Despite British insistence that there was no colour bar, the reality was quite different. It would, for example, have been unthinkable for Britain to have appointed a Black governor as happened in Guadeloupe where, in 1936, Félix Éboué became the first Black governor of a French colony (a position he held until 1938).

Across the region, the impact of the Great Depression was stark. Within the first few years, sugar prices fell from 2.18 cents per pound in 1928 to 0.57 cents by 1932. In Cuba, wages fell by as much as

75 per cent and a 1932 survey reported that wages were 'the lowest since the days of slavery'.[17] In the British West Indies, the daily rate of pay for men working in agriculture in 1938 ranged from as little as 5p in Barbados up to 17p in Trinidad. In comparison, the average minimum daily pay for agricultural labour in England and Wales in 1939 was 34.5p. While the income for the Caribbean's men was appalling, it was even worse for its women. The 17p daily rate for male agricultural labour in Trinidad compared to 9p for women.[18] In general, women labourers in Jamaica and Trinidad earned about two-thirds the wages of men. In Puerto Rico, the pay for needlework (which attracted the largest proportion of women) was between 2 to 4 cents an hour in 1938 at a time when the US had set the minimum wage at 40 cents an hour.[19]

The pay and conditions of workers were so shocking that it left a permanent impression on the twenty-six-year-old Jock Campbell, who would later become head of his family's sugar business and a prominent British Labour Party peer and advocate for social reform. On a visit to his family's sugar estate in British Guiana in 1938, Campbell was appalled by the living conditions of Black and South Asian workers in the colony. When he came across the manager of Blairmont Sugar estate he asked why his mules were housed in better conditions than the workers. The manager replied: 'Because it costs money to replace our mules'.[20]

Some workers did not even receive wages, but payment in kind. This problem was particularly acute for the forestry workers of British Honduras, where the 'truck system' was common and was regularly exploited by employers to swindle workers and drive them into a spiral of debt. So bad was this system that regulations were proposed to end it.[21]

As employment dried up, West Indian migrant workers in Panama, Costa Rica, Cuba and the Dominican Republic were forced to return home. The US, having passed the 1924 Quota Act (motivated partly by racism), had already imposed severe restrictions on immigration from the Caribbean. As a result, the numbers of West Indians leaving the US had exceeded those entering for most years between 1925 and 1937.[22] In some cases, migrant workers faced persecution and thousands of Haitian and Jamaican workers were deported from Cuba. By 1937, over 13,000 migrant workers had been deported from Cuba to Jamaica alone, and an equal number returned voluntarily as they struggled to find work.[23] In the same year, up to 20,000 Haitian sugar workers were massacred in the Dominican Republic. Such persecution was a key factor in radicalising migrant workers. In British Honduras, St Kitts, Jamaica and Trinidad, returning migrant labour were to play an active role in labour unrests.[24]

During this period, restrictions on migration were also put in place between the British West Indian islands.[25] The shutting down of employment opportunities in the wider Caribbean and the US served to both frustrate the desire of British West Indian workers to better themselves economically and force them to look more critically at how to improve the conditions within their home territory. For these and other reasons, the pressures for reform within the British West Indies would take a different shape to that of the French, Spanish and US-controlled territories. Thus, the uprisings of the 1930s were more than a protest against poor living conditions, and were described as 'a positive demand for the creation of new conditions that will render possible a better and less restricted life'.[26]

The other consequence of the closing of opportunities for overseas work was that the pace of urbanisation quickened. People flocking to escape the limitations of rural communities had only the local towns to turn to for work and an income.[27] For political organisers across the Caribbean, urbanisation was a boon – large, concentrated urban populations were much easier to reach than sprawling rural ones. If proximity made urban populations easier to reach, it was their squalid living conditions that made them receptive to arguments for radical change. An account of poverty in one urban area in Trinidad, given anonymously to an American delegation looking at conditions in the region, made for harrowing reading:

The district known as John-John in Port-of-Spain has been described by a medical man as 'an entangled conglomeration of unsightly ruinous huts and privy cesspits placed helter-skelter on a sloping, steep and slippery hillside – a danger to health, life and limb for the local residents and a menace to the surrounding city population'.

In 1939, neo-natal mortality was as high as 50 per cent, but how even those surviving ever grow to manhood and womanhood is a miracle such as Lourdes has never equalled. In single rooms that flaunt a lack of the elementary needs of decency, you will find whole families living, their diet excessively carbohydrate and decidedly deficient in animal proteins and certain vitamins.[28]

THE DECADE OF REBELLION (1930s)

Thus, one hundred years after the abolition of slavery in the British West Indies and just over a decade after the First World War, poverty, mass unemployment and political disenfranchisement fuelled a decade of industrial and political unrest. Haiti and the Dominican Republic escaped mass protests as a result of the authoritarian control exercised by their governments.[29] The French colonies of Martinique and Guadeloupe, and the Dutch colony of Suriname, all experienced unrests, but these were neither of the intensity nor impact witnessed by the Spanish-speaking and British Caribbean.[30] In Suriname, labour protests culminated in clashes with the police in what became known as the Hunger Revolt in October 1931, ending in one death, two people wounded and fifty-six arrests. Then, in February 1933, a complex mix of issues around poverty and alienation (particularly among Javanese workers) was ignited by the arrest of Anton De Kom, a Black political activist and communist who had returned from living in the Netherlands. When people assembled demanding De Kom's release, the police fired on the crowd – two demonstrators were killed and twenty-three injured. The protests faded after the authorities deported De Kom to Europe, where he would die in a German concentration camp twelve years later.[31]

In 1931, a wave of strikes in Puerto Rico affected the tobacco industry, coffee and sugar workers, women in needlework factories, road construction workers and truck drivers. Between July and December 1933, the island experienced eighty-five strikes across various sectors. By early 1934, the entire Puerto Rican sugar industry was on strike. In response, the island was subjected to 'one of the most repressive periods of US rule' according to the American economist and historian James L Dietz.[32]

A similar wave of strikes swept Cuba as its economy went into free fall (its national income had nearly halved between 1929 and 1933).[33] When the Cuban military moved against the increasingly repressive President Gerardo Machado on 12 August 1933, he fled into exile. New presidents followed in quick succession and despite political and industrial reforms introduced by the radical government of President Ramón Grau San Martín, political instability and industrial unrest continued. The turmoil of this period gave rise to the soldier turned politician, Fulgencio Batista. With American support and an increasingly authoritarian approach, Batista would dominate Cuban politics for much of the next twenty-five years.

The British West Indies saw a viral spread of unrest. The first major upheaval of the decade was on the sugar estates of Trinidad and Tobago from May to July 1934. Desperate workers who were 'close to starvation' attacked overseers, managers and police, and set fire to company buildings.[34] In October, workers in British Honduras rose in protest against their colonial government. The protests were led by Antonio Soberanis Gomez, leader of the Labour and Unemployed Association. This was the culmination of months of campaigning for unemployment relief and fair wages. Around 500 people occupied the biggest sawmill in Belize Town. Thousands raided a coconut warehouse, timber yard and the Public Works Department yard. Police fought running battles with the protesters and eventually the colony's acting governor was forced to promise some additional funds for relief to pacify the public.[35]

In January 1935, the tiny island of St Kitts (with a population of 20,000) faced a strike by sugar workers. When, at the start of the sugar harvest, it became clear that plantation owners would not increase wages, a group of workers rose up in protest and travelled around the island persuading others to join them. By the end of January, there was a virtual general strike. Following demonstrations on a plantation, the police fired on the strikers, killing three and wounding eight. As the police arrested large numbers and a British warship arrived to support the authorities, the broken and dispirited sugar workers were forced back to work with no increase in wages.[36] The following month, the oilfield workers of Trinidad went on strike followed by a hunger march to the capital Port-of-Spain. Later in 1935, as well as a coal strike in St Lucia, unrests occurred in Kingstown and Campden Park on the island of St Vincent and across various estates in British Guiana.[37]

As if there were not enough to fuel the protests, Italy's invasion of Abyssinia (Ethiopia) in October 1935 added to the mood of anger in the West Indies. After months of war, Ethiopia's Emperor Haile Selassie was forced into exile in May 1936. In an impassioned address to the League of Nations on 30 June, Selassie called for action against Italy and gave the prophetic warning: 'It is us today. It will be you tomorrow'. But world powers stood by and allowed this act of aggression to proceed unanswered. This served as yet another example of the injustice and oppression faced by Black people around the world. As Black consciousness and political awareness were further raised across the Caribbean, Trinidadian dockers refused to unload Italian ships.[38]

In June 1937, Trinidad and Tobago experienced more strikes and unrest. It started in the oilfields. While oil accounted for 60 per cent of the islands exports, the number of jobs in the industry was relatively few – sugar and cocoa employed seven times as many workers as the oil industry. Like the rest of the British West Indies, therefore, Trinidad could be considered an agricultural economy. The oil workers' strike was triggered by the rising cost of living (inflation was estimated at 17 per cent) and victimisation of workers. The strike on 19 June was led by Uriah ('Buzz') Butler, a Grenadian-born migrant worker and First World War veteran. They were soon joined by agricultural workers and others. When police tried to arrest Butler whilst he was speaking at a rally, they were thwarted by the angry crowd that erupted into violence. In response to the uprising that followed, the colonial authorities summoned the navy from Bermuda and crushed the protest. By the time most workers had returned to work on 5 July, fourteen people were dead, fifty-nine were wounded and hundreds had been arrested. Stung by the ferocity of the industrial action, the oil companies negotiated better terms with the workers and within a year a new Oilworkers' Trade Union was formed, recruiting into membership 8000 of the industry's 9000 workers. Other Trinidad unions, formed and emboldened in the aftermath of the June

1937 strikes, had mixed success over the following year. The sugar workers union led an unsuccessful strike resulting in their capitulation, but unions for seamen and workers in ports and public works proved more successful.[39]

Barbados also experienced political unrest and strikes during 1937. Led by the young, Trinidad-born political activist Clement Osbourne Payne (a friend of Uriah Butler and a member of the Trinidad Youth League), people marched on Government House calling for better working conditions. Payne was arrested and deported for his troubles. This brought large crowds onto the streets, damaging property and chasing off the police. When the police retaliated by firing live rounds into an unarmed crowd, fourteen people were killed and forty-seven wounded. They arrested more than 500 people and brutally beat several of the protest leaders whilst in police custody. Strikes and unrest spread across the island and the new mood this created resulted in the formation of the Barbados Progressive League, popularly referred to as the 'First Party of the Barefoot Man'. The league was led by Chrissie Braithwaite and Grantly Adams.[40] A young Odessa Gittens, who would later volunteer to join the Auxiliary Territorial Service in the UK during the Second World War and would become a Cabinet minister in an independent Barbados government, remembered the impact of the uprisings:

> I know that if that had not happened we would still be colonials. That was the period when the English people became sensible enough to understand that we were people like them, and I'm very glad it happened … The people who fought in that were my personal friends … I couldn't tell you that those men didn't see what I saw. God bless them.[41]

The following year, Jamaica erupted into full-scale revolt following several years of sporadic unrest. The island was by far the biggest British colony in the Caribbean (with a population of 1,123,000) and had long held the reputation for being the most politically assertive territory in the British West Indies.

Trouble started on 2 May 1938 on the Frome Estate in Westmoreland, Jamaica, where police clashed with strikers. Four striking workers were killed and nine wounded. In a series of rallies between 11 to 20 May, labour leaders Alexander Bustamante and William Grant called on workers to unite and demand higher wages. On Saturday 21 May, a strike on the docks meant that only a few ships were able to be loaded and unloaded using outside labour. By the Monday, street cleaners had joined the strike and the streets of Kingston became full of unemptied bins. Crowds started to turn over the bins and some Chinese shops were attacked with goods and money stolen. As the day went on, all shopkeepers were intimidated by the crowds into closing to release their shop assistants to join the protests. By the end of the day, full-scale rioting had broken out and rapidly spread across the island.

Over the following weeks, authorities despatched the police and army across the island in an effort to stamp out local uprisings. Eight people were killed, 171 wounded and 700 were arrested and prosecuted before the island returned to near normal by 10 June (although occasional flare ups continued throughout the year and into the following year). Two popular leaders emerged from this period – Alexander Bustamante as the leader of labour and Norman Manley as a political organiser who had aligned himself with labour interests.[42]

In this volatile atmosphere, the voice of West Indian feminism was also being heard. One example was Amy Bailey, the Jamaican women's rights advocate who, along with her sister Ina Bailey, established the Women's Liberal Club (WLC) in 1936. The WLC would advocate for the end of discrimination on the basis of sex, along with a nationalist call for Jamaicans to shape their own future. On the first day of the oral evidence session in London for Lord Moyne's royal commission on the causes of the 1930s unrest, Bailey was its second witness and the first Jamaican it heard from.[43]

THE BRITISH RESPONSE (1938 TO 1940)

As the dust began to settle, colonial governments across the British West Indies reflected on the causes of the mass protests and the fragile state of the peace that had been restored. In suppressing the uprisings, at least forty-six people had been killed, 429 injured, thousands had been arrested and prosecuted. According to West Indian historian and political leader Dr Eric Williams, 'every British Governor called for warships, marines and aeroplanes'.[44] In most of the islands where disturbances had occurred, local commissions of inquiry were appointed to consider the causes.[45] Back in London, the Colonial Office (the government department that oversaw all British colonies) was considering how to respond. Speaking in the House of Commons on 14 June 1938, the Secretary of State for Colonies Malcolm MacDonald said:

> I think we must recognise that these outbreaks express a sense of unrest which is fairly widespread in the West Indies, which arises from feelings which we must respect and which will remain as a source of further trouble unless we can do something effective, in co-operation with the local administrations, to meet the legitimate grievances of our fellow-subjects in the West Indies. These feelings of unrest are a protest against the economic distress of the Colonies themselves, a protest against some of the consequences of that economic distress: uncertainty of employment, low rates of wages, bad housing conditions in many cases, and so on.[46]

With West Indian internal security a major concern, the Colonial Office sent a report to the government's Oversea Defence Committee in April 1938. Ignoring poverty as the major factor, the report instead blamed the uprisings on 'the growth of colour feeling, the influence of strikes in America, subversive propaganda, and the Italian conquest of Abyssinia'. It went on to summarise the recommendations made by Brigadier Howlett (Inspector-General of West Indian Local Forces) in a review of security that the Colonial Office had commissioned him to undertake. The increasing sense of panic among colonial administrators and their security force was evident in Howlett's proposals. He concluded that if more disturbances were triggered by racial tensions, Black policemen and special constables could not be trusted. Maintaining a regular garrison of white soldiers in the region was essential, according to this review, and the 'arming of white minorities should be considered'.[47]

While looking at ways to strengthen its West Indian security apparatus, the government also had to calm public tensions in the region. On 5 August 1938, it appointed a Royal Commission to investigate the causes of the protests and announced that it would be chaired by Lord Moyne. The commission was specifically asked 'to investigate social and economic conditions in Barbados, British Guiana, British Honduras, Jamaica, the Leeward Islands, Trinidad and Tobago, and the Windward Islands, and matters connected therewith, and to make recommendations'.

Moyne's report was blunt in its description of living conditions across the British West Indies. On housing and public health, it noted: 'Housing accommodation for the poorer people in the West Indies is generally deplorable, general sanitation is often primitive in the extreme, and the diet of the poorer people is often insufficient and usually ill-balanced. Little improvement in the health of the people can be expected … until these serious defects are remedied'.[48] Presenting the report to the War Cabinet on 30 January 1940, Malcolm MacDonald noted that although its findings were uncomfortable, the government was obliged to publish immediately because its contents were already widely circulating across the West Indies and if publication was delayed, 'riots might ensue'. However, Prime Minister Chamberlain took a different view. Alarmed by passages from the report that MacDonald had tabled at the Cabinet meeting, Chamberlain insisted that this presented too much of a propaganda gift to the Nazis and that publication must be delayed until after the war. He also worried about how this might tarnish Britain's reputation in the eyes of the US public.[49]

While publication of Moyne's full report could be delayed, action to address the calamitous conditions faced by the West Indies could not. When Britain declared war on Germany in September 1939, there was real anxiety among colonial administrators about whether the Caribbean would rally behind the war effort or continue to protest for domestic change. Indeed, as Moyne's Commission was taking evidence in Jamaica in 1938, protest marches for jobs were still taking place in the capital.[50] The politics of how to respond to the Commission's recommendations had to be resolved in this tense and uncertain environment.

The British government concluded that although it would not publish the full report, it would publish the recommendations and its response to them. At its meeting on 15 February 1940, the War Cabinet agreed to accept all the recommendations of the West India Royal Commission, including the creation of a welfare and development fund with an annual commitment of £1.4 million. In his description of the plight of the Caribbean, MacDonald said: 'Conditions there were probably worse than in any other part of the empire, partly because, with the exception of Trinidad, they had no mineral resources and practically no secondary industries and were thus entirely dependent upon agriculture; and partly because their population was relatively sophisticated and therefore expected social services of a fairly high order'.[51] Whilst the needs of the West Indies were great and politically urgent, poverty was a major issue across the wider empire. Thus, the package of legislation to fund development in the West Indies was part of a wider Colonial Development and Welfare Act of 1940. The £5 million Colonial Development package (which included the £1.4 million for the British West Indies), would remain a largely paper commitment that the government failed to deliver throughout the war.[52]

Facing war with Germany, the last thing the British government needed was further disturbances in the West Indies. There were two strongly opposing views about how to avoid this. On the one hand, the Colonial Office pushed for inclusion of West Indians in the war effort – urging that they be enlisted in the British forces and employed in war industries to both relieve unemployment and provide outlets for West Indian patriotism. On the opposite side stood the War Office, stubbornly resisting such efforts and determined not to allow into its ranks the same Black West Indians that British regiments had been called upon to subdue in the years immediately before the war (and, indeed, in centuries preceding that). This battle within the government would play out for the remainder of the war, with Winston Churchill interjecting at regular intervals before and after becoming prime minister.

In the immediate aftermath of the rebellions, the role of a West Indian combat regiment was tied up with issues of internal security. The reconstitution of the WIR, which had been disbanded in 1927, had been proposed as a means of creating employment and greater 'discipline' among the region's young men. It was also believed by some colonial administrators that it would strengthen the internal security apparatus available to British governors. Moyne's report had dismissed the idea on the grounds of cost. But in truth, the decision not to reinstate the regiment was the result of a murky tale of mistrust and prejudice within the War Office (the government department responsible for the British army) against West Indian fighting men. Although pushing for the recruitment of Black volunteers, the Colonial Office accepted the War Office myth of the poor fighting quality of Black West Indians. It was not until the final years of the war that one of its civil servants found historical accounts of regiments that had acquitted themselves well in battle, and concluded that they had been subjected to constant racism, poor leadership and a systematic distortion of their role in history (see p137).[53] Over hundreds of years, groups of West Indian men and women had bravely fought and struggled against their imperial rulers. But history showed that at the same time, and sometimes with the same men, British West Indians had also fought in defence of the empire – and as it declared war on Germany, Britain would need West Indian men and women to do so again.

NOTES

1   Isaac Curtis, 'Masterless People: Maroons, Pirates, and Commoners', Stephan Palmié and Francisco A Scarano (eds), *The Caribbean: A History of the Region and Its Peoples*, University of Chicago Press, 2011, p150.

2   Eric Williams, *From Columbus to Castro: The History of the Caribbean 1492-1969*, André Deutsch, 1983, pp194-200.

3   Michael Craton, *Testing the Chains: Resistance to Slavery in the British West Indies*, Cornell University Press, 1982, pp335-9.

4   Eric Williams, *Capitalism and Slavery*, André Deutsch, 1964, p202.

5   Curtis, op cit, pp151-4.

6   Hilary McD Beckles, 'The Slave-Drivers' War: Bussa and the 1816 Barbados Slave Rebellion', *Boletín de Estudios Latinoamericanos y del Caribe*, No 39, December 1985, pp85-110.

7   Gad Heuman, 'Peasants, Immigrants and Workers: The British and French Caribbean after Emancipation' Palmié and Scarano (eds), op cit, pp349-351.

8   Ibid, pp351-2.

9 Sidney Mintz, *Sweetness and Power: The Place of Sugar in Modern History*, Penguin, 1985, p6.

10 Winston James, 'Culture, Labor, and Race in the Shadow of US Capital', in Palmié and Scarano (eds), op cit, pp449-451.

11 Franklin W Knight, 'The Caribbean in the 1930s', Bridget Brereton (ed), *General History of the Caribbean, Volume V: The Caribbean in the Twentieth Century*, UNESCO, 2003, p71.

12 David Olusoga, *Black and British: A Forgotten History*, Pan Books, Apple eBooks version, 2017, Chapter 12, paragraphs 37-53.

13 Rough estimate for population of the Caribbean in 1938 given in Knight, op cit, p48. Estimates for population of British West Indies in 1936 given in *The Moyne Report: Report of the West India Royal Commission*, republished by Ian Randle Publishers: Jamaica, 2011, chapter 2, paragraph 2. Population of the British West Indies in 1938 and its ethnic breakdown is provided by Arthur Lewis, *Labour in the West Indies: The Birth of a Workers Movement*, New Beacon Books, 1977, pp11-2. The flow of Spanish immigrants into Cuba is described by Elizabeth Cooper, 'The Conundrum of Race: Retooling Inequality', in Palmié and Scarano (eds), op cit, pp391-2. Estimates for the population of the Caribbean in 1937 covering Cuba, Dominican Republic, Haiti (using 1919 figures), Guadeloupe, Martinique, French Guiana, Aruba, Curaçao, Suriname, Puerto Rico and the British West Indies including British Guiana and British Honduras are contained in *Statistical Yearbook 1948*, United Nations, 1949, pp21-3. For more on the history of South Asian immigration to the Caribbean, see Gaiutra Bahadur, *Coolie Woman: The Odyssey of Indenture*, Hurst & Co: London, 2013.

14 Dannelle Gutarra, 'Body Politics of Puerto Rican Participation in the US Military during World War II', in Karen Eccles and Debbie McCollin (eds), *World War II and the Caribbean*, University of the West Indies Press, 2017, Kindle version, paragraph 6.

15 Knight, op cit, pp44, 46.

16 Esther Captain and Guno Jones, 'Inversing Dependence: The Dutch Antilles, Suriname and the Desperate Netherlands during World War II', Eccles and McCollin (eds), op cit, paragraph 4. Tables summarising property and income qualification for the vote and to be a member of the legislative councils of the various British West Indian colonies in 1938 are contained in *The Moyne Report*, op cit, chapter 22, paragraphs 10-19. Description of restriction on women's access to elected offices also in *The Moyne Report*, chapter 11, paragraph 10.

17 O Nigel Bolland, 'Labor Protests, Rebellions, and the Rise of Nationalism during Depression and War', in Palmié and Scarano (eds), op cit, pp463.

18 Daily rate of pay in British West Indian agriculture is taken from *The Moyne Report*, op cit, chapter 10, paragraph 12, and has been converted from imperial to decimal currency. The average daily rate for agricultural workers in England and Wales is taken from *Agricultural Labour in England and Wales: Part II Farm Workers' Earnings 1917-1951*, University of Nottingham School of Agriculture, 1951, p68, and converted to decimal currency. See also Stephen Broadberry and Carsten Burhop, 'Real Wages and Labor Productivity in Britain and Germany, 1871-1938: A Unified Approach to the International Comparison of Living Standards', *The Journal of Economic History*, Vol 70, No 2, June 2010, p408, which gives average pay in agriculture around 33p a day in 1937.

19 Reference to rates of pay for women in Trinidad, Jamaica and Puerto Rico can be found in Knight, op cit, p59.

20 Ashley Jackson, 'New Research on the British Empire and the Second World War: Part I', in *Global War Studies*, Volume 7, Number 1, 2010, p47, which quotes from Clem Seecharan *Sweetening Bitter Sugar: Jock Campbell, The Booker Reformer in British Guiana 1934-1966*, Ian Randall: Kingston, 2005, p52.

21 *The Moyne Report*, op cit, chapter 24 (paragraphs 27 to 29) and chapter 25 (paragraph 62(f)).

22 Fitzroy André Baptiste, 'Amy Ashwood Garvey and Afro-West Indian Labor in the United States Emergency Farm and War Industries' Programs of World War II, 1943-1945', *Ìrìnkèrindò: A Journal of African Migration*, africamigration.com, December 2003, pp94-5.

23 Richard Smith, *Jamaica Volunteers in the First World War: Race, masculinity and the development of national consciousness*, University of Manchester Press, 2004, p156-7.

24 Bolland, op cit, pp460, 465-6.

25 *The Moyne Report*, op cit, chapter 2, paragraph 6.

26 Ibid, chapter 1, paragraph 17.

27 Knight, op cit, p52.

28 Baptiste, op cit, p96.

29 Bolland, op cit, p466.

30 Ibid, pp466, 473.

31 Peter Meel, 'Anton De Kom and the Formative Phase of Surinamese Decolonization', in *New West Indian Guide*, Vol 83, Nos 3 & 4, 2009, pp249-280.

32 Bolland, op cit, pp466, 469.

33 Knight, op cit, p61.

34 *The Moyne Report*, op cit, chapter 10, paragraph 17; Peter Fryer, *Black People in the British Empire: An Introduction*, Pluto Press, 1988, p103.

35 Fryer, op cit, p103.
36 Arthur Lewis, *Labour in the West Indies: The Birth of a Workers Movement*, New Beacon Books, 1977, pp19-20.
37 *The Moyne Report,* op cit, chapter 10, paragraph 17; Fryer, op cit, p103.
38 Fryer, op cit, p103.
39 Lewis, op cit, pp28-30.
40 Fryer, op cit, pp103-5.
41 Ben Bousquet and Colin Douglas, *West Indian Women at War: British Racism in World War II*, Lawrence & Wishart, 1991, pp40-1.
42 Lewis, op cit, pp34-6.
43 Dalea Bean, *Jamaican Women and the World Wars: On the Front Lines of Change*, Palgrave Macmillan, 2018, p153; see list of witnesses in *The Moyne Report,* op cit, Appendix A.
44 Figures for death, injuries and arrests taken from Lewis, op cit, p18. Eric Williams quote taken from Williams (1983), op cit, p473.
45 *The Moyne Report*, op cit, chapter 10, paragraph 17.
46 Hansard, 14 June 1938, volume 337, column 85, https://api.parliament.uk/historic-hansard/commons/1938/jun/14/colonial-office#column_85.
47 National Archives, UK, enclosure 1, 2 April 1938, CO 318/432/3.
48 *The Moyne Report*, op cit, chapter 8, paragraph 57(8).
49 CAB 66/5/27. National Archives, UK, conclusions of War Cabinet of 30 January 1940.
50 *The Moyne Report*, op cit, chapter 10, paragraph 14.
51 CAB 65/5/42. National Archives, UK, conclusions of War Cabinet of 15 February 1940.
52 E R Wicker, 'Colonial Development and Welfare, 1929-1957: The Evolution of a Policy', in *Social and Economic Studies*, Vol 7, No 4, December 1958, pp170-192.
53 CO 968/102/4. National Archives, UK, minutes sent from E E Sabben-Clare to Colonial Office civil service colleague Mr Rogers on 9 February 1944 (5th paragraph), also Sabben-Clare minutes sent on 14 February, and 28 March 1944 in paragraph 3(iii).

2

Fighting for Empire: Britain's West Indian regiments

From early European conquest, the West Indies has had a turbulent history of slave revolts, territorial conflicts between colonial powers competing for greater proportions of the Caribbean area and its wealth, and labour uprisings and industrial unrest. Armed militia were required to protect individual territories from foreign attacks, and to suppress the local populations. Initially restricted to the white population, it soon became clear that recruitment to these militia had to be opened up to people from other ethnic backgrounds. As a result, Black West Indians, and West Indians of colour, would play a central role in propping up the colonial powers of the region. However, their role would be determined within the parameters of 'race' as it was constructed in the nineteenth and twentieth century.

THE INVENTION OF RACE AND RACISM

Race as a social construct was born out of the political and economic drive for Europeans to justify and maintain a brutal and hugely profitable system of enslavement of Africans. Modern racism was shaped on the plantations of the West Indies and North America, since the plantocracies did not want the unimaginable wealth generated on the backs of enslaved Africans to be challenged by the moral teachings of Christianity or Enlightenment ideals about freedom and equality between 'men'. By denying Africans the status of being human, they could justify the suffering and degradation visited upon them in the process of generating maximum profits from their labour as enslaved people. It was this imperative that gave rise to 'scientific racism', a pseudoscience that was promulgated across eighteenth and nineteenth-century Europe with support and funding from one of the wealthiest and most powerful lobbies of its time: the West India Lobby. The opulence of these slave-owning oligarchs would lead to the coining of the eighteenth-century phrase 'as rich as a West Indian planter'. They supported philosophers and writers whose brand of 'scientific racism' matched the interests of the lobby.[1] The effect of this distorted ideology was keenly felt in the decades leading up to the Second World War and during the war itself.

There were two aspects of racism that structured British colonial rule. The first was colourism, which further divided categories of 'races' by gradation of skin colour. In a racial hierarchy where white people placed themselves at the top, and placed Black people at the bottom, proximity to whiteness was rewarded. In West Indian and American slave societies, enslaved people were stratified by the colonial power so that those with more European blood, and therefore of lighter complexion, were given a higher status than those of darker complexion. After slavery had ended, Black West Indians of darker complexion were excluded from positions of status in the colonial or military services, whilst those who were 'lightly coloured' would be given greater opportunities – though, of course, not anywhere near equal status to white people.

The pseudoscience of race was also deployed to categorise native inhabitants across conquered territories based, in part, upon how they had resisted their European colonisers. Theorising the nature of this resistance as biological, 'fighting' characteristics were variously assigned to different groups, leading to the theory of 'martial races'. This theory divided groups of people according to their supposed warrior-like skills and propensities. During the nineteenth century, different ethnic and religious groups were ranked as fighters based on physical appearance and their history of military conflict with Britain, but mostly according to the whims and prejudices of individuals in the British military and colonial establishment. By the early twentieth century, applying this theory was proving far too restrictive when Britain's armed forces needed greater numbers of recruits. However, the prejudices upon which it was based lingered and West Indians were often seen as less suitable fighters due to the argument that they had been 'pampered' and Westernised by their European rulers.[2] The impact of racism in Britain and the Caribbean during the Second World War is set out in Section Three on recruitment into the wartime services. In Chapter Eleven we look at how the wartime colour bar was applied in Britain and the British Caribbean.

EUROPEAN BATTLES FOR THE CARIBBEAN (1600s TO 1800s)

In the centuries that immediately followed white settlement in the Caribbean, the region became an extension of European warfare and politics. The accumulation of wealth in the Caribbean would strengthen European economies, fund the expansion of their military, and bolster political prestige. It was in this context that Oliver Cromwell, keen to curb the increasing power of Spain, decided to attack its possessions in the Americas. To do this, he dispatched an expeditionary force in 1654 to take Hispaniola. Of the 2500 men who made up this force, there were only 1000 experienced soldiers. The remaining 1500 had been pressed into service from the streets of London and were described by one observer as 'largely criminals'. More soldiers were needed, so upon its arrival in the Caribbean in 1655 they recruited local men – both free settlers and those living under the yoke of servitude as indentured Europeans. Over 3000 men were drawn from Barbados and surrounding islands. The description of these recruits was not much better than those recruited in England – 'the very scum of scum' according to one witness. They were not up to the task. After two unsuccessful attacks on Hispaniola in April 1655, and the loss of 1000 men, they retreated and sailed south. Instead of the vastly richer Hispaniola, this desperate force seized control of the poorly defended Spanish island of Jamaica. The use of Caribbean recruits (free, indentured and, eventually, enslaved) continued under future British forces in the region.[3]

To conquer, control, and defend territories on the other side of the Atlantic, naval power was critical. The Royal Navy normally had several thousand men deployed in the Caribbean, but at its height (in 1782) a third of its ships, and more than 30,000 of its sailors, were stationed there. Disease and desertion left it struggling to maintain numbers, even during periods of normal deployment. These pressures, and the quality of seafarers to be found in the Caribbean, resulted in an increasing reliance on Black seamen – enslaved people and freemen. The most notable of them all was John Perkins (also known as Jack Punch), who was born into slavery around 1750 in Jamaica. He joined the navy as the slave of William Young, a carpenter, first aboard the *Grenado* in 1759 and then the *Boreas* in 1760. After stints in the navy and in private vessels, he secured his first command of the schooner *Punch* in 1778. Over the following decades, Captain Perkins' naval exploits saw him running intelligence gathering missions for Britain in Saint-Domingue and commanding a range of vessels including the Royal Naval sloop *Endeavour*, the schooner *Spitfire*, then the larger *Marie Antoinette* (a captured French vessel), the *Drake*, and the 32-gun *Tartar* (with 264 men), which he commanded from 1802 until his retirement in 1804. During what has been widely acknowledged as an accomplished naval career, he destroyed or captured hundreds of enemy ships and took 3000 prisoners, with numerous of his exploits covered in the British press. In the many newspaper reports, Perkins' 'race' was referred to only once in an 1803 article praising his accomplishments and referring to his 'mulatto' origins. Born into slavery, Perkins died in 1812 himself a slave owner and a member of the Jamaican colonial elite.[4] He was the Royal Navy's first Black officer, and it would take almost 150 years before it appointed its next.

With the region enduring constant attacks and counterattacks, its defence required more than the active engagement of professional soldiers and sailors like Perkins. Citizens of the islands had to be prepared to defend themselves. Free, able-bodied white men, aged between sixteen and sixty-five, were often required to join their local militia. Over time, the racialised restrictions on joining were eased as the increase in the Black and mixed-heritage population forced local administrators to broaden their recruitment. Thus, free Black and mixed-heritage people would also be required to serve but were generally not allowed to become officers.[5]

Despite playing an essential role in territorial defence for the empire throughout the eighteenth and nineteenth centuries, the British Caribbean militias tended to be poorly led, trained and resourced. Sir Lionel Smith, Barbados governor during 1833-6, described militias throughout the West Indies as 'disgraceful ... because there is no just excuse for want of men or means, and I can only attribute the defect to apathy or to a mistaken confidence that they can always command the services of the regular troops'.[6] Smith had a point – being able to rely on the services of the regular army was important for a colonial power. Britain needed to strengthen its Caribbean defences and a disciplined and highly effective force of Black soldiers was the way to achieve this. The need for such a force had emerged towards the end of the eighteenth century.

In 1793, a few years after toppling its monarchy, the new republic of France declared war on Britain. Two years later it had recaptured Guadeloupe and St Lucia from the British with the help of Black conscripts who had been emancipated in French colonies a year earlier. A combination of French military aggression and rebellious Maroons forced Britain to assemble an expeditionary force of 33,000 troops to strengthen its position in the West Indies (though bad weather prevented some from reaching their destination). Dispatched in waves during the spring of 1796, this was the largest expeditionary force in British history up to that point.[7] In addition to the challenge of French forces and Maroons, British troops faced a third deadly threat in the form of disease. From 1793 to 1815, half of the 89,000 white soldiers fighting for Britain in the Caribbean died, 90 per cent as a result of disease. The scale of these losses struck fear in soldiers. For the military high command, such losses were unsustainable and early in the conflict the commander of British forces in the region, General Sir Ralph Abercromby, determined that the recruitment of Black soldiers was the answer.[8]

AN ARMY OF ENSLAVED BLACK PEOPLE (1790s TO EARLY 1800s)

Abercromby and other colonial leaders saw Black people as better suited to the West Indian climate and, therefore, potentially better fighting material. The plantocracy was strongly opposed to the idea and were alarmed at the prospect of arming local Black people – its lobby in London (the West India Committee) tried to persuade the British government to block the plans. But the secretary of state for war, Sir Henry Dundas, had made up his mind that Black soldiers were needed. These soldiers would be purchased, not recruited. Dundas bought enslaved people costing up to £70 a head to create twelve fighting regiments. Faced with white slave-owners who refused to sell the fittest of their enslaved populations to the British army – or objected in principle to the arming of Black people to kill white people – Dundas was forced to purchase his soldiers from West Africa or confiscate them from slave ships.[9]

Between 1795 and 1808, Britain purchased 13,400 enslaved Black people for the West India Regiment (WIR), making the British army one of the biggest slave-owners of recent centuries. But the WIR also recruited free men – Black, mixed-heritage and even some white people – all led by white officers.[10] The Corps of Loyal Black Rangers was created as a regiment in Grenada during 1795, and during the same year eight other Black regiments were established. Black and white soldiers lived in the same type of accommodation and were paid the same. But Black recruits were considered less prone to sickness, desertion or drunkenness than their white comrades.[11]

After Nelson's defeat of the combined French and Spanish fleet off the Cape of Trafalgar in 1805, the British West Indian territories were beyond the reach of a devastated French naval force. By now, the WIR would form about a third of Britain's garrison forces, along with much better prepared white soldiers sent from Britain. With improvements in medical care, the fatality rate faced by European soldiers fell drastically from 41 per cent in 1796 to 14 per cent by 1810.[12] The terror of disease among white soldiers was well on the way to being addressed.

By the end of the Napoleonic Wars, Black West Indian regiments had won much praise and honours in three engagements: Dominica in 1805, Martinique in 1809 and Guadeloupe in 1810. With these wars behind it, Britain proceeded to reduce this colonial force and disbanded many of the West Indian regiments so that by 1816 it had gone from twelve regiments to six.[13]

Table 2 – Organisation of British army

Section: between seven to twelve soldiers, under the command of a corporal or sergeant.

Platoon (or Troop): twenty-five to thirty soldiers, split into three or four sections. Commanded by a lieutenant or second lieutenant.

Company (also a Squadron or Battery): 100-150 soldiers, and made up of at least two platoons. The company is led by a major with a captain as second in command.

Battalion: 500-1000 soldiers, and normally consists of several companies and a headquarters. Usually commanded by a lieutenant colonel.

Regiment: The regiment is the key administrative unit of the British army and tend to have a greater sense of history and permanence behind them. They are usually made up of several battalions. However, battalions from the same regiment do not usually fight together and, instead, are grouped into other fighting units. Regiments tend to be led by a colonel.

Brigade: 3000-5000 soldiers, made up of several battalions or cavalry/armoured regiments. Usually commanded by a major-general or brigadier.

Division: 10,000-25,000 soldiers, made up of three brigades along with supporting artillery, engineer, medical and logistics. Commanded by a lieutenant-general or major-general.

Corps: Made up of two or three divisions (40,000-80,000 soldiers) and commanded by a lieutenant-general.

Army: Made up of two or more corps, and was usually around 150,000 soldiers during second world war. Commanded by a general or field marshal.

WEST INDIA REGIMENT'S ROLE IN CONQUEST AND SUPPRESSION (1800s)

Britain's West Indian regiments both played an important role in defending the colonial power against foreign aggressors seeking to seize its resource-rich Caribbean territories, and were used to extend British imperial infrastructure by supporting the conquest of territories on other continents, and the control of Black populations of the British Caribbean itself. In 1865, the WIR supported colonial forces in the vicious suppression of the Morant Bay Rebellion (see Chapter One). At the orders of the island's brutal governor, the 1st and 6th regiments of the WIR were involved in crushing the uprising with arrests, destruction of property and killing of many innocent people, including some who were their friends or relatives.[14]

The role of these forces in the Morant Bay atrocities reverberated through history, contributing to a long-standing mistrust of the WIR within the Jamaican population.[15] This was neither the first nor last time they would be used against West Indian populations – they had been used to suppress earlier Jamaican civil disturbances and had also helped to put down the Bussa rebellion in Barbados and British Guiana uprising during 1816.[16] Their effectiveness in controlling local uprisings was matched by their impact in imperial wars in Africa.

Whilst fighting in the Asante Wars of 1873-4 and the Sierra Leone conflict of 1898-9, the WIR won praise from their European commanders. But this praise was laden with racist stereotyping. One such officer, Alfred Ellis, claimed that Black West Indian soldiers fighting in the Asante War marched two to three times the distance of white soldiers and could carry out equal work on half the food rations. He said of Black West Indians: 'The English-speaking negro of the West Indies is most excellent material for a soldier. He is docile, patient, brave, and faithful'. He believed that harsh treatment that would drive English soldiers to insubordination would provoke no more than 'passive obedience and a stubborn sullenness' from West Indian soldiers.[17]

According to the accounts of many of their officers, these were brave fighters almost to the point of recklessness. The first Black soldier to win a Victoria Cross was Samuel Hodge, from the British Virgin Islands, who died fighting with the WIR in Gambia in 1866 (just ten years after the award was introduced by Queen Victoria). Another conflict in the Gambia resulted in the award of a Victoria Cross in 1892 to a young Jamaican, Lance-Corporal William Gordon.[18] If, at times, they displayed a sense of over-confidence and invincibility on the battlefield, it would also show in their behaviour at home as they swaggered through the streets of West Indian towns and villages. This was a further reason for them to stand apart and be looked upon with a mixture of respect, fear, suspicion and hostility among the local Black populations.

Table 3: British Military Ranks

Army	Royal Navy	Royal Air Force
Field Marshal	Admiral of the Fleet	Marshal of the Royal Air Force
General	Admiral	Air Chief Marshal
Lieutenant General	Vice Admiral	Air Marshal
Major General	Rear Admiral	Air Vice Marshal
Brigadier	Commodore	Air Commodore
Colonel	Captain	Group Captain
Lieutenant Colonel	Commander	Wing Commander
Major	Lieutenant Commander	Squadron Leader
Captain	Lieutenant	Flight Lieutenant
Lieutenant	Sub Lieutenant	Flying Officer
Second Lieutenant	Midshipman	Pilot Officer
Non-commissioned ranks		
Warrant Officer Class 1	Warrant Officer 1	Warrant Officer
Warrant Officer Class 2	Warrant Officer 2	
Staff Sergeant	Chief Petty Officer	Flight Sergeant
Sergeant	Petty Officer	Sergeant
Corporal	Leading Seaman	Corporal
Lance Corporal		Senior Aircraftman
	Able Seaman	Leading Aircraftman
Private	Ordinary Seaman	Aircraftman

Among the white population, there was very little trust for the regiment despite their aggressive willingness to defend the status quo. The government in London had grave concerns about the loyalty of the WIR and sought the views of its West Indian governors on the matter. The governor of Jamaica (Charles Henry Darling) responded in January 1861 and made clear his absolute confidence in the Regiment, based on his experience of using them to stamp out anti-colonial resistance twice during 1859 in Jamaica and once in St Lucia in 1849 when he was its then governor. He wrote:

> … it would be difficult to find Troops who not only display a more thorough and even ardent desire to execute their duty upon occasions in which they are brought in contact with the population of their own color, but whom it is on such occasions, more necessary to control and restrain in order to prevent unnecessary violence and Bloodshed.

However, he admitted that his was a minority view among West Indian governors and the white Jamaican population. He suggested that among the Black population, it was the Black soldiers of the WIR that they feared the most – not white European soldiers.[19]

White suspicion of the WIR was not helped by occasional incidents of disorder such as in 1802 when its 8th battalion, which was stationed in Dominica, mutinied after the men were ordered to carry out manual work and then not given the pay they were entitled to. It was one of a number of incidents that would be used to pin a reputation on the WIR as a 'troublesome' force to lead.[20] Caribbean history has seen many incidents of mutiny and disorder among white soldiers, but rebelliousness among Black soldiers tended to stick in the memory of colonial governments.

THE GREAT WAR AND THE BRITISH WEST INDIES REGIMENT (1914 TO 18)

By the beginning of the twentieth century, the West India Regiment was a well-established military force with a declining garrison role. With the outbreak of the First World War on 4 August 1914, there was widespread support for Britain across its Caribbean colonies. Marcus Garvey encouraged West Indians to enlist and expressed his support in a letter to the Secretary of State for Colonies six weeks into the war. But there was no flood of volunteers as there was in Britain or the white Dominions, and support was not universal. Some Black West Indians expressed the view that this was a 'white man's war', although this sentiment was roundly condemned across the Caribbean press.[21] This was also a remote war. Only briefly was the West Indies directly touched by the conflict when the German light cruiser, *Karlsruhe*, attacked and sunk ships in the Caribbean during 1914 before being destroyed by an internal explosion.[22]

In the early months of conflict, there was no sense of urgency from the War Office to encourage Caribbean recruitment. Despite this, a trickle of West Indians were already making their way to England to volunteer. Arthur Cipriani, who would become a prominent Trinidadian politician and labour leader, launched a personal crusade to encourage the recruitment of local men. The first batch of Trinidadian volunteers left for England, at their own expense, to enlist in early December 1914, and Cipriani describes the send-off they received as 'the most remarkable witnessed in the history of the Colony and was a very fair show of the feeling of the Colony's entire population'. It took him until the autumn of 1915 to get the island's government (along with local businesses) to support local recruitment efforts, with 450 volunteers sailing for England in September and picking up over 400 more recruits from Grenada, St Vincent and Barbados en route.[23]

By late 1915, recruitment efforts were also picking up in other parts of the British West Indies. The War Office opened recruitment to all West Indian men and recruitment meetings were being held even in Jamaica's more remote districts.[24] The change in policy had occurred in the spring of that year with the decision to create a new regiment of Black West Indian soldiers. It was the result of lobbying from the people and governors of the British West Indies to persuade a reluctant War Office. The Colonial Office, and its West Indian governors, feared that without local recruitment the region's population would grow frustrated at a lack of opportunity to demonstrate their loyalty to the empire and its war effort. This lobbying benefited from the considerable support of King George

V who took an early interest and discussed the matter with Lord Kitchener, the Secretary of State for War, in April. On 19 May approval was given to the formation of a new regiment, and the British West Indies Regiment (BWIR) was formed.[25]

The BWIR was seen as an army of patriotic citizens rather than the professional soldiers who made up the West India Regiment. Thus, many of the BWIR recruits saw themselves as a cut above the WIR and its tough soldiers who usually came from the poorer sections of society.[26] As a new regiment, the BWIR did not carry the baggage of brutality and race-betrayal that the WIR had accumulated through its history of conflict with local populations, including the quashing of the Morant Bay rebellion.

In addition to considerable lobbying for the West Indies to play an active role in the war, there was another factor at play. Since the Boer Wars in the late 1800s and beginning of the 1900s, there were real concerns about the physical health of men across the UK and their suitability to serve in the armed forces. Poverty and malnourishment had taken its toll on the British working class, and the army would see the results. A range of commentators and eugenicists had bemoaned what they saw as the enfeeblement of British manhood. As the war proceeded, this would be compounded (in their view) by the further loss of the nation's 'fittest' men who were being killed in the trenches whilst the 'weakest' were left at home to further dilute an already degraded gene pool. This 'crisis in masculinity' meant the army struggled to find recruits capable of enduring the physical or mental demands of war.[27] The scale of losses in the trenches was huge. On the worst day of the Somme (1 July 1916) Britain suffered over 57,000 casualties, which include 19,240 fatalities. This was a level of loss the nation could not carry on its own. Thus, increasing numbers of recruits would be needed from across the empire.

In contrast to anxieties about the state of British manhood, there was a growing fascination with, and fetishization of, Black masculinity. A range of colonial administrators and military figures, including Field Marshal Haig (Commander-in-Chief of the British Armies in France) and Major General Sir W. J. Murray (British Commander-in-Chief in Egypt) commented on the 'fine' or 'exceptional' physique of the new West Indian recruits. These observations were reflected in British press articles describing West Indian volunteers on parade in towns across the country.[28] But the sturdy, muscular soldiers of the BWIR were not an accurate reflection of the physical state of the wider West Indian population, which had also been blighted by poverty, malnourishment and poor public health. It is estimated that around 60 per cent of the 26,667 Jamaican volunteers for military service were rejected as medically unfit.[29] The position in Britain looked no better at the start of the war, with estimates suggesting between 40 to 60 per cent of the male population were unfit for military service – a position that was not believed to have improved since the turn of the century.[30]

THE TABOO OF THE BLACK SOLDIER IN EUROPEAN COMBAT (1915 TO 18)

As young West Indian men enlisted in their tens of thousands, the military command had to decide how best to use them. The thought of arming Black soldiers to kill white people (even if those white people were German enemies) was unpalatable across the British establishment. This attitude would prevent the recruitment of West Indian and African soldiers to combat roles in European theatres of war, instead deploying them in the Middle East and Africa, where European powers were fighting proxy wars through native colonial armies. Where BWIR troops were deployed in Europe, it was, in effect, as labour units – moving ammunition for white British troops. As the devastation of trench warfare brought losses on a scale that British armies had not seen before, more voices were raised in favour of using Black soldiers from across the empire in combat roles. Among those voices was Winston Churchill (more than twenty years later Churchill would again throw his weight behind this argument during the Second World War).[31] But the War Office and military high command were stubborn and would not easily yield on this point.

The US, like Britain, struggled with the idea of using Black soldiers in combat roles. The American position on race was illustrated in the deployment of the 15th New York National Guard Regiment, made up of African American troops led by white and Black officers. Formed in 1916 by New York governor, Charles

Whitman, the unit was deployed in France in January 1918 as the 369th Regiment. The regiment would be more popularly known as the 'Harlem Hellfighters'. They were initially given manual and labour tasks, but lobbying from their commander finally persuaded the military authorities to give them a combat role. However, to avoid leading a Black regiment into battle, General John Pershing (commander of the US expeditionary forces in Europe) handed over command of the Hellfighters to the French army. They entered the trenches on 15 April 1918 and suffered heavy bombardment from the Germans. They would endure more time in front-line combat (191 days) than any other American unit of their size.[32]

Despite the formal refusal to give the BWIR any combat role in Europe, things were often different in the heat of battle. Thus, whatever their official role, Black West Indian soldiers would engage the enemy when the need and opportunity arose. George Blackman, who was born in Barbados in 1897 and served in the 4th Battalion of the BWIR in Europe, said: 'They called us darkies ... But when the battle starts, it didn't make a difference'. In one encounter, he recalled giving orders to engage the enemy:

> I made the order: 'Bayonets, fix', and then 'B Company, fire'. You know what it is to go and fight somebody hand to hand? You need plenty nerves. They come at you with the bayonet. He pushes at me, I push at he. You push that bayonet in there and hit with the butt of the gun – if he is dead he is dead, if he live he live.[33]

For Black people born and living in Britain, the application of the colour bar was more confusing. The army's approach to recruitment was inconsistent, with some recruitment centres refusing to admit Black British volunteers and others accepting them. This inconsistency also applied to Black West Indians and Africans who made their way to the UK and approached recruitment centres to volunteer.[34] A number of Black Britons led men into battle as officers – including the notable figure of 2nd lieutenant Walter Tull. Born in 1888 in Kent to a Black Barbadian father and white English mother, Tull became a professional footballer and joined up as part of the 17th battalion of the Middlesex Regiment – better known as the 1st Football Battalion – after the outbreak of war. A popular and respected officer, he died in battle in March 1918 and those who fought with him tried repeatedly to recover his body from No Man's Land under heavy fire.[35] Tull was widely believed to have been the first Black officer in the British army until the story of Lieutenant Euan Lucie-Smith came to light – a mixed-heritage officer in the 1st Battalion of the Royal Warwickshire Regiment who was commissioned in September 1914 and was killed in action on 25 April 1915 during the Second Battle of Ypres.[36]

DISTINCTION IN BATTLE (1914 TO 18)

From the outset of war, British imperial forces were pitted against Germans in a struggle to acquire enemy territory on the African continent. West Indians were part of these battles. In Cameroon the bravery of the 2nd battalion of the WIR was commented on in the battle of Wum-Biagas in October 1915 when it was reported that whilst the machine gun section was under heavy fire, 'the discipline and morale of the rank and file ... was all that could be possibly desired'.[37] In April 1917 a small detachment of the 2nd battalion (numbering around fifty men) came under heavy attack from the enemy whilst in the German East African territory of Tanganyika (now known as Tanzania) and was said to have 'repulsed, with considerable loss, a determined attack ... by a superior enemy force'. A Military Cross and Distinguished Conduct medals were awarded to several members of the battalion.[38] Seven months later, still in Tanganyika, the battalion was involved in battles during early November. In their war diaries, it was reported that the men had 'behaved excellently' and it was noted that such was their keenness and bravery that several of them had to be reprimanded 'for exposing themselves unnecessarily' to enemy fire.[39]

The deployment of the BWIR was more confused and problematic. Initial training was in England in autumn and winter of 1915-16, resulting in large numbers being hospitalised and dying from pneumonia brought on by the cold weather. They were eventually moved to Egypt where an outbreak of measles, mumps and meningitis resulted in more hospitalisation and deaths. It was eventually decided to split up the regiment. Around 500 men from the 1st, 2nd and 3rd battalions of the BWIR were sent to East Africa as reinforcements for the WIR. A hundred men from the 2nd battalion were sent to Mesopotamia (part of modern-day Iraq), and men from the 3rd and 4th battalions were sent to France to become ammunition carriers and, in effect, to work as a labour unit. Subsequent recruitment to the BWIR was used to deploy more men to Europe to work as ammunition carriers and labourers in a war zone that was in desperate need of men.[40] In the Middle East, the BWIR fought in the Palestine campaign and took part in raids on Turkish trenches in July 1917. In a message to the BWIR, Major-General Sir E. W. Chaytor (commander of Australian and New Zealand forces in Palestine) gushed that '... all the troops of my division report that they like to fight alongside you; in fact, they could never wish for anybody better'. Chaytor was equally positive about the BWIR in a letter sent to a battalion commander in October 1918: 'Outside of my own Division there are no troops I would sooner have with me than the BWI, who have won the highest opinion of all who have been with them during our operations here'.[41]

Over 15,500 recruits (including 397 officers) served in the eleven battalions of the BWIR. In total, 185 were killed in action and 697 wounded. But sickness was by far the bigger killer, accounting for an additional 1071 deaths. The regiment received a range of distinctions, including five Distinguished Service Orders, nine Military Crosses, eight Distinguished Conduct Medals, 37 Military Medals and 49 mentions in dispatches.[42]

Despite limited opportunity to display their ability in combat, and praise from those who observed them under fire, the performance of the BWIR would largely be judged on two incidents. In the first, they were victims of inept planning and leadership, and in the second they were forced to stand up against the most blatant racism.

COLD CLIMATE IN HALIFAX AND COLD RECEPTION IN TARANTO (1916 AND 1918)

The third contingent of Jamaican recruits to the BWIR were sailing to Britain on board the *Verdala* troopship when, in March

1916, they were caught in a blizzard and diverted to Halifax in the Canadian province of Nova Scotia. The ship had no steam heating and the 1115 West Indian soldiers and twenty-five white officers had to cope with the bitter cold. For the officers, this was made much more bearable by the fact that they had winter clothing. The Black West Indian soldiers, however, were left in tropical, light-weight khaki clothing – completely inappropriate for the climate. In his history of the BWIR, Captain Cipriani describes the metal freezer that the *Verdala* had become and how its frozen passengers were forced to resort to using razors and knives to cut their own arms and legs in order to 'get a blood-flow to ease their agony'. Once they arrived at Halifax, their evacuation from the ship was further delayed. It was not until gangrene had set in and strong protests were made about the need for urgent action, that the sick were taken off the ship 'and all the available doctors in neigh-bouring hospitals devoted themselves to the alleviation of these men's tortures'.[43]

In fact, winter clothing for all the men was onboard, but inex-plicably they had not been issued to the Black Caribbean soldiers. Of the more than 600 men who suffered from frostbites, five of them died and 106 had limbs amputated. They were all returned to Jamaica where the outcry against their suffering was compounded when the disabled soldiers' pensions were delayed.[44]

As the war ended, the battalions of the BWIR were transferred to a military camp in Taranto in Italy awaiting their repatriation and formal demobilisation. The Black soldiers faced discrimination and racist abuse in the camp and, yet again, were used as labourers. In addition, there was a dispute over a pay increase of six pence a day that had been given to British soldiers and was owing to West Indians. However, the War Office ruled that West Indians should not receive this pay increase because they were 'natives'.[45] On 6 December 1918, following these indignities and injustices, the men of the 9th battalion mutinied and attacked their officers. The breaking point was an order from Lieutenant-Colonel Willis, commander of the 9th battalion, for his men to clean the latrines used by Italian labourers. A number of his men surrounded his tent and slashed it with their bayonets. The following day the 9th and 10th battalions of the BWIR refused to carry out work.[46] In response, the local commander disarmed all BWIR battalions and called for heavily armed white troops to bring order back to the camp. The pay rise owing to the West Indian soldiers was eventually granted by the War Office in February 1919 after the Colonial Office had urged a change of policy.[47]

The damage done to the morale and loyalty of West Indian soldiers after the experience of Taranto, and years of mistreatment during the war, was immense. Following the mutiny, between fifty to sixty sergeants of the BWIR formed the 'Caribbean League' committed to fighting for the rights of Black people and independence for the Caribbean.[48] These men, and other West Indian veterans of the Great War, would play an important role in the radicalising of the West Indies during the inter-war years.

The Halifax and Taranto incidents would reinforce two prejudices in the minds of the British army and War Office. First, that West Indians could not cope with cold European climates – even though the conditions in Halifax were arctic and the Black soldiers who were subjected to it had been dangerously under-dressed. The second prejudice was a belief that West Indians were 'troublesome' – despite the fact that the mutinous behaviour had been provoked by years of injustice and insult. To add insult to injury, West Indian soldiers would be labelled as poor fighters, despite the experience of the First World War (and over a hundred years of the WIR) proving otherwise.

NOTES

1 Writings on the origins of racism include: Peter Fryer, *Staying Power: The History of Black People in Britain*, Pluto: London, 1985, pp133-190; Ben Bousquet and Colin Douglas, *West Indian Women at War: British Racism in World War II*, Lawrence & Wishart, 1991, pp6-14; Ruth Benedict, *Race and Racism*, Routledge & Kegan Paul: London, 1983; 'The invention of whiteness: The long history of a dangerous idea', *The Guardian*, 20 April 2021, www.theguardian.com/news/2021/apr/20/the-invention-of-whiteness-long-history-dangerous-idea.

2 For descriptions of the martial race theory and how it applied to the West Indies, see Michael S Healy, *Empire, Race and War: Black Participation in British Military Efforts During the Twentieth Century*, PhD thesis, Loyola University Chicago, 1998, pp27-36; also Anna

Maguire, *Colonial Encounters during the First World War: The Experience of Troops from New Zealand, South Africa and the West Indies*, Kings College London, 2017, pp89-100.

3   David A J Wells and The West India Committee, *The West Indian Soldier: A brief history of the British Army and the Caribbean*, West India Committee, 2015, pp2-4.

4   Douglas Hamilton, '"A most active, enterprising officer": Captain John Perkins, the Royal Navy and the boundaries of slavery and liberty in the Caribbean', in *Slavery & Abolition: A Journal of Slave and Post-Slave Studies*, Vol 39, No 1, 2018, pp80-100. Also see 'John Perkins: A Black Commander on the Jamaica Station' in *The Naval Review*, 23 February 2023, www.naval-review.com/news-views/john-perkins-a-black-commander-on-the-jamaica-station.

5   Wells and The West India Committee, op cit, p5.

6   Ibid, p7.

7   Humphrey Metzgen and John Graham, *Caribbean Wars Untold: A Salute to the British West Indies*, University of the West Indies, 2007, pp42-4.

8   Ibid, pp44-8.

9   Wells and The West India Committee, op cit, pp45-6; Metzgen and Graham, op cit, pp47-8.

10   Wells and The West India Committee, op cit, p46.

11   Metzgen and Graham, op cit, p48.

12   Ibid, pp49-50.

13   Ibid, p70.

14   Ibid, p78.

15   Richard Smith, *Jamaican Volunteers in the First World War: Race, masculinity and the development of national consciousness*, University of Manchester Press, 2004, p57.

16   Metzgen and Graham, op cit, p75.

17   Smith, op cit, p57.

18   Metzgen and Graham, op cit, pp79-80.

19   CO 137/353/18, National Archives, UK, letter from Charles Darling to the Duke of Newcastle dated 24 January 1861.

20   Metzgen and Graham, op cit, p71.

21   Glenford Howe, *Race, War and Nationalism: A social history of West Indians in the First World War*, Ian Randle Publishers: Kingston, Jamaica, 2002, p16; Marcus Garvey's letter to Colonial Secretary referred to in John Siblon, *Caribbean Soldiers on the Western Front*, African Heritage Forum, 2016, p11; reference to scale of West Indian enlistment compared to the white Dominions is contained in Metzgen and Graham, op cit, p89.

22 Metzgen and Graham, op cit, p91.

23 Arthur A Cipriani, *Twenty-Five Years After: The British West Indies Regiment in the Great War 1914-1918*, Trinidad Publishing Company, 1940, pp8-9.

24 Smith, op cit, p39.

25 David Olusoga, *Black and British: A Forgotten History*, Pan Books, Apple eBooks version, 2017, op cit, chapter 12, paragraph 12; see also Metzgen and Graham, op cit, pp91-2.

26 Michael S Healy, 'Colour, Climate and Combat: The Caribbean Regiment in the Second World War', *International History Review*, Vol 22, No 1, March 2000, pp70-1.

27 Smith, op cit, pp13-24.

28 CO 318/344, National Archives, UK, 'A Short History of the British West Indies Regiment in Egypt' referring to the 'fine physique', p117; later in the file, p170, a separate report from Field Marshal Haig on 'Services of Battalions of the British West Indies Regiment' refers to the 'exceptional' physique of the men. See also reference to press coverage of West Indian troops in Britain in Olusoga, op cit, chapter 12, paragraph 14.

29 Smith, op cit, pp15-6 and 100-117, the figure of 26,667 volunteers is mentioned on p103.

30 Olusoga, op cit, chapter 12, paragraph 22; see also Smith, op cit, p15.

31 Metzgen and Graham, op cit, p90; Olusoga, op cit, chapter 12, paragraphs 15-21, 24-25; Smith, op cit, pp59-61.

32 Erick Trikey, 'One Hundred Years Ago, the Harlem Hellfighters Bravely Led the US into WWI', *Smithsonian Magazine*, 14 May 2018; Claire Barrett, 'Over a Century Later, Harlem Hellfighters to be Awarded Congressional Gold Medal', *HistoryNet*, 16 August 2021; 'Remembering the Harlem Hellfighters', National Museum of African American History & Culture; Harlem Hellfighters Congressional Gold Medal Act, August 2021.

33 Simon Rogers, 'There were no parades for us', *The Guardian*, 6 November 2002, www.theguardian.com/uk/2002/nov/06/britishidentity.military.

34 Olusoga, op cit, chapter 12, paragraphs 27-30.

35 Stephen Bourne, *Black Poppies: Britain's Black Community and the Great War*, The History Press, 2014 and 2019, chapter 2. See also 'The Empire Needs Men: Background Information', published as part of a multi-media resource pack *The Empire Needs Men!*, the Imperial War Museum, 1998, pp5-6.

36 Mark Bridge, 'Euan Lucie-Smith: Plaque for first black officer rewrites history of First World War', *The Times*, 27 October 2020,

https://www.thetimes.co.uk/article/euan-lucie-smith-plaque-for-first-black-officer-rewrites-history-of-first-world-war-vnkdwgbgg.

37   Smith, op cit, p90.

38   CO 318/344, op cit, see pp160-2.

39   WO 95/5370/8, National Archives, UK, diaries of 2nd Battalion West Indian Regiment entry for 9 November 1917.

40   Siblon, op cit, p22-3.

41   Olusoga, chapter 12, paragraphs 15-16 refers to the role of the BWIR in the Middle East; the quotes from Chaytor are taken from Metzgen and Graham, op cit, p96, and Cipriani, op cit, p26.

42   CO 323/1673/3, National Archives, UK, document 2, p2.

43   Cipriani, op cit, p46.

44   See Siblon, op cit, p22; and Metzgen and Graham, op cit, p93.

45   W F Elkins, 'A Source of Black Nationalism in the Caribbean: The Revolt of the British West Indies Regiment at Taranto, Italy', *Science & Society*, Vol 34, No 1, Spring 1970, pp99-103.

46   Smith, op cit, p130.

47   Siblon, op cit, p28.

48   Elkins, op cit, pp101-2.

II

The Caribbean Home Front
in the Second World War

3

First years of war in the Caribbean

In 1939, Britain had cause to worry about the history of rebellions in its West Indian colonies. Would they swing behind the war against Nazi Germany? The answer to this question would quickly come through, but then events of the war in Europe took a series of dramatic turns as Germany invaded the Netherlands and France. This would have a major impact on Dutch and French colonies in the Caribbean and would intensify US anxieties about the impact of the war within its hemisphere.

The US defined its hemisphere, the western hemisphere, as all the North and South American land masses and the North and South Atlantic and territories of Greenland, Bermuda and the Falklands (but not Iceland or the Azores). In the Pacific, the hemisphere encompassed Alaska, the Aleutians, and all islands east of the 180th meridian – which included Hawaii and an area beyond, and south to (but not including) New Zealand.[1] This would be the focus of US military strategy during the war and the years leading up to it.

The early years of the Second World War were crucial ones for the Caribbean. They set the political and military landscape for the region within which the remainder of the war would play out.

THE HYPOCRISY OF THE COLOUR BAR (1938 TO 1940)

As war approached, the British armed forces began to build their strength. They looked at the West Indies as a source of recruitment. However, it was decided that these recruits had to be of 'pure

European descent' – somewhat ironic given the Nazi ideology that they were preparing to fight against. By 1938, a range of legislation and regulations had formalised the colour bar for recruitment into the armed forces. This placed the Colonial Office in an uncomfortable position as it sought to avoid sparking further racial tensions across the empire. The British government was particularly concerned about the position in the West Indies, which was just starting to calm after several years of intense industrial and political upheaval. Despite these concerns, an important part of Whitehall (the War Office) saw the West Indian upheavals as an illustration of why Black people had no place in the army. Since the army would have to play a major role in policing the empire, the War Office believed that Black people should be kept out of the ranks. In short, they could not be trusted to police their own 'race'.[2]

After Britain and France declared war on Germany on 3 September 1939, the Colonial Office continued to lobby for the removal of the colour bar on military recruitment. These restrictions also affected people of colour born and living in Britain. When British born twenty-two-year-old Charles (Joe) Moody applied to join the army, he was dismayed to be rejected because of his ethnicity. His father was the prominent Black, Jamaican-born activist Dr Harold Moody, president of the League of Coloured Peoples (LCP), which he had founded in 1931. The LCP was the main voice for people of African descent living in the UK and would count among its members such prominent figures as the West Indian broadcaster and feminist Una Marson, the Marxist writer and historian C L R James, and the African nationalist Jomo Kenyatta. Dr Moody would be a constant voice of protest about British racism (at home and abroad) during the war.

Three weeks into the war, the Ministry of Information wrote to the Colonial Office expressing its concerns about the colour bar and the negative publicity this was generating throughout the empire. The letter cited the exclusion of West Africans from commissions in the Royal Air Force (RAF), the refusal to accept a Jamaican dentist into the RAF, and the case of Joe Moody. The ministry feared that these, and other cases, could '... constitute a serious handicap to British wartime propaganda, which in colonial territories must be based in no small measure on the contrast between

Nazi racial theories and our own ...' It offered to throw its weight behind the Colonial Office's efforts to change government policy.[3]

A few weeks later, the efforts of the Colonial Office had paid off and the colour bar was lifted in October. But this would only be a pause for the duration of the war. The efforts of the Colonial Office had been supported by another government department – the India Office. Following a similar announcement in the Lords by the secretary of state for India, the Colonial Office issued a press statement on 19 October:

> His Majesty's Government have decided that, during the present emergency, British subjects from the Colonies and British protected persons who are in the country, including those who are not of pure European descent, are to be on the same footing as British subjects from the United Kingdom as regards eligibility for voluntary enlistment in the armed Forces and for consideration for the grant of emergency commissions in those Forces.[4]

Whilst welcomed by most West Indian governors, the decision provoked horror in other parts of the empire. In South Africa, the British High Commissioner summarised local newspaper reaction to the change: 'French have no colour feeling and Kaffirs, Moors, and Indians will lodge together. Those are conditions that will face South African troops if, as appears daily more possible, they are sent to France'.[5] The racist sensitivities of Briton's dominion territories (particularly the southern hemisphere nations of Australia, New Zealand and South Africa) would be a factor in shaping London's policy towards the use of non-white troops.

The formal removal of the colour bar did not mean that discrimination was ended. An internal Colonial Office memo made clear that the change would '... not, of course, mean that British subjects who are obviously men of colour will in practice receive commissions'. Instead, the changes would mean that alternative reasons would be found to reject Black recruits. At the beginning of January 1940, the Cabinet was informed that Colonial governors were under instructions to discourage non-white British subjects from travelling to the UK to enlist.[6] And although the requirement of 'pure European descent' was lifted, the 'British parent' rule was not – all three services still required candidates to be British-born sons of British-born parents, clearly in the hope that this would limit the numbers of people of colour entitled to apply.[7]

Whilst the RAF would eventually relax its position on race, the army and particularly the Royal Navy would continue to ignore the pause on the colour bar. Not content with refusing to recruit Black West Indians into its ranks, the Royal Navy would rub salt into the wound by seeking the support of Caribbean colonies to identify white West Indians with maritime experience who could serve as officers.[8]

PUBLIC MOOD IN BRITISH WEST INDIES AT THE OUTBREAK OF WAR (1939)

In the days immediately after the declaration of war, the British Government waited anxiously for news on the mood of the population of the West Indies. West Indian governors were quickly reporting that Britain's colonial subjects were fully behind King and country. But it was the telegram from Jamaica's governor, Sir Arthur Richards, which drew most attention within the Colonial Office. Richards was fulsome in his praise for the response of the local population and their political and labour leaders:

> The reaction in Jamaica has been unanimously loyal. The way in which all classes have publicly expressed their loyalty and their desire to help is most gratifying and has completely belied the prophesies of unrest. For example Manley and followers of the national party have called off all meetings and political agitation and have publicly said that this is no time for domestic strife. Bustamente [sic] in private correspondence and in published letter has placed the services of himself and the labour unions unreservedly at my disposal.

But he also warned about the urgent need to find an outlet for this surge in patriotism: '... I am apprehensive lest the absence of a means of service should lend colour to the feeling they are not considered good enough to serve their King in war. Last war left many bitter memories of this kind'.[9]

Support for the war effort was bolstered by strong anti-Nazi sentiments among labour leaders. In Trinidad, the trade union movement was issuing strong denunciations of this racist ideology within the early months of the war, stating that: 'Fascism and Naziism [sic] are repugnant to the class conscious workers throughout the world'.[10]

With such strong public support for the war effort, and despite widespread poverty across the region, financial support would flow freely from the British West Indies both through public funds and individual donations. By the summer of 1940, the people of Barbados had already contributed £12,000 towards a 'Win the War' fund. Contributions to purchase bombers and other aircrafts included £7,000 from residents of Georgetown in British Guiana, £20,000 from the people of Jamaica, £5,000 from a local association in the Windward Islands, and £21,000 as a first instalment of contributions from the people of Trinidad and Tobago. By the end of 1942, Trinidad and Tobago (whose oil production placed it among the wealthiest of the Caribbean islands) was proposing an additional $2.5 million (over £500,000) interest free loan to the UK government. This was on top of $5.2 million of loans the territory had already made, and a commitment to make further funds available from any budget surplus in future years.[11]

Among newspapers of the British West Indies, support was virtually universal. Indeed, the first newspaper across the empire to launch a fund to buy aircrafts for the RAF was the *Jamaican Gleaner* in its 'Gleaner bomber fund'.[12]

In Whitehall, Colonial Office civil servants pondered the pros and cons of raising a West Indian fighting unit and one suggested that it might not be worth the effort since their value 'in the last war was considered very low'. It appeared that the history of the British West Indies Regiment and the West India Regiment in the First World War had already been re-written. One senior civil servant (Sir Henry Moore, the Deputy Under-Secretary at the Colonial Office) even suggested giving Britain's West Indians troops to the French: 'I suppose we could not offer the French, who are less susceptible in such matters, to send some W.I. battalions to serve side by side with French Colonial troops'. This suggestion was taken no further.[13]

Despite the reservations of some of his civil servants, the Secretary of State for Colonies Malcolm MacDonald was persuaded by the views expressed by Arthur Richards and others – namely, the political consequences of not involving the West Indian population would be disastrous. In his second report to the War Cabinet, MacDonald gave an update on colonial manpower. He singled out the West Indies as requiring the opportunity to serve in a combat unit and asserted that this was 'of the first political importance'.[14] But despite the call for urgent action, the issue of recruitment into combat units would drag on for years. The Colonial Office's negotiations with the War Office, Air Ministry and Admiralty would prove long, meandering and largely frustrating, with occasional moments of success.

THE DUTCH AND FRENCH CARIBBEAN RESPOND TO NAZI CONQUEST IN EUROPE (1940)

The hopes of the government of the Netherlands to remain neutral were dashed when Germany invaded on 10 May 1940. As its queen and government fled into exile in London, the Dutch state entered a virtual reality for the remainder of the war. It would exercise power through its overseas avatars in the East Indies (Indonesia) and in the West Indies. When, eventually, the Dutch East Indies was conquered by Japan all that remained of Dutch power was its Caribbean colonies: Suriname, Aruba, Curaçao, St Maarten, St Eustatius, Saba and Bonaire. When it came to international relations, its Caribbean colonies had always been an afterthought for the Netherlands.[15] As its global role shrunk to governance of these Caribbean territories the Dutch state would struggle to decide how best to play this hand.

German troops swept into France during the summer of 1940, posing the challenge to French colonies (including those in the West Indies) to choose between supporting de Gaulle's Free France resistance or the puppet Vichy government that had reached an accommodation with the Nazis. With few exceptions, the French colonial establishment chose Vichy. One exception was Félix Éboué, the governor of Chad. Born in French Guiana, Éboué had served as acting governor of Martinique and was subsequently appointed governor of Guadeloupe before the war – the first Black man to serve in such a prominent role in any French colony. He would play a critical role in rallying Chad and France's other central African territories behind Charles de Gaulle and his Free French movement. But Éboué's French Caribbean successors did not follow his example. Instead, Admiral Georges Robert, who in September 1939 had been appointed as France's high commissioner to the western hemisphere and was based in Martinique, imposed a rule of uncompromising loyalty to the new Vichy government.

The early defeat of the Netherlands and France would complicate the geopolitical landscape of the Caribbean. As we will see in the next chapter, it created military and diplomatic challenges for the US and UK, who would not always agree on their approach to the French and Dutch Caribbean territories.

PATRIOTS, ADVENTURE SEEKERS, ANTI-NAZIS AND DISSENTING VOICES

Although West Indian support for Britain was overwhelming, there were dissenting voices. The RAF-veteran and historian, Robert N Murray, describes how some West Indians considered support for Britain as akin to support for imperialism and oppression.[16] Indeed, at the extremes there were instances of hatred for Britain resulting in indiscriminate support for other foreign powers. In Trinidad and Tobago, where disciplinary action against Black recruits in the local navy would result in imprisonment in separate and poorer conditions than white naval ratings, the wall of one prison cell was scrawled with anti-British graffiti: 'God bless Hitler, God bless Uncle Sam and fook [sic] the TRNVR [Trinidad Royal Navy Volunteer Reserve] Navy'. In the period leading up to the war, there were reports of customers at cheap Trinidadian cinemas cheering at newsreel footage of Hitler and Mussolini, refusing to stand for the national anthem 'God Save the King', and praising American visitors, who were seen as different from British colonialists.[17]

But pro-German attitudes were unusual across the region. Indeed, Nazi-sympathisers (or those suspected of such sympathies) faced public hostility and much worse, as was illustrated in one story of a Hitler and Mussolini supporting rail worker who was beaten up by a local man, reported to the police and arrested for treason.[18] Overwhelmingly, West Indians supported Britain because they hated Nazis and felt a sense of loyalty to the 'mother country'. Those who volunteered for military service often had a strong patriotic motivation, but they were also spurred on by a yearning for adventure, peer pressure, a desire to better themselves with new skills or the need for a stable income.

Gerald Beard was a Jamaican carpenter, working with his father, before he joined the RAF:

> I was not all that much interested until one of my friends said to me, 'Why not join up! Join along with me?' He was a very good friend, so I thought I'll do it ... When we were in Jamaica we thought that Britain was the Motherland, so I thought I would be doing a good service in that respect.[19]

Stanley Hodges, a cabinet-maker and son of farmers from the Kingston area of Jamaica, was frustrated with the lack of opportunities available to him: 'West Indians were invited to volunteer for the army and the RAF. My life then seemed to be at a standstill, and when I thought of the possibility of coming to England, the Motherland as we knew it then, I decided to volunteer for the RAF'.[20]

Odessa Gittens was a schoolteacher in Barbados when she heard news that the Auxiliary Territorial Service (the women's branch of the army) was recruiting. She joined the ATS and served in Britain: '... beside my love of Britain (because we were British), I wanted to further my studies and I was not able (because my father and mother had died) to pursue courses which you had to pay for. And I thought this was a good opportunity to do my duty to Britain and to myself'.[21]

Another Barbadian recruit was Marjorie Griffiths. Having heard on the radio about the opportunity to join the ATS in Britain, Marjorie volunteered simply because she 'wanted a challenge'. She explained: 'I'd never even gone to another West Indian island when I left home. I was at the age when I was thinking of doing that, going away on a holiday, and it just never happened'.[22]

When Japan's conquest of the Dutch East Indies, in March 1942, left the Caribbean as the only part of the globe flying the Dutch flag, this had great significance within the region. One volunteer in the Surinamese military reflected:

> Of great importance is that Suriname and the Dutch Antilles remained the only territories on which the Dutch flag still waved freely when the Netherlands was invaded. Suriname and the Dutch Antilles held full responsibility. The Netherlands had fallen out. This territory [Suriname] and the Dutch Antilles were free and we were holding aloft the Dutch flag. For this reason there was a lively awareness that 'we need to join the fight'.[23]

In the French islands of Martinique and Guadeloupe, elected officials attempted to join the Free French forces under de Gaulle, but they were quickly reined in by local Vichy forces under Admiral Georges Robert. The small Jewish community was targeted by the authorities and victimised through property confiscation and dismissals from employment. And as the authoritarian grip intensified, dark rumours spread of a possible return of slavery – a nightmare that particularly resonated in the French West Indies with the history of slavery's abolition in 1794 and reintroduction by Napoleon Bonaparte in 1802.[24]

POVERTY AND INDUSTRIAL ACTION DURING WAR (1939 TO 1945)

The economy of the Caribbean was in a precarious state during the 1930s. For most of the region, the war would bring greater hardship. As a result, industrial and social conflict was inevitable despite early promises by labour and political leaders to curb such actions. The sugar industry, so important to the region, struggled during the early years of war as a result of shipping shortages, rationing and German blockades.[25] In the earliest of his monthly reports to the British War Cabinet on conditions in the colonies, the secretary of state for colonies was informing colleagues that strikes had broken out on the sugar estates of British Guiana, triggered by rumours among workers that their bosses were looking to profit from the war. They returned to work after a modest increase in wages and promises that such profiteering would not occur. A few months later, in January 1940, Trinidad oil and sugar workers were ending their unofficial strike having secured wage increases to address the cost of living pressures.[26]

Labour action to improve pay and working conditions was much wider than a Caribbean issue. In May 1940, in one of his last acts as Secretary of State for Colonies, Malcolm MacDonald was informing the War Cabinet that the development of trade union movements across the empire 'has confronted the Colonial Governments concerned with a whole range of new problems ... For a long time past in the Colonial Office we have been aware of this new problem looming up ...' His report went on to describe a protest involving 600 workers in Cyprus, a strike among Indian labour on the tea estates in Ceylon, and provided an update on the copper miners' strike in Northern Rhodesia earlier in the year, where thirteen strikers were shot and killed by the authorities after 3000 workers attacked the mine company's offices.[27] Nor was industrial action restricted to the poorer parts of empire. Australia, too, saw a wave of strikes and industrial action during the opening year of the war.[28]

Bouts of industrial unrest would continue throughout the war as West Indian populations struggled to maintain the most basic living conditions. In Jamaica and the Bahamas, strikes and unrest occurred in 1942 as unemployment levels rose when construction work on the US military bases neared completion.[29] The numbers of unemployed or underemployed in Jamaica was estimated at between 150,000 and 200,000 by the end of the year.[30]

The landscape of industrial conflict increased anxiety among big businesses about maintaining order and control of labour. This anxiety was exacerbated, among some businesses, by concerns about the loss of white supervisors who they saw as critical to controlling the Black workforce. Within a month of the outbreak of war, the Board of the Demerara Company were lobbying the UK government to encourage white employees to remain on its sugar estates in British Guiana rather than travelling to the UK for national service. The loss of such white staff, they felt, would 'affect the working of the Sugar Estates, and ... the control of native labour, which ... has shown evidence of considerable unrest during the past twelve months'. The governor wrote to sugar estates in the territory requesting that they inform their European employees that the government wanted them to remain on the estates.[31]

For Britain's colonial authorities in the Caribbean, the industrial and political climate made it more urgent to engage the population in the war effort through military service or war-related work. In their view, this would inject greater discipline into the local population, increase gainful employment, and reduce poverty.

PLANS TO RE-IMPOSE FORMAL COLOUR BAR FOR BRITISH ARMY (1940 TO 1941)

Despite the political imperative for Caribbean recruitment, Whitehall was soon discussing the reinstatement of the colour bar for the postwar armed forces. When Dr Harold Moody wrote to the Colonial Office in May 1941 to raise concerns about these proposals, he received an evasive response.[32] Civil servants and ministers in the department were debating how far to press this issue within government. They eventually decide to push the War Office (along with the Air Ministry and Admiralty) to make no commitment to reinstate the colour bar without a formal government position on the matter. The War Office responded in mid July insisting that re-enlistment into the peacetime army would be available only to 'British subjects of unmixed European descent' and that this was necessary because

> ... a large part of the Army served abroad, and that it was undesirable to have coloured men in the ranks of British units in India, Egypt, Singapore, and so on. It is especially undesirable that British battalions and regiments in India in peace, whose role is internal security, should have West Indians or similar coloured people in their ranks. If this was allowed, there would appear to be no reason why Indians should not be permitted to serve in the British Service in India.[33]

The Colonial Office's Welfare Officer, John Keith, had little sympathy with the War Office's arguments and wrote in an internal minute to his colleagues that they should not accept a policy through which 'colonial people of non-European race must be discriminated against to prevent their association with the "master race" in the eyes of coloured people like the Egyptians'. But his colleague, John Calder, argued that they had to accept the War Office's concerns around internal security because the Colonial Office itself insisted on 'the maintenance of a white garrison in Jamaica for internal security duties'. Calder did not stop there, suggesting that in terms of promotion into the officer ranks, the Colonial Office should oppose discrimination on paper, but not in practice: 'I presume we wish the regulation debarring coloured men abolished without expecting that coloured men will actually be given permanent commissions in British military, naval and air units'.[34]

These tensions between those Colonial Office civil servants who argued for a more strident push against racial discrimination, and others who argued for a more cautious approach, would continue throughout the war and beyond. But regardless of the position adopted by the Colonial Office, the Admiralty's response on this issue exemplified the scale of the challenge in winning over departments responsible for the military services. The Admiralty, with great pomposity, made clear that although it understood that the colour bar on recruitment had been lifted for the duration of the war, the recruitment standards for the Royal Navy would 'debar all, or nearly all coloured applicants, even if the bar on their entry were theoretically removed'. This was because, particularly during peacetime, the navy would accept 'only the best material'. [35]

By the beginning of 1942, the Colonial Office conceded defeat and accepted that the War Office would continue with a recruitment policy for the permanent, postwar army that excluded people of colour. All that the War Office conceded was that it would not be possible to predict future policy on the matter.[36] John Keith, clearly disappointed with the outcome, penned another minute to his colleagues in February 1942:

It should I think be decided once and for all as a matter of Cabinet policy whether people of all races who are citizens or sojourners in this country are or are not ranked equal with 'Europeans'. If the answer is yes, and I cannot believe that it would be otherwise, there can be no question that any Department of Government should now or in the future base a policy on racial discrimination.[37]

Keith's expectation that non-discrimination would be a feature of domestic government policy would prove to be wishful thinking for many years to come. In Section Three (Chapters Six to Eleven) we will see the huge efforts it took to make small dents in such policies.

NOTES

1   Stetson Conn, Rose C Engelman and Byron Fairchild, *Guarding the United States and its Outposts*, Centre of Military History, US Army, 1964, p3.

2   Marika Sherwood, *Many Struggles: West Indian Workers and Service Personnel in Britain (1939-45)*, Karia Press, 1985, pp1-2, 4-5.

3   CO 323/1673/5, National Archives, UK, letter from Ministry of Information to A H Poynton at Colonial Office dated 29 September 1939.

4   CO 323/1673/3, National Archives, UK, press statement entitled 'Recruitment of British Subjects from the Colonies in the Armed Forces of the Crown', issued on 19 October 1939.

5   Ibid, newspaper article referred to in telegram from UK High Commissioner in South Africa dated 21 October 1939.

6   CO 323/1673/6, National Archives, UK, minute by Mr Lee dated 14 October 1939; CAB 68/4/6, National Archives, UK, pp2-3.

7   Sherwood, op cit, pp7-8.

8   CO 850/178/8, National Archives, UK.

9   CO 323/1672/3, National Archives, UK, document 2 is a telegram from Governor of Jamaica to Secretary of State for Colonies dated 6 September 1939.

10   Ronald Williams, 'The Exchange: Imperialism and the Impact of World War II on Trinidad and Tobago', in Karen Eccles and Debbie McCollin (eds), *World War II and the Caribbean*, University of the West Indies Press, 2017, Kindle version, paragraph 29.

11   See section 43 in CAB 68/7/1, section 31 in CAB 68/8/13, and minute from Mr Caine dated 18 December 1942 in CO 968/101/10, National Archives, UK.

12 The Gleaner bomber fund is referred to in the wartime leaflet 'Jamaica for Victory', produced by the UK Ministry of Information around 1943 and reproduced as document 'H' in *TOGETHER*, an information and education pack published by the Imperial War Museum in 1995.

13 CO 323/1672/3, op cit, minute from Mr F G Lee on 11 September 1939 and Sir Henry Moore on 13 September 1939.

14 CAB 68/1/31, National Archives, Kew, UK, section 2 on utilisation of manpower.

15 Gert Oostindie and Inge Klinkers, *Decolonising the Caribbean: Dutch Policies in a Comparative Perspective*, Amsterdam University Press, 2003, see chapter 5 'The Dismantling of the Dutch Empire, 1940-1954'.

16 Robert N Murray, *Lest We Forget: The Experiences of World War II Westindian Ex-Service Personnel,* Nottingham Westindian Combined Ex-Services Association, 1996, pp24-5.

17 Pro-Hitler and anti-British graffiti is mentioned in Daniel Spence, *Imperialism and identity in British colonial naval culture, 1930s to decolonialisation*, PhD thesis, Sheffield Hallam University, UK, 2012, p108; reference to cheering for Hitler and Mussolini is in David J Bercuson and Holger H Herwig, *Long Night of the Tankers: Hitler's War Against Caribbean Oil*, University of Calgary Press, 2014, p25.

18 Murray, op cit, p20.

19 Ibid, p23.

20 Ibid, pp23-4.

21 Ben Bousquet and Colin Douglas, *West Indian Women at War: British Racism in World War II*, Lawrence & Wishart, 1991, p108.

22 Ibid, pp110-2.

23 Esther Captain and Guno Jones, 'Inversing Dependence: The Dutch Antilles, Suriname and the Desperate Netherlands during World War II', Eccles and McCollin (eds) op cit, paragraph 5.

24 Eric T Jennings, 'The French Caribbean in World War II: Upheavals, Repression and Resistance', in Eccles and McCollin (eds), op cit, chapter 5. Paragraph 2 refers to opposition from elected officials, paragraph 29 refers to persecution of Jews, and paragraph 32 refers to rumours of reintroduction of slavery.

25 Ligia T Domenech, *Imprisoned in the Caribbean: The 1942 German U-Boat Blockade*, iUniverse, 2014 in Google Books version, pp43-4.

26 See section 7 of file CAB 68/1/31, and section 7 of file CAB 68/4/47, National Archives, UK.

27 CAB 68/6/17, National Archives, UK. See section 38 on the state of industrial relations in the empire, section 40 on copper miners' strikes

in Northern Rhodesia, section 42 on the Cyprus demonstrations, and section 44 on the strike of Indian labour in Ceylon tea estates.

28   R C Wilson, 'Strikes in Wartime', *Australian Quarterly*, Vol 13, No 1, March 1941, pp73-9; CAB 68/6/44, National Archives, UK, section 5 refers to strikes in Australian coalmines and fears of Communist infiltration of the labour movement.

29   Fitzroy André Baptiste, 'Amy Ashwood Garvey and Afro-West Indian Labor in the United States Emergency Farm and War Industries' Programs of World War II, 1943-1945', *Ìrìnkèrindò: A Journal of African Migration*, africamigration.com, December 2003, pp94-5.

30   Sherwood, op cit, p55.

31   CO 323/1673/3, op cit, documents 15 to 19 (from 27 September 1939 to 4 October 1939) are correspondence between the Demerara Company, Colonial Office and governor of British Guiana on concerns about the loss of white overseers from the sugar estates.

32   CO 968/38/10, National Archive, UK, extract of letter from League of Coloured Peoples to Lord Moyne dated 24 April 1941, letter from Harold Moody to Moyne on 21 May 1941 and response from Colonial Office dated 30 May 1941.

33   Ibid, letter from War Office to Colonial Office dated 12 July 1941.

34   Ibid, minutes from J L Keith dated 22 July 1941; file note from J. A. Calder dated 10 November 1941.

35   Ibid, letter from Admiralty to Colonial Office dated 28 July 1941.

36   Ibid, letter from Colonial Office to War Office dated 7 January 1942; letter from War Office to Colonial Office dated 15 January 1942.

37   Ibid, minute from J L Keith dated 25 February 1942.

4

War comes to the Caribbean

Preparations for the possibility of military conflict reaching the Caribbean started as soon as Britain and France declared war on Germany. But before construction work commenced on the US military bases (see Chapter Five), much of the region was not much affected by these preparations. Things were different, of course, in the French and Dutch West Indies where, for the local colonial authorities, their *modus operandi* would change during the summer of 1940. For the rest of the Caribbean, the remoteness of the war would not last.

There were three reasons why the West Indies was too important a region for the Germans to ignore. First, with the onset of war the Caribbean would become a source of vital natural resources for the Allies – resources that were essential for modern warfare. In addition, it was a vital trading route through which vast amounts of goods and materials were shipped across the Atlantic to the UK and up the eastern seaboard of the US. And finally, it was an important strategic location that provided access to the resource-rich southern states of the US through the Gulf of Mexico. All these factors made the Caribbean a strategic target, but there was another reason why the region was important to Britain. The obvious importance of the Caribbean to the US allowed Britain to use it as leverage to draw America further into the war well before the Japanese attack on Pearl Harbor. Because of the region's importance, the West Indies was at the centre of military action during the middle years of the war. Although the history of the Battle of the Caribbean has been told by a number of historians, particularly some prominent West Indian historians, it remains understated in its importance to the outcome of the wider war.

RAW MATERIALS FROM THE CARIBBEAN

War is expensive. It costs vast amounts of money, requires the commitment and sacrifice of huge numbers of people (in the military services and as labour in war production), and consumes an endless supply of the raw material needed to produce and run military hardware. By the end of the 1930s, the Caribbean held no significant economic importance for Western powers. But the region had an abundance of two raw materials that were critical for the Allied war effort. Caribbean oil refineries accounted for around 7 per cent of the global supply of petroleum by 1941, and the heart of this production was the refineries of the Dutch islands of Aruba and Curaçao (refining crude oil from Venezuela) and the British colony of Trinidad.[1] On the eve of war, these Caribbean producers were the largest suppliers of oil to Britain (accounting for around a third of its supply) and Germany (accounting for more than 40 per cent of its supply). As war commenced, Germany would have to seek other suppliers to replace the Caribbean refineries. Trinidad was refining 28 million barrels of oil a year and had the largest oil refinery in the British empire (at Pointe-à-Pierre). It was not just the quantity of oil produced by these refineries but the quality that was important. They produced high quality aviation fuel that achieved better performance from combat aircrafts.[2]

In a BBC broadcast on 22 June 1941, Winston Churchill described the German military as a machine that 'must be fed not only with flesh but with oil'.[3] But oil was also needed, in huge quantities, to keep Britain's machinery of war moving. By early 1942, Britain required four oil tankers every day. These tankers came from across the Atlantic – mainly from the oil fields of Trinidad and Venezuela, via the refineries in Point-à-Pierre and the world's largest refinery on the island of Aruba.[4] The Atlantic supply route was essential to Britain's survival, and the Caribbean played a major part in feeding into the Atlantic chain.

In addition to oil, the Caribbean would supply Britain with almost all the bauxite required for producing aluminium, the key material for aircraft and munitions production. At the outbreak of the war, British Guiana and Suriname ranked alongside the US and France as the biggest global producers of bauxite. The mineral accounted for 20 per cent of the export earnings of British Guiana – Suriname was an even greater exporter. Together, these two territories supplied the bulk of US bauxite imports, which was why the US established a controlling interest in the region's bauxite industry through the Aluminum Company of America (ALCOA) and its Canadian offshoot Aluminum Limited of Montreal, Canada (ALCAN).[5]

In a report on the strategic importance of Caribbean bauxite, US intelligence officer Lieutenant Colonel Chester noted that just one plant at Mackenzie, in British Guiana, produced 90 per cent of the British Empire's supply, which was equivalent to a million tons in 1941. Chester wrote: 'With war's prosecution increasingly dependent on aircraft, and aircraft dependent on aluminium, the bauxite from the Guianas has become the strategic raw material par excellence. Its only competitor, petroleum, can be obtained elsewhere – bauxite, in needed quantity and quality, cannot'.[6]

As a result, Chester recommended the full-blooded military defence of these vital resources. This defence, he said, should be at whatever cost was needed to make them fault-proof. The importance of the region was obvious to all. It was also an important location for the extraction (or transportation) of other key materials such as tungsten, manganese, chromite, copper, tin, industrial diamonds, mica, platinum, nickel and quartz. These were designated as key raw materials, or 'strategic minerals', that were on a list of dozens of materials critical to the successful execution of warfare.[7]

However, despite the importance of the region, Britain's overstretched military struggled to defend the Caribbean and other corners of its empire. This situation was not eased until the US entered the war. But even before its entry, Churchill was keen to persuade America to take on the defence of British (and Dutch) Caribbean territories. As well as easing the pressure on overstretched British forces, there were wider political, economic and strategic benefits in drawing the US closer to the Allied cause.[8]

THE FALL OF EUROPE (1940)

As Germany swept through the Low Countries in May 1940, the fate of the bauxite-rich, oil-producing Dutch Caribbean territories was an immediate concern for the British and French allies. They could not afford to delay. With the reluctant support of the Dutch government that had fled into exile in London, British troops were sent into Curaçao and French troops into Aruba to defend them against a potential German attack. The troops sent to Curaçao were a regular British battalion that had been stationed in Jamaica. Reflecting its continued anxiety about internal security, Britain insisted on replacing the battalion of white troops it had taken from Jamaica with white Canadian forces.[9]

The US had a strong political interest in the West Indies and in European activities in the region. The Monroe Doctrine, enunciated by the United States 117 years earlier, made clear that any European military encroachment on the continents of the Americas would be viewed as an act of aggression against the US. As a result, Washington viewed the British and French military action in Curaçao and Aruba with a mix of annoyance and relief. The annoyance was at being placed in an awkward diplomatic position by two friendly European states that were testing the Monroe Doctrine to the limit. This was compounded by the diplomatic backlash from Latin American states against Allied military action in the region, and concern by the US about how Japan might react across the Pacific. But there was some relief that prompt Anglo-French action had avoided the need for a swift military response from the US to protect these two key Caribbean islands and American business interests.[10]

Before Britain and the US had come to terms with the occupation of the Netherlands, they were rocked by the fall of France the following month (see pp77-9). As this was happening, Italy joined the war in an Axis alliance with the Nazis (Japan would formally join forces with the Axis at the end of the following year). Britain was now facing a period of maximum peril with Hitler in control of a vast stretch of the European coastline, including the French naval ports along the English Channel. The defeat of British forces on mainland Europe, and their evacuation from Dunkirk, had inflicted further loss and damage upon an already battered Royal Navy.[11] The position of the navy was increasingly perilous as it struggled to find sufficient ships to protect the convoys of merchant vessels that provided a transatlantic lifeline to Britain. Faced with this shortage of warships, the Caribbean would shortly play a crucial role in securing for Britain a fleet of fifty American First World War destroyers in exchange for military bases in the British West Indies (see Chapter Five).

In the first nine months of the war, Britain had been able to draw on the supply of French bauxite to support war production, but the defeat of France changed this and made Caribbean bauxite even more vital. As Britain reviewed the security arrangements for the bauxite areas of British Guiana, the security risks were obvious. Although some improvements were made, London took the view that the US authorities were best placed to look after the security of the Suriname bauxite facilities (given the scale of US interest in that territory) and that any improvements made there were also likely to benefit British Guiana.[12] Not for the first or last time, Britain would stand back in the hope that the US would address the challenges involved in defending the Caribbean.

The fall of France also meant that a new solution was required for the defence of Aruba. The new French government withdrew its troops from the island whilst British forces moved in to replace them. As European powers collapsed, many in the US military were anticipating that Britain would be next. Washington's immediate concern was whether the powerful British and French naval fleets could be kept out of German and Italian hands. Although the United States military viewed war with Germany as an inevitability, they were not ready in 1940 and needed time to build a navy capable of fighting across two oceans (the Atlantic and Pacific). Military plans developed at the end of June, and submitted to the president at the beginning of July, predicted that if the Allied navies fell into Axis hands the Nazis would encroach upon the western hemisphere. This, in turn, would embolden Japan who would make aggressive moves across the Pacific area.[13]

In this doomsday scenario, the plans submitted to Roosevelt assumed that the US could not rely on the support of North and South American states (except for Canada). As a result, Roosevelt was advised that there were two key milestones on the path to war. First, the date at which the French or British fleets (or both) fell into enemy hands. The second date would come six months after this, and it marked the point at which the Axis powers would be ready to launch a naval assault on the western hemisphere (it would take six months to carry out repairs to their enlarged but war-damaged fleet). Based on these milestones, Roosevelt was told that the loss of the French or British fleets should automatically trigger the United States' mobilisation for war.[14]

CARIBBEAN GEOPOLITICS AND PAN-AMERICANISM (1940)

The Monroe Doctrine was not only a guiding principle for the US, it also had a strong appeal to many of the independent republics of South and Central America. They saw it as protecting the nations of the Americas from the interference and military jockeying by European colonial powers that had created conflict and instability over centuries. And so, as the turmoil in Europe swept across the Atlantic to reshape the politics of the Dutch and French Caribbean, independent republics of America restated their interests in the affairs of Europe's colonies. The US convened an urgent Pan-American conference, which was held in Havana (Cuba) from 21 to 30 July 1940 and attended by the twenty-one republics of the Americas. The purpose was to consider the implications of the rising Nazi threat in Europe and its impact on the Caribbean. This was not only about the Dutch and French colonies in the region – it was also about the British West Indies. With the rapid march of Germany through Europe during the summer of 1940, many believed that Britain would be the next to fall, creating uncertainty about its West Indian possessions.

The Havana Conference concluded at the end of July by adopting the 'Act of Havana', which agreed that the nations of America could not be transferred from one European power to another. Therefore, in the event of the collapse of Britain and other European powers, their Caribbean colonies would be administered by an inter-American force until the end of the war, at which point they would either be returned to their former colonial ruler or become independent. For the governments of Britain, the Netherlands in exile, and the new Nazi-collaborating administration in France, the Havana agreement was an unacceptable interference in their colonial affairs. However, they had no choice but to accept it. The negotiations that produced the Act of Havana proved to be a precursor to the 'Atlantic Charter', which was signed by the US and UK in August 1941 (four months before the US entered the war).[15] The charter set out a postwar vision that included the rights of all people to choose their own form of government. Despite being a co-signatory, Britain tried to play down many aspects of the Atlantic Charter, particularly those that spoke to the aspirations for independence and economic justice in its colonial empire. This was yet another compromise that the British were willing to make to keep the US happy. In his single-minded focus to strengthen wartime cooperation with the US, Winston Churchill and his government would have to swallow this and many other bitter pills.

VICHY'S CARIBBEAN SATELLITES (1940)

On 16 June 1940, just before its final capitulation to the invading German army, the French government of Paul Reynaud had ordered the evacuation of the gold reserves from the Bank of France. The intention was to ship the gold to Canada where it would be kept out of German hands and, instead, could be used to fund the French resistance. The naval cruiser *Emile Bertin* set off with her cargo of gold, escorted by a fleet that included her sister ship *Jeanne d'Arc*, the aircraft carrier *Béarn*, the destroyer *Le Terrible*, armed merchant cruisers, tankers and cargo ships. The fleet was also carrying 2000 French troops. However, by the time it reached Canada the French government had collapsed and was in the process of being replaced by a puppet government of Vichy France, headed by Marshal Philippe Pétain and operating under strict terms laid down by

Germany. The captain of the *Emile Bertin* received new orders from France to sail to Martinique and, after a brief stand-off with the Canadian government, he was allowed to do so.

Arriving on 24 June, the French fleet and its gold cargo was placed under the control of Admiral Georges Robert, the French High Commissioner to the Western Hemisphere, who was based in Martinique. Admiral Robert saw his role as securing the full support of French colonies for the new Vichy government. Operating as the ultimate regional authority, he would play different ethnic and social groups against each other and undermine the institutions of colonial government to suppress opposition to Vichy. In addition to the 2000 troops who arrived on 24 June with the convoy, Martinique already had a garrison of several thousand French troops. Estimates vary about the quantity and value of the gold cargo, and historians have suggested that it could have been as high as $300 million.[16] In 2022 prices, this would be the equivalent of just under $6 billion.

Thus, the French gold reserves and a significant part of its naval fleet were under the protection of the Caribbean arm of the technically neutral Vichy regime. Germany and Britain were anxious to keep these valuable assets out of their opponent's hands. From 5 July 1940, British naval ships imposed a blockade on Martinique, checking every vessel entering and leaving the island.[17]

The system of government in French Caribbean territories was multi-layered. Each had a governor appointed by the French government. Each governor was supported by a group of advisers drawn primarily from local establishment figures. In addition, there were councils headed by mayors in each commune, and there was a local assembly for each territory that approved the budgets and voted on other major issues. Finally, each territory was represented in the National Parliament in France by two deputies and a senator. The local assemblies (or Conseils Généraux) tended to be dominated by Black and mixed-heritage professionals, acted as a counterbalance to the local colonial government, and were bitterly resented by the small white French Caribbean community known as the *békés*. It was the local assemblies and mayors, unsurprisingly, that spoke out against the Vichy regime.[18] In Guadeloupe, Councillor Paul Valentino spoke at an extraordinary meeting of the local assembly on 1 July 1940 and declared: 'I belong to a race that is loathed by Nazism, and Hitler is now in France. He had announced that he would place France under tutelage and wipe non-aryans from its soil. A misery greater than that we experienced prior to 1789 awaits us'.[19]

During September and October, Caribbean opposition to the Vichy regime was loudest in French Guiana. Aware that the territory was on the verge of swinging behind General de Gaulle's Free French movement, Admiral Robert despatched additional troops to French Guiana to strengthen its political and military authorities and silence the opposition. Having asserted his authority, Admiral Robert would continue to apply an authoritarian grip across the French Caribbean. The authorities under his control stamped out opposition through the detention of opponents and by dissolving the institutions of government.[20]

ROOSEVELT'S VICHY GAMBLE (1940 TO 1942)

Within months of the fall of France, the US government had decided to deal with Vichy France in a way that was at odds with the more strident position adopted by the UK government. Washington had identified two factions within Pétain's Vichy regime. On one side were figures like General Maxime Weygand, the Minister of National Defence, who argued that France should stick strictly to the neutrality terms in the armistice agreement signed with Germany in June 1940. The opposing faction wanted closer collaboration with Germany. In what became known as Roosevelt's 'Vichy Gamble', Washington would try to bolster Weygand and his faction.

The gamble sought to hold France to its position of neutrality, denying Axis powers the resources, equipment and support that might further tip the balance in their favour (at least for long enough to give the US time to prepare for war). And if Weygand's faction could not hold the line, Washington hoped that they might split from the rest of Vichy, taking the remaining element of the French naval fleet with them as they set up a splinter government.[21]

Washington's approach to the new French regime shaped its approach to the Vichy satellites in the Caribbean. As Britain imposed a blockade, Washington negotiated an agreement with Robert that restricted the movement of French naval ships and aircrafts from Martinique, committed them to taking no warlike actions, and prevented the movement of the French gold reserves. Admiral Robert would also allow US military observers to make regular inspections to confirm compliance with the agreement. In return, Washington agreed to ease restrictions on access to frozen French government bank accounts in the US, to be used exclusively to purchase a limited range of supplies such as food, medicines and essential industrial materials. Such were the restrictions applied by the US that Admiral Robert's initial clampdown on French Guiana in September 1940, as he tightened his grip across the French Caribbean, could not have happened without US approval.[22] Washington continued to rely on this agreement, diplomacy and economic pressure to neutralise the French Caribbean. These efforts were continuing after the US entered the war, and after German U-boats took the war to the seas of the Caribbean.

THE BATTLE OF THE CARIBBEAN BEGINS (FEBRUARY 1942)

On Monday 19 January 1942, three German U-boats set off from the French port of Lorient on their way across the Atlantic. Under the codename operation Neuland (German for 'New Land'), they were the first wave that would spearhead a major assault on shipping in the Caribbean. In command was Captain Werner Hartenstein, sailing in U-boat U-156. He was accompanied by Captain Gunther Muller-Stockheim in U-67 and Jurgen Von Rosenteil in U-502. By a twist of fate, on the same day in Whitehall, London, Major Thomas Haddon (Assistant Secretary to the Joint Intelligence Sub-Committee of the War Cabinet) was forwarding a note to the War Office which concluded that 'an enemy "offensive" in the Caribbean is improbable'. Civil servants and military leadership in London and Washington would continue to labour under that false belief until the U-boats struck their first blow a month later.[23]

Whilst the US was formally neutral, Hitler held back from attacking its coastline or the Caribbean for fear of tipping

Washington into the war. However, the Japanese attack on Pearl Harbor on 7 December 1941 changed everything, bringing the United States into the war and making its coastline, and the zones that it controlled, legitimate targets. First, German U-boats targeted the American east coast on 12 January 1942. The attack, codenamed Operation Paukenschlag (or 'drumbeat'), was meant to start on 14 January, but when the first U-boat arrived two days early its captain was so amazed at the lack of American defences that he started the attack immediately. The coastline and merchant shipping, with no naval protection and all brightly lit up like neon targets, presented easy pickings. The freighter *Cyclops* was torpedoed and sunk with the loss of eighty-seven lives. Over the next nineteen days in January, the U-boats sunk thirty-nine ships, including sixteen tankers. The US navy failed to spot a single U-boat. Despite observing the struggles of the British navy during the first two years of the war, including improvements it had made by implementing convoy systems, the US navy was completely unable to protect its coastline and the seas around it.[24] U-boat attacks on the American east coast would continue throughout the year.

It was whilst operation Paukenschlag was in full swing that Germany's U-boat commander (Admiral Karl Dönitz) had despatched the first U-boats to the Caribbean. Departing Lorient in January, they were in the Caribbean and ready to attack by mid February. The Battle of the Caribbean started at around 2am on the morning 16 February 1942 when Werner Hartenstein ordered his crew of U-156 to torpedo the 4000-ton British tanker, *Pedernales*, in the San Nicolas harbour in Aruba. A few minutes later, they torpedoed the *Oranjestad* – another British-registered oil tanker. With both ships leaking their cargo of burning fuel into the sea, the *Oranjestad* did not take long to sink whilst the *Pedernales* burned all night before being towed away to be salvaged.[25]

Hartenstein and the crew of U-156 had not yet finished their night of terror. Just over an hour and a half after attacking the *Pedernales* and *Oranjestad*, they turned their fire on another tanker – the 6400-ton *Arkansas* – sending two torpedoes into it. More burning fuel poured into the harbour as the *Arkansas* sank to the bottom. With mayhem all around them, Hartenstein ordered his

U-boat to surface and fire its deck gun at the oil refinery on the shore. But the U-boat crew made a fatal mistake. In their rush to attack the refinery the crew had forgotten to remove the heavy watertight cover from the muzzle of the 105mm deck gun, as a result the barrel exploded and ripped apart when the gun was fired. The deck gun explosion killed Seaman Heinrich Büssinger and left Lieutenant Dietrich von dem Borne seriously injured. The submarine beat a hasty retreat under fire from the big Allied guns onshore.[26]

The other U-boats continued the onslaught and by the end of the first day of the Battle of the Caribbean, three German submarines had sunk five tankers in the seas around Aruba and Curaçao (the *Oranjestad*, *Arkansas*, *San Nicolas*, *Tia Juana* and *Monagas*) and damaged a further two (the *Pedernales* and *Rafaela*). The attack killed fifty-six people. The only damage to the U-boats was the self-inflicted injury to U-156 caused by its exploding deck gun.[27]

As well as feeling the economic consequences of the war, the Caribbean was now seeing the human costs close-up. U-boat attacks were horrific, as shown in one description of the carnage after a vessel is hit by a torpedo: 'Unarmed crew members who somehow survived the initial torpedo blast and managed to stay afloat in the acrid water suffered a fate worse than death, as frantic chaos reigned amid burning "oil scum ignited by signal flares on life preservers, men attempting to swim in a heavy viscous layer of fuel oil, [and] men trying to swim underwater to avoid flames"'.[28]

A few days into the Battle of the Caribbean (on 19 February) the supply ship *Scottish Star* was torpedoed and sunk by the Italian submarine Luigi Torelli around 600 miles from Barbados, on the Brazil to New York shipping lane. Over sixty crew members managed to scramble into the four lifeboats. Among them was twenty-two-year-old Sid Graham, born in the east end of London to a Barbadian father and English mother. He described the moment the torpedo struck:

> I was having a bath in a bucket and when we got torpedoed I went up in the air and hit my ribs on the washbasin ...

busted 'em ... I got up on the companionway and that's when the submarine started to shell us. Wasn't going down quick enough for him. I was badly hit in the arm. I went in the lifeboat and we got away from the ship and the ship went down ... Luckily enough we were in the Caribbean, not in the cold, but we didn't know where we were going.

Sid's lifeboat sailed for eight days before its survivors were picked up by a Barbadian fishing boat.[29]

The survivors of submarine attacks alerted local populations that the Axis forces were operating in the seas around them. However, these stories were not widely told by West Indian press and radio. News coverage was heavily censored by the Allies and the scale of the German U-boat campaign would be downplayed and largely hidden until well after the war. Although Allied forces were well aware of the devastating impact of the U-boat campaign, they could not keep track of all local shipping that was lost. In the opening days of Operation Neuland, more U-boats arrived in the Caribbean. On the same day that the Italian submarine torpedoed and sunk the *Scottish Star*, the U-boat U-129 (captained by Nicoli Clausen) torpedoed the Norwegian tanker *Nordvagen* two miles off the north-eastern tip of Trinidad. The tanker exploded and sank immediately, with no time to send a distress signal. The authorities had no idea the *Nordvagen* had been the victim of a U-boat attack.[30]

On 26 January, US naval intelligence informed their Caribbean command that a large number of German submarines were entering the Caribbean, but this was ignored.[31] As a result, in the first days of the February attacks, there was confusion across the Caribbean military commands as they tried to identify where the boats had come from. It was widely believed that German U-boats did not have the range to sail from German-controlled ports in Europe and operate in the Caribbean. Instead, immediate suspicion turned to the possibility that the submarines had been sent from Martinique.[32] It did not take long for the Allies to identify that the U-boats had, indeed, sailed from Europe. However, a few days later the role of Martinique in the U-boat campaign would trigger major tension between the Allies and Vichy France.

THE MARTINIQUE INCIDENT (21 FEBRUARY 1942)

The explosion of the blocked deck-gun during the 16 February attack had left Lieutenant Dietrich von dem Borne's right leg so badly injured that it had to be amputated just above the knee and he needed urgent medical attention. Luckily for him, his father was a prominent figure in the German Admiralty. This probably helped when Hartenstein sought permission from U-boat command to take von dem Borne to Martinique for treatment. The German authorities put pressure on the Vichy regime in France, who then instructed Admiral Robert to allow von dem Borne to disembark. Robert duly obliged, although he must have understood the problems this would cause. Having delivered Lieutenant von dem Borne into Martinique medical care, U-156 was back out to sea on 21 February.[33]

The Allied reaction was immediate. Winston Churchill, his Foreign Secretary Anthony Eden, US Under-Secretary of State Sumner Welles, and President Roosevelt were all angered by Admiral Robert's action. But Churchill and Eden were also frustrated that the US had ignored their warnings about the complicity of the French Caribbean regime. For Roosevelt, this could hardly have come at a more awkward time given criticism about his diplomatic approach to Vichy France. The Washington press corps had picked up rumours that a U-boat had dropped off a Nazi officer in Martinique for medical treatment, and when they asked Roosevelt on 24 February whether it was true, he flatly denied it. By now, Washington was issuing strong warnings to Admiral Robert. He was told to guarantee that Axis forces would not be allowed to use French Caribbean bases, otherwise the US would take economic and military action against his regime.[34]

With wider intelligence that Vichy was preparing to render military support to the Germans, Washington demanded that Admiral Robert immobilise all his naval vessels and fighter planes by removing essential parts. On 13 May, he agreed to comply with the US demands.[35]

The Martinique incident was an important point in the deterioration of trust between Washington and Admiral Robert. The relationship continued a downhill path until his eventual (forced) resignation. Roosevelt's administration certainly considered the option of removing Robert by force, but the cost of doing so was too high. A US war department plan for an invasion of Martinique estimated that it would take 21,000 infantry troop, supported by seventy-five fighter aircraft, forty bombers, four cruisers and sixteen destroyers. It assumed that casualties would be anything from 250 to 18,000 men.[36] Even if they were inclined to invade, the US forces in the Caribbean were preoccupied trying to defend merchant shipping against a rampaging fleet of U-boats. For now, they were not ready to act.

SHIPPING LOSSES IN THE CARIBBEAN (FEBRUARY TO DECEMBER 1942)

Operation Neuland got off to a devastating start. After sinking and damaging seven tankers on the first day of the campaign, the Axis forces (mainly German U-boats, but also an Italian submarine) sunk twenty-two ships in the Caribbean by the end of February 1942. This was half of all ships sunk by submarines in the western hemisphere during that month. More importantly for the Germans, seventeen of the twenty-two ships were tankers.[37] And this was only the first thirteen days of the campaign. Admiral Dönitz, commander of all German U-boats, was delighted with the early results. Whilst his submarines were able to inflict such huge losses, and suffer little damage themselves, he resolved to continue the campaign.

After the havoc of February, the Germans and Italians continued their heavy assault on merchant shipping in the Caribbean during the first half of March. The first wave of U-boats was on its way back to the Lorient base when the next wave was despatched to replace it. The sinkings continued in April. The deadly year of 1942 saw many highs for the Axis campaign in the Caribbean, and lows for the people and Allied forces in the West Indies. But of all the months, May was the happiest for the Germans.

For now, the lack of an effective convoy system, ineffective use of anti-submarine aircraft, and poor coordination between the different forces, made life easy for the submarines. The simple strategy of Admiral Dönitz was to sink more merchant ships, of greater size and capacity, than the US and Britain could build. Reducing the merchant shipping capacity would choke the Allies' supply lines. And for now, whilst sinking 700,000 tons of Allied shipping each month, this strategy seemed to be working. During the month of May, one estimate suggests that the Caribbean accounted for 78 per cent of all Allied shipping losses to U-boat attacks. Another estimate suggests that twenty U-boats operated in Caribbean waters during the month, sinking fifty-three merchant ships and damaging a further four, and four U-boats passed through the Caribbean into the Gulf of Mexico where they sank nineteen ships and damaged six.[38] It is not surprising that U-boat crew referred to this period as 'the merry month of May'. The effectiveness of the Caribbean strategy forced merchant shipping to avoid the area and sail further out into the Atlantic. As a result, the submarines adapted their strategy and widened their Caribbean net to ensnare nearby Atlantic shipping too.[39]

But it was not just the effectiveness of their attacks on merchant vessels that made May so fruitful for U-boat captains and their crew. It was also that they were in the warm Caribbean Sea, facing hardly any effective Allied anti-submarine activities. Much better than operating in the freezing north Atlantic, facing the constant threat from naval convoys supported by co-ordinated, anti-submarine air support. On their days off, U-boat crew would hunt, bathe and fish on the many uninhabited islands in the Bahamas or the Virgin Islands. This would not last. The appeal of Caribbean sunshine is obvious when, in off duty hours, you can sunbathe in it. But it would be a very different matter when Allied defences improved and U-boat crew were forced to stay submerged for long periods of time or were not allowed out of the boat when it moved on the surface. Instead, under constant threat of air attack, they endured soaring temperatures as these steel submarines baked under the Caribbean sun.[40]

Table 4: Key Wartime Milestones

Caribbean	Britain, empire & Europe	US	Wider world
War begins in Europe (3 September 1939)			
	Colour bar to British Armed Forces lifted (19 October 1939)		
	Winston Churchill becomes British Prime Minister (10 May 1940)		
Germany invade Netherlands on 10 May 1940, forcing Dutch government to flee and retain control over West Indian colonies whilst in exile (15 May 1940)			
	Italy enters war in support of Germany (10 June 1940)		
France surrenders after German invasion putting French West Indies under control of Vichy France (22 June 1940)			
	Battle of Britain (10 July 1940-31 October 1940)		
	Germany, Italy and Japan formally enter military alliance under Axis Agreement or Tripartite Pact (27 September 1940)		Germany, Italy and Japan formally enter military alliance under Axis Agreement or Tripartite Pact (27 September 1940)
	Slovakia, Hungary and Romania join the Axis forces (November 1940) [Bulgaria join in March 1941]		
RAF start recruitment and training of West Indian aircrew (November 1940)			
US Destroyers for Bases Agreement signed (27 March 1941)			
	USSR join Allied forces after Germany launch attack (22 June 1941)		USSR join Allied forces after Germany launch attack (22 June 1941)

Caribbean	Britain, empire & Europe	US	Wider world
		US declare war following Japanese attack on Pearl Harbor the day before (8 December 1941)	
	Germany and Italy declare war on US (11 December 1941)		
Battle of the Caribbean (16 February to 30 November 1942)			
African American troops deployed in Trinidad (May 1942 to December 1943)		African American troops deployed in Trinidad (May 1942 to December 1943)	
U-boats redirected from Caribbean to support North Africa (November 1942)	'Operation Torch' – Allied invasion of French North Africa (8 November 1942)		
Britain agrees to recruit West Indian women into the ATS (May 1943)			
Admiral Robert forced to resign. This marks the end of Vichy French Caribbean (30 June 1943)			
US start deployment of Puerto Rican troops in British West Indies (late August 1943)		US start deployment of Puerto Rican troops in British West Indies (late August 1943)	
	Italy surrenders to Allies and Germany occupies northern Italy (September 1943)		
British War Cabinet agree to create the Caribbean Regiment (6 January 1944)			
RAF start recruitment of West Indian groundcrew (26 January 1944)			
Caribbean Regiment established (1 April 1944)			
	D-Day Landings in Europe (6 June 1944)		
VE Day – Allied Victory in Europe (8 May 1945)			
VJ Day – Victory in Japan and end of war (2 September 1945)			

The loss of merchant shipping was so severe that during the latter part of May the US was worried that the carnage at sea would embolden the Vichy French naval fleet in Martinique to join forces with the Germans. As a result, the US navy was instructed to blockade the harbour in Martinique's capital city, Fort-de-France. At the same time, Germany instructed two of their U-boats to blockade the harbour because they feared that Admiral Robert and his regime in Martinique would turn against them.[41]

Throughout the year, the scale of the losses inflicted upon the Caribbean was immense. From 16 February to 30 December 1942, a total of 337 ships (totalling 1.87 million tons) were sunk in the region, with an estimated loss of 7000 merchant seamen. One estimate suggests that it accounted for a third of worldwide merchant shipping losses during that year.[42] For periods of 1942, the Caribbean was the most dangerous shipping area in the world.[43] Whilst the U-boats roamed almost at will across the region, some areas of the West Indies (main shipping routes and the seas around strategic locations such as oil refineries) were more hazardous than others. Between 1942 and 1943, a 150-mile area around Trinidad suffered the greatest concentration of shipping losses of anywhere during the Second World War.[44]

British imports of refined petroleum, for motor vehicles and aviation, fell from 4768 tons a week in 1941 to 4114 in 1942, despite an increase in demand.[45] As the loss and damage to Allied shipping mounted, Churchill grew more concerned and regularly expressed his frustration to Roosevelt and his advisers. The wartime prime minister would later reflect in his history of the Second World War:

> The only thing that ever really frightened me during the war was the U-boat peril ... I was even more anxious about this battle than I had been about the glorious air fight called the Battle of Britain ...
>
> How much would the U-boat warfare reduce our imports and shipping? Would it ever reach the point where our life would be destroyed? ... The high and faithful spirit of the people counted for nought in this bleak domain. Either the food, supplies, and arms from the New World and from the British Empire arrived across the oceans, or they failed.[46]

It was not only Britain that had reasons to worry about the impact of the U-boat campaign in the Atlantic and the Caribbean. The US was dependent on Caribbean sea lanes. Although it was by far the biggest oil producer in the world, the US required tankers to transport vast volumes of oil, from its southern oil producing states, through the Caribbean to its oil-thirsty east coast. It did not have the inland pipelines, railway or road haulage capacity to feed its eastern seaboard. Thus, with severe restrictions on merchant shipping, the US was forced to drastically cut oil production destined for these states from an average of 1.42 million barrels a day in 1941 to just 391,000 barrels a day in 1942. It also imported oil from the Dutch islands and Trinidad. General George C Marshall, Chief of Staff to the US Army and Roosevelt's top military adviser, told a senior naval colleague: 'The losses by submarines off our Atlantic seaboard and in the Caribbean now threaten our entire war effort'.[47] Canada suffered as well, relying on a significant portion of its oil imports being transported by tankers through the Caribbean.

IMPACT ON CARIBBEAN LIFE (1942 TO 1943)

Small schooners, transporting goods between islands, were also attacked by U-boats. Large numbers of Caribbean seamen (and non-Caribbean merchant sailors passing through the region) lost their lives. Shortages of common foodstuff and essential materials became the norm.

Caribbean governments were forced to impose rationing, including on products and materials that the region was exporting. During 1942, the supply of fuel across the region was severely restricted, with a reduction of up to 60 per cent. Within the British West Indies, Jamaica was hit the worst. So acute was the shortage that Jamaica's governor, Sir Arthur Richards, was forced to restrict the use of private cars on the island and instructed that horse and carts be used to transport food to the capital, Kingston. Richards did not exempt himself and gave up the use of his official car, which he replaced with a pony and carriage.[48] One local resident, Bertha Williamson, remembered the impact of the oil shortage: 'In the country places where we didn't have electricity we have to use kerosene oil and this became scarce. Sometimes you go out to get half a pint and you have to wait in a queue for the whole day ... And sometimes you have to go home without'.[49]

London was sufficiently worried about the impact on Jamaican unemployment, and the social unrest that this could trigger, that they promised additional financial relief for the island.[50] With Atlantic cargo capacity at a premium, the Caribbean could not export as much of its cash crops. This further aggravated an already bleak economic situation.

In Puerto Rico, around 100,000 tons of food and other supplies were imported each month from the US during normal times. But during the U-boat attacks of early 1942, this fell to between 10,000 and 20,000 tons. In September, it was only 7000 tons. There were reports of fights breaking out over discarded and rotting food, and of hundreds of people converging on the San Juan Crematorium each day looking for food in the garbage. Despite the local government's estimates suggesting that the island's minimum monthly import requirement was 56,000 tons, Washington decided to allocate only 30,000 tons of cargo. The governor, Rexford Tugwell, poignantly described the increasing desperation on the island: 'We sat helplessly on our island while ship after ship coming to us with food, medicines, fire equipment, munitions, and all the other necessities was sunk. Our losses gradually came to exceed survivals. Our hospitals were filled with rescued passengers and seamen; our warehouses were gradually emptied of food'.[51]

For merchant seamen, the threat was very immediate. By March 1942, the number of vessels lost to U-boat attacks was having a major impact on morale. In Curaçao, Chinese sailors who worked for a local shipping company threatened to go on strike. These were non-union workers without citizenship rights, operating as stokers on local tankers. They demanded a pay rise, a war bonus for dangerous work, repatriation to China at the end of their contracts and, most importantly, Allied warships providing convoy protection for their tankers. When they mounted a peaceful demonstration on 14 March, the local Dutch authorities ordered police and military trucks to detain the stokers in a local camp. As other Chinese stokers joined them in an act of solidarity, the numbers interned in the camp swelled to 420. After a month, a riot broke out in the camp on 18 April and the authorities opened fire on the inmates, killing fifteen and wounding forty.[52]

Concern about the willingness of merchant sailors to continue to sail was more widespread than the Caribbean. Referring to Allied shipping losses in the western Atlantic, President Roosevelt's adviser (Harry Hopkins) warned him in April 1942 that: 'I believe the bad effect on the crew, not only of ships in this area but other areas as well, cannot be over-estimated. It is going to be difficult to keep these men at work if the sinkings continue, particularly if they have no escort ...' (see Chapter Eight, pp169-171).[53]

Whilst shipping losses and the pressures of war brought rationing and hardship to people across the Caribbean, the impact in the Vichy-controlled French Caribbean was devastating.

DRIVING VICHY OUT OF THE CARIBBEAN (1943)

The deterioration in US-Vichy relations never recovered after the Martinique incident (see pp84-5). The result was a tightening of the blockade and further restrictions on imports. This was in addition to supply problems, which were already severe. Since November 1940, interruptions in the supply of flour meant that there were periods when the island ran short of bread. In late 1941, meat was only available three days a week, and by 1943 much of the population of Fort-de-France were without meat or fish for weeks at a time (rationing had been introduced in 1942). As food and supply problems grew worse during 1943, the authorities on Martinique assigned 350 soldiers to support agricultural production.[54]

The lack of food was made worse by discrimination in its distribution, with the local population receiving less because more was given to the military. As an example, of the twenty-seven tons of vegetables arriving in Fort-de-France each day in late February 1943, eighteen tons went to the military and five tons to hospitals. This left only four tons to be distributed among the civilian population and even this was skewed disproportionately towards local supporters of Admiral Robert. And within the military, the mainly white navy enjoyed better rations than the mainly Black infantry.[55] Later that year, Robert's bias towards the navy would come back to haunt him when the army failed to rally to his support at his moment of greatest need.

When the Allies launched their successful invasion of North Africa on 8 November 1942, known as Operation Torch, this marked the beginning of the end for the Vichy regime. The forces of Vichy France in North Africa stepped back to allow the Allies to take the region. Germany responded by breaking its armistice treaty and marching its troops into southern France (in preparation for an Allied attack on the Mediterranean coast) effectively undermining any remnant of credibility for the regime of Marshal Pétain.

There was now no need for any type of compromise with a Vichy government that was so clearly under the control of a German occupying force. For the Caribbean arm of Vichy, this brought the end game even closer. During early 1943, Admiral Robert's grip loosened as the French West Indies started to anticipate the liberation of France. First to make its move was French Guiana, announcing its split from Robert on 17 March 1943.[56] In Guadeloupe, street protests across the island culminated in local police and soldiers firing on crowds on the night of 26 April, wounding several people. The US decided that this was the time to move against Admiral Robert. It broke off diplomatic relations and started planning for an invasion. Washington's preparations for an attack were widely leaked by them in order to unnerve the Martinique regime, which worked.[57] As the island teetered on the edge of civil war, the trickle of refugees fleeing Martinique for Dominica, many keen to enlist in de Gaulle's Free French, had turned into a flood – between 2500 and 3000 had arrived by the end of May and numbers were increasing at a rate of 100 a day.[58] During the final weeks of June, Admiral Robert's army deserted him as massive public demonstrations took place in support of de Gaulle.[59] His loss of control and the imminent US invasion left Robert no option but to announce, on 30 June, that he would step down.

THE ALLIES TURN THE TIDE ON CARIBBEAN U-BOATS (1942 TO 1943)

The first three and a half months of the U-boat onslaught inflicted a heavy cost on the American economy and war effort. The risks to US oil supplies became clear within the first three weeks of the campaign as the main supply routes, from the Dutch islands and Trinidad to New York, were attacked. President Roosevelt was lobbied by American oil barons who warned him that there would be insufficient oil to sustain the war effort beyond 1942 if the early shipping losses continued.[60]

By June 1942, the Allies were starting to get the infrastructure in place for good anti-submarine defences. But as the month dragged on, the battle figures still looked very one-sided. By 23 June, the Axis forces had sunk their millionth ton of shipping in the Caribbean (a total of 160 Allied ships) and had lost just one U-boat.[61] By September, Admiral Dönitz was acknowledging that great improvements had been made in the Caribbean defences: 'After the disappearance of single-ship traffic, the area no longer bears fruit. Strong aerial surveillance makes an attack approach against a convoy difficult, if not impossible'.[62]

Towards the end of the year, two military successes on the other side of the Atlantic helped to further improve the Caribbean's defence. In February 1942, German U-boats had received changes to the Enigma machines that were used to encode messages before transmitting them. These, and the changed codes, meant the earlier breakthrough made at Bletchley Park by Alan Turing and his team of code-breakers had been rendered virtually redundant. Previous German changes to Enigma codes had thrown intelligence gathering into the dark until they could break the codes again. However, the February changes would result in the longest intelligence blackout since the initial breaking of Enigma in 1940 and the more complex German naval version in 1941. It would take ten months for the Allies to achieve a breakthrough. That breakthrough occurred on 30 October 1942 in the Mediterranean when U-559 was fatally damaged by a coordinated Allied attack. As the U-boat surfaced to evacuate its crew, it was boarded by a team of three Royal Navy sailors from *HMS Petard* who retrieved vital codebooks before two of them drowned in the sinking submarine. Two months later, the Bletchley code-breakers were using this catch to re-establish the flow of vital intelligence on U-boat movements.[63]

The second success was the Allied invasion of North Africa – Operation Torch – in November. In response to instructions from

Hitler, the next wave of U-boats on their way to the Caribbean were called off and diverted to provide support to Axis forces in North Africa and the Mediterranean. Of the eight U-boats already operating in the Caribbean, six remained during November and managed to sink twenty-four ships – for the rest of the war this monthly tally would not reach double digits.[64] This reprieve allowed the Caribbean's defenders time to regroup, strengthen their defences and prepare for the next onslaught.[65] When the Germans did return in significant numbers eight months later, they found West Indian defences had been much improved.

With his U-boats facing unrelenting attacks from Allied air and naval forces in the North Atlantic, Admiral Dönitz moved thirteen of his fleet to the Caribbean in July 1943, expecting it would be safer and more productive for them. The thirteen managed to sink six Allied vessels. But in return, four U-boats were destroyed in the Caribbean.[66] The carnage was even greater because more U-boats had been despatched to the Caribbean but were sunk in the Atlantic whilst trying to get through, and many of those that made it through would perish on their return voyage. Gaylord Kelshall suggests that a total of thirty-two U-boats were committed to the July offensive in the Caribbean, and more than half were lost, mainly on the outward or return journey from their Lorient base.[67] By now it was clear that the Axis powers had definitively lost the Battle of the Caribbean. The shipping losses inflicted during 1942 would never be repeated in the region. Forty more merchant vessels would be sunk in the Caribbean over the remainder of the war, bringing the combined losses to around 400 totalling two million tons.[68]

Whilst other global events had contributed to Allied success in the Caribbean, it was equally true that victory in the Caribbean would contribute to overall victory in the Second World War. Many historians have reflected on the importance of the Battle of the Atlantic and the catastrophic consequences for Britain if it had been lost. The Caribbean zone could be seen as an ancillary to the Atlantic battle. If key parts of the Caribbean had been lost at an early stage in the war (or, at least, turned into hotly contested territories) Britain would have been starved of vital oil, bauxite and other resources. But it would also have changed the American dynamic.

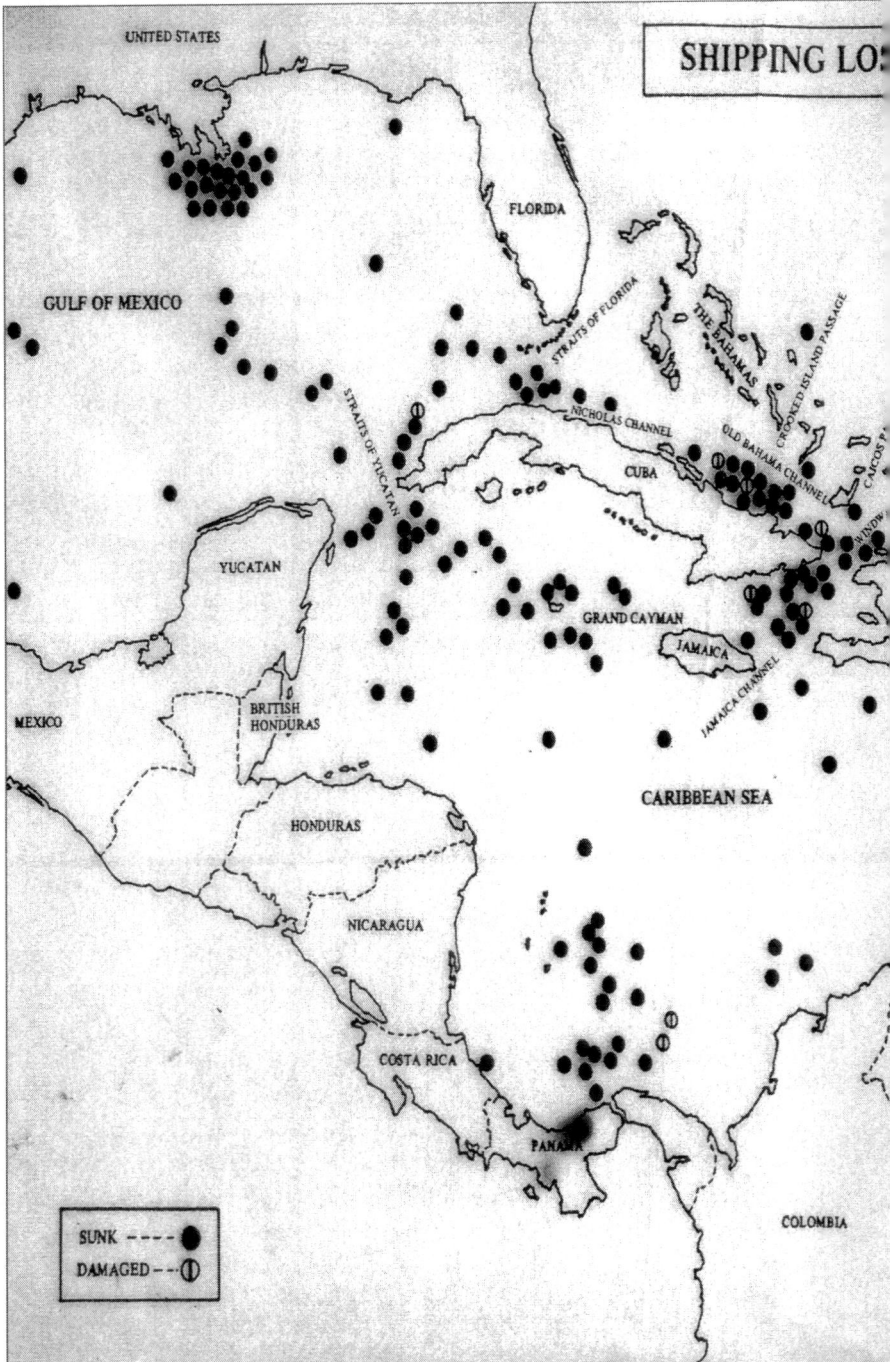

SHIPPING LO[SSES]

Legend:
SUNK ---- ●
DAMAGED --- ◑

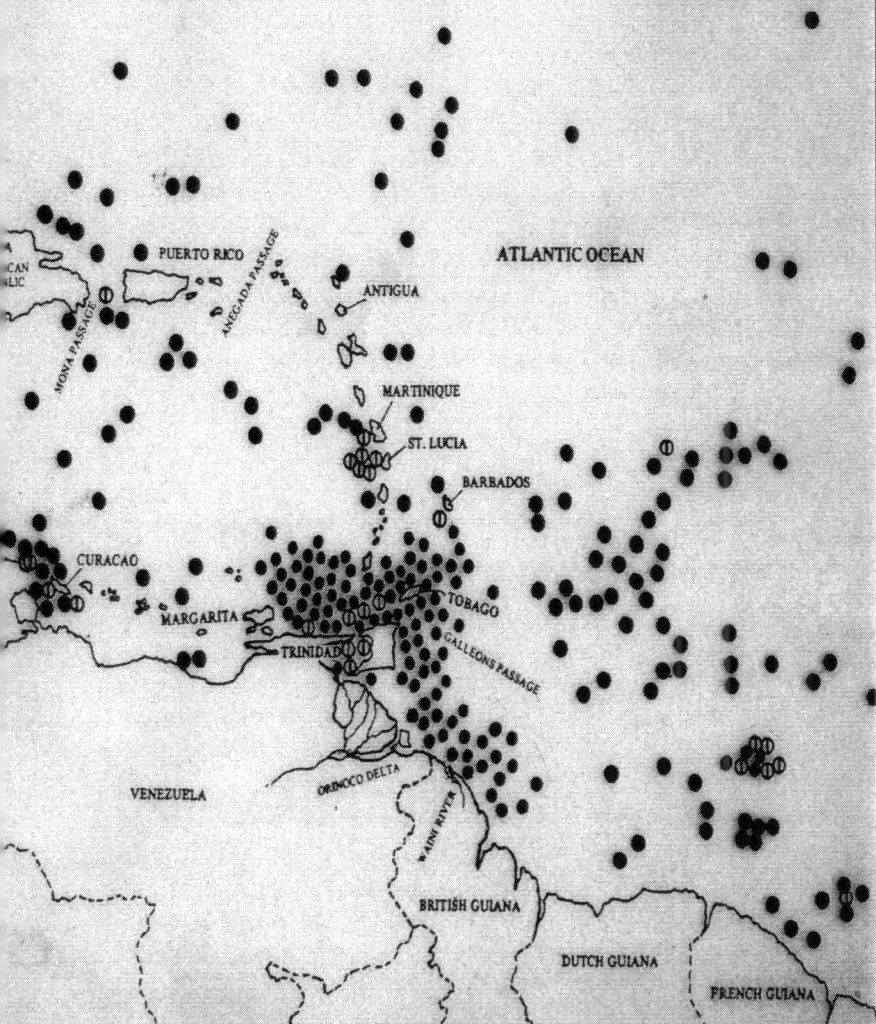

Map of shipping losses in Caribbean theatre in G Kelshall,
U-boat War in the Caribbean (1988). Courtesy Paria Publishing

Upon entering the war, the US had committed to a Europe-first strategy, with the aim of defeating the Axis forces on mainland Europe before turning to the Pacific and Japan. It is inconceivable that they could have stuck to such a strategy had Axis forces occupied parts of the West Indies. The Caribbean is the entry point to the Gulf of Mexico and the underbelly of the US. At all costs, the US would have had to defend its own borders before turning to Europe. It is difficult to believe that Germany could have mounted a successful invasion of key parts of the Caribbean. Although this was a scenario that the Allies had considered (Britain scoffed at the idea but the US gave it serious consideration), the sheer weight of American response to such an event would surely have stretched German military capacity to the limit.[69] However, as the Battle of the Caribbean illustrated, it may have taken time for the US to galvanise its military response. This would have prolonged the war and left Britain in an even more precarious position.

Britain had relied upon the US armed forces (especially its air and sea power) to defend the Caribbean. But for much of 1942, the American military failed to live up to these expectations. This was not surprising because until Pearl Harbor, the US was largely a war spectator – albeit cheering on the British side. Although it had started to build up its war machine, the US had no experience of just how tough and disciplined Germany's modern fighting force had become, whilst Britain (by the end of 1941) already had more than two years' experience. While initially British advice on naval tactics was often ignored (which appeared to be more out of US pride than good judgement), this later changed after hard lessons of failure. Among the most impressive aspects of the US response was the astonishing industrial might that it brought to bear upon the war effort.

Even before its entry into the war, the US had been building its industrial muscle by supplying vital war materials to aid Britain. Through Lend-Lease, America provided a range of military equipment including seven million Enfield rifles, 8250 tanks and antitank guns, 3400 antiaircraft guns and 2100 pieces of artillery (see p180).[70] Aid was also provided to the Soviet Union following the Nazi invasion in June 1941. At the same time, the US was arming itself in preparation for war. This increased industrial output was the final economic stimulant that helped to end the lingering impact of the Great Depression. Therefore, when America formally entered the war, it had already transformed its production capabilities and was ready for the next push. US manufacturers provided a decisive advantage for the Allies and accounted for 310,000 aircraft, 41 billion rounds of ammunition, 100,000 tanks and armoured vehicles, and 2.4 million other vehicles.[71] Their shipbuilders were producing three vessels a day – a much faster rate than German U-boats could destroy them.[72]

America's contribution was not just a matter of numbers. They helped to ensure that the quality of the Allied military machine was constantly improving. There were improvements made in US and UK anti-submarine technology and discipline that managed to outpace German advancements in the stealth, range, and firepower of its U-boats. In the Caribbean, and around the globe, the Axis forces simply could not withstand the immense power of the combined Allied forces that stood against them.

As the dominant Allied partner, America would exert great influence on the affairs of the West Indies in this period in all aspects of life – military, political, economic and social.

NOTES

1 Fitzroy André Baptiste, 'The Exploitation of Caribbean Bauxite and Petroleum, 1914-1945', in *Social and Economic Studies*, Vol 37, Nos 1 & 2, March-June 1988, p122.

2 See Fitzroy André Baptiste, *War, Cooperation, and Conflict: The European Possessions in the Caribbean, 1939-1945*, Greenwood Press: Connecticut, US, 1988, pp9, 30-1, Table 1 61-2; also David J Bercuson and Holger H Herwig, *Long Night of the Tankers: Hitler's War Against Caribbean Oil*, University of Calgary Press, 2014, pp8-10.

3 Full text of the speech is on the International Churchill Society website at: https://winstonchurchill.org/resources/speeches/1941-1945-war-leader/alliance-with-russia. See also Bercuson and Herwig, op cit, p279.

4 Gaylord T M Kelshall, *The U-Boat War in the Caribbean*, Paria Publishing Company Ltd, Trinidad, 1988, p18.

5 Baptiste 1988, *Social and Economic Studies*, op cit, pp110-2.

6 See FO 371/30723, National Archives, UK, report by Sir Connop Guthrie and Colonel Stratton on bauxite production in the Caribbean

dated 27 February 1942, it includes an annex by Lieutenant Colonel Chester of US Intelligence.

7   Bercuson and Herwig, op cit, p10; also Baptiste 1988, *Social and Economic Studies*, op cit, pp107-9.

8   Winston Churchill, *The Second World War (Volume 2): Their Finest Hour*, Cassell & Co Ltd: London, 1949, pp357-8, 362-3.

9   CO 323/1787/74, National Archives, UK, minute by Arthur Poynton dated 28 June 1940.

10 Stetson Conn, Rose C Engelman and Byron Fairchild, *Guarding the United States and its Outposts*, Centre of Military History, US Army, 1964, pp328; also Fitzroy André Baptiste, *War, Cooperation, and Conflict: The European Possessions in the Caribbean, 1939-1945*, Greenwood Press: Connecticut USA, 1988, pp33-7.

11 Humphrey Metzgen and John Graham, *Caribbean Wars Untold: A Salute to the British West Indies*, University of the West Indies, 2007, pp162-3.

12 Baptiste 1988, op cit, *War, Cooperation and Conflict,* p116.

13 Ibid, p41.

14 Ibid.

15 Ibid, pp45-7.

16 Jolien Harmsen, Guy Ellis and Robert Devaux, 'St Lucia and the "Time of the Americans"', in Karen Eccles and Debbie McCollin (eds), *World War II and the Caribbean*, University of the West Indies Press, 2017, Kindle version, paragraphs 6-7; also Bercuson and Herwig, op cit, pp74-6; Baptiste 1988, *War, Cooperation and Conflict*, op cit, pp63-5.

17 Harmsen, Ellis and Devaux, op cit, paragraph 7.

18 Baptiste 1988, *War, Cooperation and Conflict*, op cit, pp66-8.

19 Eric T Jennings, 'The French Caribbean in World War II: Upheavals, Repression and Resistance', in Eccles and McCollin (eds), op cit, second paragraph.

20 Baptiste 1988, *War, Cooperation and Conflict*, op cit, pp199-200.

21 Ibid, pp70-1.

22 Ligia T Domenech, op cit, p53; also Baptiste 1988, *War, Cooperation and Conflict,* op cit, pp71-4, 171-8.

23 WO 32/10092, National Archive, London, letter from Thomas Haddon of the Office of the War Cabinet to Lieutenant Colonel J Y E Myrtle dated 19 January 1942 attached to a note from Denis Capel-Dunn to Colonel Stirling about Caribbean defence; Bercuson and Herwig, op cit, p36 refers to the U-Boats setting off from Lorient on 19 January 1942.

24 Kelshall, op cit, pp12-3.

25 Baptiste 1988, *War, Cooperation and Conflict*, op cit, p142; Bercuson and Herwig, op cit, pp52-3; Kelshall, op cit, pp28-9.

26 Kelshall, op cit, pp29-31; Bercuson and Herwig, op cit, pp52-4.

27 Baptiste 1988, *War, Cooperation and Conflict,* op cit, p143; Kelshall, op cit, pp33-4.

28 Geoff Burrows, 'Puerto Rico and the Caribbean Sea Frontier During the Nazi U-boat Campaign of 1941-1943', in Eccles and McCollin (eds), op cit, paragraph 17.

29 Stephen Bourne, *The Motherland Calls: Britain's Black Servicemen & Women 1939-45,* The History Press, 2012, chapter 2, 'Sid Graham: The Call of the Sea'; Peter Burton, 'Sid Graham, A forgotten Bajan WWII hero (1920-2017)', *BajanThing,* 6 September 2015, www.bajanthings.com/sid-graham-a-forgotten-bajan-wwii-hero; Peter Burton, 'British Ship: SS Scottish Star Torpedoed – 19th February 1942', *BajanThing,* 19 February 2017, www.bajanthings.com/british-ship-scottish-star-torpedoed-19th-february-1942.

30 Kelshall, op cit, pp46-7.

31 Bercuson and Herwig, op cit, p55.

32 Domenech, op cit, pp21-2.

33 Bercuson and Herwig, op cit, pp61-3, 73-4; Baptiste 1988, *War, Cooperation, Conflict,* op cit, pp143, 180.

34 Bercuson and Herwig, op cit, pp77-8; Baptiste 1988, *War, Cooperation, Conflict,* op cit, pp180-2.

35 Baptiste 1988, *War, Cooperation and Conflict*, op cit, pp182-6; Bercuson and Herwig, op cit, pp79-80.

36 Bercuson and Herwig, op cit, p75.

37 Kelshall, op cit, p57.

38 Bercuson and Herwig, op cit, pp154-5 estimate that 78 per cent of sinkings were in Caribbean; Kelshall, op cit, p89 gives estimate of 20 U-boats in Caribbean and four in Gulf of Mexico, respectively sinking fifty-three and nineteen ships.

39 Kelshall, op cit, pp89-90.

40 Ibid, pp84-5, pp326.

41 Ibid, p86.

42 Ibid, pxiv, pp250-1.

43 Metzgen and Graham, op cit, p2; Kelshall, op cit, p112; Burrows, op cit, paragraph 14.

44 Baptiste 1988, *War, Cooperation and Conflict*, op cit, p144.

45 Bercuson and Herwig, op cit, p199.

46 Churchill, 1949, op cit, p529.

47 Bercuson and Herwig, op cit, p199.

48 Domenech, op cit, p41.

49 Oliver Marshall, *The Caribbean at War: 'British West Indians' in World War II*, The North Kensington Archive, London 1992, p14.

50 CAB 68/9/43, National Archives, UK, see paragraph 92.

51 Domenech, op cit, pp90-1, 104.

52 Bercuson and Herwig, op cit, pp120-2.

53 PREM 3/385/5, National Archive, UK, pp297-8 of the file is a telegram from Harry Hopkins to President Roosevelt dated 14 April 1942.

54 Jennings, op cit, paragraphs 13-15.

55 Ibid, paragraph 18; Baptiste 1988, *War, Cooperation and Conflict,* op cit, p198.

56 Baptiste 1988, *War, Cooperation and Conflict,* op cit, pp200-2.

57 Conn, Engelman and Fairchild, op cit, pp439-440; Harmsen, Ellis and Devaux, op cit, paragraph 28; Bercuson and Herwig, op cit, p80.

58 CAB 66/38/11, National Archive, UK, see paragraph 126.

59 Baptiste 1988, *War, Cooperation and Conflict,* op cit, pp211-2.

60 Kelshall, op cit, p58; Domenech, op cit, p26.

61 Kelshall, op cit, p108.

62 Bercuson and Herwig, op cit, p233.

63 Hugh Sebag-Montefiore, 'The boarding of U-559 changed the war – now both sides tell their story', *The Guardian,* 21 October 2017, www.theguardian.com/world/2017/oct/20/enigma-code-u-boat-u559-hms-petard-sebag-montefiori; Bercuson and Herwig, op cit, pp42, 232; Kelshall, op cit, p308.

64 Kelshall, op cit, p239.

65 Metzgen and Graham, op cit, p203.

66 Conn, Engelman and Fairchild, op cit, p437; Bercuson and Herwig, op cit, pp253-4.

67 Kelshall, op cit, pp308-414.

68 Metzgen and Graham, op cit, p159; Kelshall, op cit, p446; Domenech, op cit, p123.

69 See Kelshall, op cit, pp11 where he considers US attitude towards a German invasion, pp17-18 where he speculates about outcome of war had Battle of the Atlantic been lost, pp179-182 where he looks at the scenario of a German invasion of Barbados, and p430 where he considered impact upon the war of Allies having to commit resources to the defence of the Caribbean. Also see Bercuson and Herwig, op cit, pp16 and 31-6 where he looks at US concerns about unlikely attack from German aircraft carrier.

70 Thomas D Morgan, 'The Industrial Mobilization of World War II: America Goes to War', published in *Army History,* No 30, US Army Center of Military History, Spring 1994, p32.

71 Ibid, p34.

72 Domenech, op cit, p28; also Kelshall, op cit, p16.

5

US in the Caribbean

Franklin Roosevelt was describing the strategic importance of the Caribbean to US defence, and predicting the threat of a German submarine assault on the region, seventeen years before he became president and a quarter of a century before the first U-boats launched the Battle of the Caribbean. In 1916, in a submission to the House Naval Committee, he warned that if America entered the First World War, Germany would launch submarine attacks in the Caribbean and Western Atlantic. As the then Assistant Secretary of the Navy, Roosevelt argued for the strengthening of Caribbean defences as a means of bolstering US defences.[1] His predicted threat to the West Indies would not emerge during the First World War but, instead, materialised in the Second.

US DEFENCE STRATEGY (1930s TO 1942)

The Monroe Doctrine, which shaped US defence and foreign policy, was an assertive defence posture. It treated as an aggressor any outside power that engaged in military activity within the western hemisphere. In effect, the Caribbean and South America were seen as buffer zones for the purpose of defending the mainland US. However, its limited military capacity meant the US could not, initially, extend its defensive reach into its Caribbean and South American buffer. As a result, from 1939 Washington had to focus on the defence of the continental United States whilst maintaining significant military outposts only in Panama and Hawaii.[2]

The United States' lofty ambition to act as defender of its hemisphere (for its own self-interest) required armed forces that could cover a huge geographical area. It would take a few years to build this capacity. In the interim, America depended on Britain's Royal Navy remaining intact and sharing the burden of providing a global defence against the Axis forces. The fate of the British naval fleet, and the prospect of the UK capitulating to Germany, was a major worry for Roosevelt's administration during the first eighteen months of Britain's war. Much of the American fleet was stationed in the Pacific to deter Japanese aggression, leaving it unable to muster the strength needed to provide full coverage of the North and South Atlantic. In October 1940, General George C Marshall (US army Chief of Staff), said: 'As long as the British fleet remains undefeated and England holds out, the Western Hemisphere is in little danger of direct attack'. He warned that if the British fleet was lost, the situation would change dramatically.[3] Clearly, Marshall was not anticipating the U-boat attack that would be launched upon the Caribbean a year and a half later.

As Germany swept through Europe in 1940, US anxieties were heightened. Washington's military strategists planned their response to a doomsday scenario where the capitulation of Europe would trigger a revolution in Brazil led by Nazi sympathisers, Japan squaring up to the US in East Asia, and an emboldened Germany launching attacks within the western hemisphere.[4] But Britain held out, and by April 1941 America's military establishment was more confident that the UK could avoid defeat and would be a valuable ally when (as was looking more inevitable) the US entered the war.[5]

As the United States built up its military resources, its defensive perimeter was extended and by 1941 outposts stretched along the Atlantic front to cover Greenland, Newfoundland, Bermuda, Puerto Rico and Trinidad.[6] By July 1942 America had 800,000 soldiers involved in an active military theatre or defence commands. Of this number, around three quarters (approximately 600,000 troops) were deployed in defending the US and the western hemisphere. These defensive forces were split equally between the continental US and garrisons across its hemisphere, including a network of Caribbean military bases.[7] Its bases were necessary to achieve a defensive strategy of engaging Axis forces before they could land on its coasts. Better to have naval and air bases from which it could intercept the enemy ships and aircrafts out at sea – in the Caribbean through its West Indian bases, in the mid Atlantic through its bases in Newfoundland and Bermuda, and in the Pacific through its bases in Hawaii, Alaska and the Panama Canal Zone.[8] In essence, the US would make no significant move to advance the fight in Europe before ensuring that its own borders (and the territories around it) were properly secured. As we will see in the section below, the trading of First World War destroyers to the UK in exchange for military bases in the Caribbean was a deal that benefited both nations. It would also have a major impact on the British Caribbean societies that accommodated these bases.

DESTROYERS FOR BASES AGREEMENT (1940 TO 1941)

It was clear that the Royal Navy was in urgent need of destroyers. At the end of the First World War in 1918, Britain had more than 400 destroyers in its fleet. But by September 1939 this had fallen to a mere 153. Although a shipbuilding programme would address the shortage, it was going to take time.[9] By the summer of 1940, Britain had 171 destroyers but almost half were out of action because of damage inflicted by the German U-boats and Luftwaffe.[10] Churchill made a desperate appeal to Roosevelt on 15 May 1940 for help, asking for old destroyers that could be converted to provide additional convoy support. He wrote to the president again on 11 June, stressing that: 'Nothing is so important as for us to have the thirty or forty old destroyers you have already reconditioned … The next six months are vital'. At the end of the following month, he wrote again, cataloguing the four destroyers lost to U-boat attacks and seven that had been damaged (all over the previous ten days), and stressing his urgent need for the old US destroyers: 'Mr President, with great respect I must tell you that in the long history of the world this is a thing to do *now*'. If this help was not forthcoming, '… the loss of destroyers by air attack may well be so serious as to break down our defence of the food and trade routes across the Atlantic'.[11]

The Dunkirk evacuation further exposed the British fleet as it suffered grave damage and destruction. By the end of the year, the Royal Navy was enduring unsustainable losses. During 1940, twenty-one new destroyers had been built but thirty-four had been lost.[12]

It was not only American destroyers that Britain desperately needed. Indeed, these old destroyers were in such poor condition (having been laid up rusting on the Atlantic coast) that it would take a lot of work to make them battle ready.[13] What London really needed was a US military commitment that would relieve overstretched British forces. Handing the US a network of West Indian bases, along with even greater responsibility for defending the region, achieved this goal. In the hope of America assuming a bigger role, the UK had already been turning its back on the Caribbean to focus military efforts elsewhere. Churchill also hoped that drawing the US further into the war would send a clear geopolitical message that Britain had a strong ally that was 'neutral' in name only. He even hoped that the destroyer deal might provoke Hitler into declaring war on the US, formally pulling it into the conflict – but he recognised this was highly improbable.[14] When eventually a deal was announced, a furious Hitler considered retaliating by invading Gibraltar and seizing French, Spanish and Portuguese territories in Africa and the Atlantic. He gave up on the idea and turned his attention instead to planning for the invasion of the Soviet Union.[15]

Whilst Roosevelt was determined to secure the Caribbean bases needed for his defence strategy, his decision to link them to the transfer of old destroyers to the Royal Navy was a matter of convenience. Restrictions imposed on the US federal government by Congress (through a series of legislation on neutrality) meant that the president was not able to simply give the destroyers to the UK.[16] Instead, he needed a transaction that showed America was receiving something of at least equal value. Ninety-nine-year leases on Caribbean bases achieved this. Churchill, on the other hand, had considerable qualms about this arrangement – he felt it looked too much like a grubby deal and, in any case, the leases were of far greater value than the old destroyers. But Roosevelt insisted that this was the only way to proceed.[17]

The agreement was reached on 2 September 1940 and finally signed, after detailed site surveys, on 27 March 1941. It was a tough series of negotiations which was concluded with Churchill, essentially, capitulating to all the considerable demands made by the American side. Among the most contentious aspects of the agreement was that the US authorities would have criminal jurisdiction over their military bases in the British Caribbean, all personnel working on them, and American soldiers whether on or off base. In exchange for fifty old destroyers, the US received ninety-nine-year leases for land to build bases in eight British territories. In addition to Bermuda and Newfoundland, bases were established in six British West Indian territories – Antigua, Bahamas, British Guiana, Jamaica, St Lucia and Trinidad. Earlier in the month, the US Congress had passed the Lend-Lease Act, allowing the president to lend, lease or gift vast amounts of military equipment to Britain and, eventually, other Allies.[18]

The first US troops, a force of 432 men from the 1st Bomber Squadron, arrived in Trinidad and Tobago on 24 April 1941 and set up camp at Piarco Field. Two weeks later, the ground forces from the 252nd Coast Artillery and the 11th Infantry arrived, setting up camp at Queens Park on the outskirt of Port of Spain and bringing the total garrison strength up to 1487 men. The speed of their deployment, so soon after the final agreement was signed and before construction had started, was an indication of growing concern in Washington at the pace at which the German threat was building.[19]

Although the focus of America's presence in the Caribbean was Panama, Puerto Rico and six British West Indian territories, Washington also had an eye on the Dutch territories of Curaçao and Aruba. Immediately after its entry into the war, the US persuaded the exiled Dutch government to invite its forces to replace British troops guarding these important oil refining islands. On 11 February 1942, a US force of 2300 men arrived on the islands and replaced the 1400 strong British force. The American forces, and their artillery, were not properly installed before the first U-boats struck the islands five days later.[20]

For the duration of the war, the numbers of US troops in the Caribbean peaked at around 110,000 by the end of 1942, but around half were stationed in Panama to guard the canal. With the Battle of the Caribbean turning in the Allies favour from this point onward, the size of the American forces dropped to around 91,000 at the end of 1943 and 67,500 when the war in Europe ended.[21] The leased bases were a vital part of the Allied defence infrastructure, but they would not stay in place for ninety-nine years and were handed back in the 1950s and 1960s.[22]

From the end of 1941 through to the end of the war, the US would play a much greater role in the British West Indies than it had ever done before. This was particularly evident in four aspects of life: race relations, military strategy and planning, economic life, and criminal justice jurisdiction.

US SOLDIERS AND RACE RELATIONS IN THE CARIBBEAN (1941 TO 1945)

As tens of thousands of American soldiers arrived in the Caribbean, the issue of race would inevitably surface. Indeed, local politicians were expressing anxieties before their arrival. Speaking in Trinidad's legislative council on 17 January 1941, Adrian Cola Rienzi said: 'I hope, Sir, that the Americans in coming to Trinidad will not bring to this colony some of the objectionable practices in the Southern States of America. I refer to "Jim Crowism"'.[23]

During these years, there were many stories of American racism in the Caribbean. However, it was no more regular an issue than that of British, Dutch and French racism in the region, it was simply more blatant. One cause of tension between Americans and local men was anger and confrontation over relations with local women.[24] In British Guiana, Colonel Campbell (the commanding officer of the US base) issued written instructions to his officers describing the type of women it was appropriate for them to go out on dates with. He described four racial categories: (a) British White, (b) Portuguese, (c) mixed Portuguese, and (d) mixed Coloured. He made clear that: 'Officers' dates should derive from (a) above and to a very limited extent the upper group of (b) above ... It has been observed in the past that Officers have been seen in Georgetown with eminently undesirable companions'.[25]

Campbell's note, issued in 1943, was circulated around the capital, Georgetown, and produced an immediate public backlash.

The Colonel was forced to issue a swift apology and conduct a round of interviews and meetings with newspaper editors repenting his error. A letter from Mr Kirkpatrick (a Georgetown resident) to a friend in London, described the damage Campbell's note had inflicted on relations with the American forces: 'I'm afraid the harm's already done and no amount of apologies can heal the breach ... The name of the Yank is at present mud in this colony'. Kirkpatrick went on to quote a newspaper article on the matter that said of the Americans: 'it was difficult on mixing with them to tell who was the enemy'.[26]

Whilst the deployment of white GIs generated racial tensions in the region, it was Washington's decision to deploy African American and Puerto Rican soldiers that provoked the most extreme of reactions from British colonial administrators. In May 1942, 2484 African American soldiers of the 99th Coast Artillery Regiment were sent to Trinidad, making up just over 10 per cent of US forces there. The island's governor, Sir Hubert Young, was outraged and made his views clear to local American commanders (who supported his objections) and London. There was concern that higher paid African American soldiers would get into conflict with local men, particularly over relationships with women – which they did. Washington suspected that some of Britain's objections were also about not wanting to expose the Black population of Trinidad and Tobago to much better paid and better educated Black Americans. At the heart of British concerns was simple racism. The local colonial administration did not rate Black soldiers – certainly not in preference to white troops – and nor did the senior US command.[27]

Washington had its own domestic policy challenges on the recruitment and deployment of people of colour in its military. Roosevelt faced constant lobbying from liberal groups on the issue. But he also faced objections from the territories where he sought to deploy Black American soldiers. British, Free French and Dutch Caribbean territories objected to the presence of African American or Black Puerto Rican soldiers.[28] When the US tried to station the 65th Infantry Regiment (a Puerto Rican unit) in Panama to relieve white US soldiers, the Panamanian government expressed concerns. But after the deployment went ahead in January 1943, US authorities were happy with the regiment's performance. The army went on to deploy a small detachment of Puerto Rican troops to guard Batista Field in Cuba in late March. With the Cuban deployment also proving successful, Washington was ready to deploy Puerto Rican soldiers across its network of Caribbean bases to replace its white soldiers.[29]

At the beginning of April, US commanders approached governors of several British West Indian territories to inform them of the plan and get their views. The governor of Jamaica (Sir Arthur Richards) was alarmed and voiced his strong objections, saying any such deployment would be 'a major public calamity, with political and social repercussions of incalculable extent'. With such dire warnings from Kingston, it was hardly surprising that the British Cabinet was being told that the proposals might trigger public disorder in the colony. Jamaicans already had to accept other military units coming from overseas (from Britain, Canada and the US) to protect them from possible enemy attacks, and yet they had not been given the full opportunity to enlist and protect themselves. But in Richard's view, at least these other overseas units were white, whereas the Puerto Ricans would introduce an additional layer of racial complexity and tension.[30]

By now, the Black American GIs of the 99th Coast Artillery Regiment had been stationed in Trinidad for almost a year. It had been an uncomfortable stay – clashes with white American soldiers and Black Trinidadians were common. The island's governor, Sir Bede Clifford (he had replaced Hubert Young the previous year) saw the Puerto Rican issue as an opportunity and a threat. The opportunity was to accept them in exchange for the Americans removing the 99th regiment. But if not, the threat of having to accommodate both African American and Puerto Ricans soldiers was too much for him to bear. When a major fight broke out in mid April between locals and men of the 99th (with seventeen Trinidadians being hospitalised) Sir Bede changed his mind about objecting to the Puerto Ricans and, instead, advised the Colonial Office that he was happy to have them so long as all African American soldiers were removed from Trinidad.[31]

The British government took the matter up with Washington, making clear that it would object to Puerto Ricans being stationed in its West Indian territories. London's genuine anger at the proposals was heightened by increased tensions within the British government over a long running disagreement about the creation of a West Indian combat unit. The presence of Puerto Rican soldiers in the British West Indies would highlight the lack of progress on this issue (see Chapter Six).

Having pushed the matter during May and June, London managed to get commitments from the Americans that the soldiers would be 'white Puerto Ricans', with good levels of English, and would be sent only to Trinidad, St Lucia and British Guiana. The Latin American historian Geoff Burrows believes the US military created a specific category of 'Puerto Rican white' or 'Portorican white', in part, to facilitate this commitment to the British government.[32] The US had also listened to the strong objections from Sir Arthur Richards and decided not to send these troops to Jamaica (or, at least, not in the initial wave). But the British government pushed for more concessions and asked Washington to promise that these arrangements would last only for the duration of the war, the African American troops would be withdrawn from Trinidad, and the UK government would be consulted before Puerto Ricans soldiers were sent to any other British territory. As the first 200 Puerto Rican troops landed in British Guiana on 25 August, London continued to press Washington for further concessions. A note from the Foreign Office in London to the War Department in Washington alarmed the Americans by the willingness of the British government to put its racist objections to the Puerto Rican deployment on paper. Worried that such a document would be made public, the State Department asked the Foreign Office to withdraw it, which they agreed to do (although London was bemused by the sensitivities of the Americans to the points made in the note).[33]

With Britain having overplayed its hand, Washington refused to make any further concessions and the remaining Puerto Rican troops arrived in St Lucia and Trinidad during September 1943, with no reported problems. At the end of October, the US State Department informed Sir Ronald Campbell (a senior British diplomat) that it now planned to send Puerto Rican troops to Jamaica and Antigua. Jamaica's new governor (Sir John Huggins) was thrown by the announcement, and warned London that the local press were already making unfavourable comparisons between the opportunity the US was giving Puerto Ricans whilst Britain refused to give Black Jamaicans similar opportunities to enlist and serve overseas.[34] As we will see in Chapter Six, this issue would provoke Britain's secretary of state for colonies into making a strong, final push to persuade his colleagues in the War Cabinet (and particularly the secretary of state for war) to create a Caribbean combat unit. Despite the warnings of tensions and the risk of major unrest, Jamaica and other colonies reported no problems, and there were descriptions of the Puerto Ricans as having settled in well.[35] The African American soldiers of the 99th were transferred out of Trinidad at the end of 1943, the regiment would be broken up and disbanded the following year.[36]

AGREEING MILITARY STRATEGY AND PLANS (1941 TO 1945)

With vast numbers of men and resources deployed in the region, the US asserted its responsibility for deciding Caribbean military strategy and local defence plans. This created some tensions with Britain's West Indian governors who often found it difficult to defer to American military commanders. Formal arrangements had been agreed for the local British colonial and military authorities to work closely with the US military on defence planning. This would be achieved through the 'local combined defence committees' being convened by the governor of each territory. Despite Churchill's efforts to insert into the US bases agreement a greater degree of British involvement in local military decisions, all he was able to achieve was a set of words in the preamble that referred to the US and UK working in a 'spirit of good neighbourliness' and through 'friendly cooperation'.[37] But this was little more than lip service – in reality, it would be the American military commander who made defence decisions regardless of the views of the local governor or British military.[38]

There were clear differences of views between Britain and its American partners. Churchill's primary concern was the trade routes from the Caribbean into the Atlantic which provided the lifeline to the UK. On the other hand, Roosevelt (although recognising the importance of these trade routes for the UK and the US) was heavily focused on the Panama Canal, and this distorted his strategy for the region's defence.[39] The Canal Zone was a key point connecting Pacific and Atlantic trading routes, and was crucial for enabling the US navy to move quickly between the two oceans.[40] Washington fixated on the risk of a Japanese attack on the canal and ploughed great resource and planning into its defence. In 1941, the UK remained keen for the US to take on the defence of the Caribbean, but believed that America tended to exaggerate the scale of the Japanese and German threats to the region. The consequence of this exaggeration was that too much military resources would be '... locked up in these out-of-the-way places ...'[41] In Britain's view, America needed to scale back its plans, not least because the more ambitious they were the more British military resources would be tied up in supporting them. Britain would change its tune when the Battle of the Caribbean was launched and would then consider American defence strategy and tactics inadequate.

It would be wrong to think that the British authorities in the region were constantly trying to tone down American defence plans. The allies were often able to agree on local plans that were extreme to the point of being callous. In planning for an invasion or raid by Axis forces, British territories had to produce a 'scorched earth plan', setting out how they would destroy local infrastructure and hamper daily life for an invading army. The plan for Jamaica was brutal – not just for the enemy but, more importantly, for the local population. Included in the list of planned destruction across the island was food crop, cattle and horses, food stores 'in excess of day-to-day requirements', and water pumping installations. This would have produced unimaginable hardship for the population. The Colonial Office in London was alarmed by the plans and consulted the War Office for their views. Although both departments agreed the plans went too far, the War Office only believed they were excessive because Jamaica should have planned for a raid – implying that the plans would be fine in response to a full invasion. This left Colonel Rolleston, a Colonial Office civil servant, astonished at the acceptable scale of the destruction, writing to a colleague: 'To my mind the whole [plan] appears unrealistic ... Also, even in the case of invasion, do they mean to destroy food stocks?'[42] But London's main concern was how to tone the plan down without offending their US ally since the local combined defence committee which had agreed them included American senior officers. The Colonial Office sent a carefully worded letter to the Jamaican colonial government suggesting amendments to the plan, and pushed no further when it received a fairly noncommittal response from Kingston informing them that some minor adjustments had already been made.[43]

JOBS AND LOCAL ECONOMIES (1940 TO 1945)

The US had long been a powerful economic force in the Caribbean. Its business interests in the region included the mining of important minerals, and it used migrant West Indian labour in American agriculture and the construction of the Panama Canal. The Second World War would see a further extension of this economic influence. With American agriculture facing a labour shortage as men went off to war, the US government recruited from the Caribbean to fill these vacancies. It is estimated that up to 64,000 men from the British West Indies were recruited to work in the United States during the war.[44] The high levels of unemployment in these colonies meant its people were grateful for all the employment the US could provide. However, the conditions and treatment of Black labour, particularly in America's southern states, were a concern for West Indian workers. At times, even the journey to the US could be fraught with danger and racial antagonism. One example of such racism was the harrowing journey aboard the SS Shanks taking workers from Jamaica to New Orleans in May 1943. With 4000 passengers crammed aboard a vessel with a capacity of 1900, the ship ran out of food and water, and the sewage system failed. It was reported that a Jamaican passenger was 'forced over-board and not accounted for' by the white military police, who were also reported to have abused and beaten other Jamaican passengers. So bad were conditions that one Jamaican organisation compared the experience to the slave ships during the Middle Passage.[45]

In addition to American industries, the US was also creating jobs within the Caribbean through the major construction programme for its military bases. The cost of building the bases in the six West Indian territories (Antigua, Bahamas, British Guiana, Jamaica, St Lucia and Trinidad) was $139.4 million.[46] Washington took great efforts to ensure that American businesses were the first to benefit, therefore most of the construction material was purchased from US suppliers. Indeed, the US War Department took the principle of buying American (a stipulation of the Buy American Act of 1933) to extremes, even though it was allowed to apply exemptions. As a result, fuel was initially imported from the US to supply their Trinidad bases despite the local US commander, General Ralph Talbot, pointing out (with great understatement) that there was an 'adequate' local gasoline supply on the island – it was, after all, the largest oil supplier in the British Empire.[47] The jobs created by the construction of the bases were predominantly local. At the end of October 1941, 44,900 people were employed on the six Caribbean and two non-Caribbean bases, and 7400 were American. In Jamaica, 93 per cent of workmen were locally recruited and in Antigua it was 81 per cent – all the other Caribbean territories fell somewhere between these two figures. For St Lucia, the second smallest construction programme, it meant that the 5215 jobs (at its peak) were filled by 4615 locals and 600 Americans.[48]

With rising costs of living, unemployment, and rampant poverty, the population of the region needed the jobs and pay cheques that US investment provided. However, Britain was keen to avoid importing the inflated rates of pay that came with US labour. As a result, American workers received US wage rates plus an addition for overseas service, whilst local recruits received a significantly lower rate related to the local labour market. This created massive differences in pay. In British Guiana, for example, an American tractor driver would receive $10 a day but a local recruit, doing the same work, would receive only $2.80. Inevitably, this created tension, with local workers striking for fairer pay. There were similar issues in other territories. US troops were called in to control the population when disorder and unrest broke out in British Guiana and Jamaica.[49]

Not only were workers receiving pay way below that of US workers, they were also facing inflation driven in part by the much higher pay cheques of Americans. This was most extreme in Trinidad, which housed the largest complex of military bases in the Caribbean, employing 26,000 people. In addition, the U-boat attacks across the region and its disruption to trade drove prices up even further and inflation was running at around 46 per cent in the British West Indies by mid 1942.[50] In these circumstances, industrial action and unrest in pursuit of better pay and conditions was to be expected. However, paranoid senior US military commanders did not see it this way and suspected that Nazi infiltrators in the local labour movement were manipulating a gullible Black workforce.[51]

If the impact of the American bases' construction programme on local wages was double-edged, the same could be said about its impact on local infrastructure. The concentration of large numbers of workers into communities around construction sites placed great pressure on housing and basic amenities. In St Lucia, construction work on the base at Vieux Fort meant that by mid 1942 its population had quadrupled from 2000 to somewhere between 8000 and 9000 people. The local government failed to match this rapid increase in population with the additional housing, water supply, garbage disposal and other necessary infrastructure. Instead, the town's increased population depended on a muddy and ever more polluted Vieux Fort River (reported to be dark blue in colour) as the main source of drinking water. Residents also faced substantial increases in rent for overcrowded and inadequate accommodation. The area became a breeding ground for pulmonary tuberculosis, venereal disease and gastrointestinal diseases. The last months of 1942 saw the island's greatest outbreak of typhoid, affecting 233 and killing forty-seven people in the town of Vieux Fort.[52]

Although the investment in US military bases across the British West Indies had a mixed impact for Caribbean people, the new jobs it created were welcomed as an antidote to the chronic underdevelopment of the region under British colonialism. Britain's Caribbean colonies were in a dreadful economic state at the beginning of the war. As the war commenced, their immediate future was even bleaker under a colonial ruler that (without American military and economic support) was facing bankruptcy. Given America's stronger economic position and greater interest in the stability of a region that was crucial to its defence strategy, it is unsurprising that it would continue to exert its influence to shape Caribbean economic policy. The Anglo-American Caribbean Commission, formed in March 1942, was a tool through which this influence was exerted. The commission set as its task the development of Caribbean infrastructure, trade, industry, agriculture and education. It was co-chaired by Charles W Taussig (an American sugar entrepreneur) and Sir Frank Stockdale (a British agriculturalist and the head of the West Indian welfare and development fund). Taussig was not only the co-chair of the commission, but also a close friend of Roosevelt. His influence with the British government was illustrated when the red carpet was rolled out for him on a visit to the UK at the end of 1942 during which he met the king, lunched with the prime minister, and was in constant contact with the secretary of state for colonies.[53] The commission advised on the distribution of $25 million a year of US funds, in addition to the funds already committed by Britain for regional development (see Chapter One).[54]

Puerto Rico had a more direct relationship with Washington and benefited from Roosevelt's New Deal with significant investment in local infrastructure and industry. Additional investment from wartime expenditure (construction of bases, building of military infrastructure and recruitment of large numbers of military personnel) added a much-needed cash injection for the economy. On top of these sources of investment, the island received an unexpected bonanza in revenue from rum taxes, particularly during the latter part of the war.[55] Under the guidance of powerful and effective political leaders – Governors William D Leahy followed by Rexford Tugwell, and President of the Senate Luis Muñoz Marín – the island's 'Little New Deal' was implemented with lasting impact.[56] The Puerto Rico Reconstruction Administration, created under the New Deal, spent over $1.36 billion during its first twenty years in operation, with the bulk of this during the period between 1935 and 1943.[57] There is no doubt that Puerto Rico's economy benefited from the various sources of US investment during the war. In return, America's preparation for the defence of the Caribbean (although far from perfect) was in better shape than it would have been without the investment in Puerto Rican military and civil infrastructure.

THE RULE OF LAW IN CARIBBEAN TERRITORIES WITH US BASES (1941 TO 1945)

When the American armed forces arrived in the British West Indies, along with their military equipment, accommodation and transport infrastructure, they brought their own judicial system. The US bases (and all those who worked on them) operated under the jurisdiction of the American military's legal system, with an inbuilt bias towards American forces. US personnel were subject to American legal jurisdiction whether they were on or off the military base. On occasions, American GIs would (literally) get away with murdering local people of colour. Their behaviour produced outrage and brought them into regular conflict with local populations, and generated frustration and anger within British colonial governments that had to deal with the tensions that these actions caused.

In September 1941, a corporal in the US forces was charged with the murder of an Antiguan outside the leased base area in St Johns. A month later, in Trinidad, another American soldier was charged with murder, having shot and killed a local resident. Both cases were tried by the American authorities through court-martials. After the soldier was acquitted in Trinidad, the local colonial authorities reported back to London that a Trinidadian court would have convicted on the evidence. Whilst Trinidad was reeling from this injustice, a second citizen of the small island of Antigua (a population of only 33,000 people) was shot and killed by another American soldier.[58] In the climate of distrust and fear that these incidents provoked, the Antiguan authorities were relieved when Christmas and New Year passed without any further incidents between the local population and American forces.[59]

Trinidad saw another American charged with the murder of a local in April 1942, this time in Arima, near Fort Reid. The case became a cause célèbre, with street demonstrations demanding justice, and thirty-three protesters being arrested. The island's governor, Sir Hubert Young, demanded that the American be turned over to the colonial authorities to face justice in a Trinidadian court, but the US military authorities ignored the demand and proceeded with a court-martial, resulting in another acquittal.[60] The incident drove relations with US forces on the island to a low point.

In British Guiana, a 'posse' of US military police (MPs) raided a Georgetown boarding house and assaulted the owner's son. Their excuse was that they were looking for US personnel who they suspected of being there illegally. The report of the incident described the group of MPs as coming from a station with a record of brutality. As a result of the incident, $550 had to be paid in compensation to the owner of the boarding house and the MPs were charged and brought up in front of a court-martial. Authorities in the colony also reported that there had been several cases of US soldiers raping local women. In these cases, soldiers had avoided prosecution either by getting transferred away from the colony, or by putting pressure on the woman (if she was pregnant) to marry the soldier, who would then file for divorce after the birth of the child.[61]

With America's ever-increasing influence in the region (over defence, the economy, culture and political direction) Britain's colonial leaders felt threatened. Such was the concern that when the Anglo-American Caribbean Commission was launched in March 1942, President Roosevelt felt obliged to issue a categorical denial that the US was seeking sovereignty over the British West Indian colonies with American bases.[62] This did not stop the continuing speculation. In truth, this was not a question of legal sovereignty, but one of power and influence. In that respect, the Rubicon had been crossed and there was no going back on the greater role the US would play in shaping the Caribbean. The Second World War significantly accelerated this trend.

NOTES

1   Claus Füllberg-Stolberg, 'The Caribbean in the Second World War', in Bridget Brereton (ed), *General History of the Caribbean, Volume V: The Caribbean in the Twentieth Century*, UNESCO, 2003, pp83-4. See also Fitzroy André Baptiste, *War, Cooperation, and Conflict: The European Possessions in the Caribbean, 1939-1945*, Greenwood Press: Connecticut, USA, 1988, p2; and Ronald Williams, 'The Exchange: Imperialism and the Impact of World War II on Trinidad and Tobago', in Karen Eccles and Debbie McCollin (eds), *World War II and the Caribbean*, University of the West Indies Press, 2017, Kindle version, paragraph 3.

2   Stetson Conn, Rose C Engelman and Byron Fairchild, *Guarding the United States and its Outposts*, Centre of Military History, US Army, 1964, pp7-8.

3   Ibid, p9.

4   Baptiste, op cit, p40.

5   Conn, Engelman and Fairchild, op cit, pp385-6.

6   Ibid, pp8-9.

7   Ibid, p15.

8   Ibid, pp8-9.

9   Baptiste, op cit, p51.

10 Humphrey Metzgen and John Graham, *Caribbean Wars Untold: A Salute to the British West Indies*, University of the West Indies, 2007, p162.

11 Winston Churchill, *The Second World War (Volume 2): Their Finest Hour*, Cassell & Co Ltd: London, 1949, pp353, 356-7.

12 Gaylord T M Kelshall, *The U-Boat War in the Caribbean*, Paria Publishing Company Ltd: Trinidad, 1988, p2.

13 Churchill, op cit, p535.

14 Ibid, pp358, 362-3; also Baptiste, op cit, p10.

15 Baptiste, op cit, p59.

16 Ibid, pp52-4; Churchill, op cit, p363.

17 Baptiste, op cit, p58.

18 Conn, Engelman and Fairchild, op cit, pp354, 366-375; Metzgen and Graham, op cit, pp162-3; Baptiste, op cit, pp86-100.

19 Conn, Engelman and Fairchild, op cit, pp387-390.

20 Ibid, pp415-6.

21 Ligia T Domenech, *Imprisoned in the Caribbean: The 1942 German U-Boat Blockade*, iUniverse, 2014, Google Books version, p34 estimates US forces in the Caribbean were 110,000 by November 1942; Baptiste, op cit, p215 estimates US forces fell from 110,000 in June 1943 to 91,000 by December 1943, then 67,500 by VE Day; Conn, Engelman and Fairchild, op cit, on p414 give a higher figure of 119,000 and estimate that more than half were based in Panama.

22 Kelshall, op cit, p5; and Jolien Harmsen, Guy Ellis and Robert Devaux, 'St Lucia and the "Time of the Americans"', in Eccles and McCollin (eds), op cit, paragraph 30.

23 Williams, op cit, paragraph 7.

24 David J Bercuson and Holger H Herwig, *Long Night of the Tankers: Hitler's War against Caribbean Oil*, University of Calgary Press, 2014, p188.

25 CO 968/17/6, National Archives, UK, letter from Governor to Secretary of State for Colonies dated 3 July 1943.

26 CO 968/17/6, op cit, Postal & Telegraph Censorship dated 24 July 1943.

27 Domenech, op cit, p63; Bercuson and Herwig, op cit, pp190-1; Füllberg-Stolberg, op cit, pp97-9; Ben Bousquet and Colin Douglas, *West Indian Women at War: British Racism in World War II*, Lawrence & Wishart, 1991, p68.

28 Geoff Burrows, 'Puerto Rico and the Caribbean Sea Frontier during the Nazi U-boat Campaign of 1941-1943', in Eccles and McCollin (eds), op cit, paragraph 28.

29 Conn, Engelman and Fairchild, op cit, pp440-1.

30 CO 968/17/4, National Archive, UK, telegram from Sir Arthur Richards to Secretary of State for Colonies dated 6 April 1943. Also CAB 66/37/25, National Archive, UK, paragraph 90.

31 CO 968/17/4, op cit, see telegrams from Sir Bede Clifford to Secretary of State for Colonies dated 12 and 19 April 1943.

32 Burrows, op cit, paragraph 28.

33 CO 968/17/4, op cit, see telegram from British Guiana on 29 August 1943 about arrival of Puerto Rican troops; telegram from Foreign Office to UK Embassy in Washington dated 27 May 1943; covering note from British Embassy in Washington to Foreign Secretary dated 1 September 1943 and enclosing a copy of the Aide Memoire, dated 14 July 1943, sent by the Embassy to US State Department.

34 CO 968/17/4, op cit, telegrams about arrival of Puerto Rican troops from Trinidad on 3 September 1943, and Windward Islands on 18 September 1943; telegram from British Embassy in Washington to Foreign Office on 4 November 1943; telegram from Jamaica dated 8 November 1943.

35 CO 968/102/3, National Archives, UK, extract from letter from Mr Sabben-Clare on 12 April 1944 saying that the Puerto Rican troops had settled down peacefully and been accepted by the local population; minute dated 17 August 1944 from Mr Kennedy noting that they had received no reports of any problems from Jamaica, this was more than eight months after the arrival of Puerto Rican troops.

36 William C Gaines, 'Coast Artillery Organisational History, 1917-1950, Part I, Coast Artillery Regiments 1-196', *The Coast Defense Journal*, Vol 23, No 2, May 2009, p50, https://cdsg.org/wp-content/uploads/pdfs/FORTS/CACunits/CACreg1.pdf.

37 Conn, Engelman and Fairchild, op cit, pp373-4.

38 Baptiste, op cit, pp111-3.

39 Kelshall, op cit, p6.

40 Bercuson and Herwig, op cit, p14; Burrows, op cit, paragraph 18; Kelshall, op cit, p6.

41   WO 32/10092, National Archives, UK, letter from Offices of the War
     Cabinet to the War Office dated 1 October 1941.

42   CO 968/83/9, National Archives, UK, minute from W.R. Rolleston
     dated 30 September 1942.

43   CO 968/83/9, op cit, see telegram from Secretary of State for Colonies
     to colonial governments dated 29 January 1942 and then revisions
     to these instructions sent on 1 May 1942, letter from Governor of
     Jamaica to Secretary of State on 8 July 1942 enclosing scorched earth
     plan, correspondence between Colonial Office and War Office dated
     15 August and 4 September 1942, minute from T K Lloyd dated
     2 October 1942, letter from Colonial Office to Jamaica dated 14
     October 1942 and response from Jamaica on 14 December.

44   Domenech, op cit, p58 estimates 30,365 were recruited from
     the Bahamas, Barbados, British Honduras and Jamaica. In the
     'Background Information: Some Facts and Figures' leaflet in
     TOGETHER (published by Imperial War Museum, London, 1995)
     an estimate is given of 40,000 West Indians working in the US during
     the war. In Fitzroy André Baptiste, 'Amy Ashwood Garvey and Afro-
     West Indian Labor in the United States Emergency Farm and War
     Industries' Programs of World War II, 1943-1945', *Ìrìnkèrindò: A
     Journal of African Migration*, 2003, pp102-4 provides an estimate of
     just under 64,000 recruits from the Bahamas, Jamaica and Barbados
     between 1943-5.

45   Baptiste 2003, op cit, p108.

46   Conn, Engelman and Fairchild, op cit, pp377-8.

47   Ibid, pp379, 403-4.

48   Conn, Engelman and Fairchild, op cit, p381 for percentage of local
     recruitment across the Caribbean territories; also Harmsen, Ellis and
     Devaux, op cit, paragraph 32 provides numbers for St Lucia.

49   Conn, Engelman and Fairchild, op cit, p381.

50   Baptiste 2003, op cit, p98; the 46 per cent inflation figure is from
     Marika Sherwood, *Many Struggles: West Indian Workers and Service
     Personnel in Britain (1939-45)*, Karia Press, 1985, p55.

51   Conn, Engelman and Fairchild, op cit, pp382-3; also Bercuson and
     Herwig, op cit, p30.

52   Harmsen, Ellis and Devaux, op cit, paragraphs 33-5.

53   CAB 66/33/40, National Archives, UK, section 122 on pp14-5.

54   Domenech, op cit, pp35-9.

55   José L Bolívar Fresneda, 'The War Economy of Puerto Rico, 1939-
     1945', in Jorge Rodríguez Beruff and José L. Bolívar Fresneda (eds),
     Island at War: Puerto Rico in the Crucible of the Second World War,
     University Press of Mississippi, Kindle Version, 2015, paragraphs 1-2.

56 Füllberg-Stolberg, op cit, pp134-5; also Fresneda, op cit, paragraphs 4-5.

57 Burrows, op cit, paragraphs 5-8.

58 CAB 68/8/62, National Archives, UK, section 27 on p11. Also CAB 68/9/5, National Archives, UK, section 33 on p15.

59 CAB 68/9/10, National Archives, UK, section 28 on p13.

60 Bercuson and Herwig, op cit, p193.

61 CO 968/17/6, National Archive, UK, a three-page report on 'US Forces in British Guiana' attached to a letter from the Governor to the Secretary of State for Colonies on 31 May 1943.

62 CAB 68/9/22, National Archives, UK, section 31 on p17.

III

Serving Overseas

6

The fight for a combat role

The strategy of the UK government was one of total warfare. All the resources available to Britain and its empire would be focused on the battle against the Axis forces. The role of the empire in this struggle should not be understated. It was an immediate source of support during the struggle. It was also a backstop so that if Germany had occupied Britain, the empire could continue the fight. In his famous 'We shall fight on the beaches' speech delivered in the House of Commons on 4 June 1940, the Prime Minister described the unbending determination with which Britain would resist Nazi Germany. But it is the last sixty-five words of Churchill's speech that are often overlooked. They articulated the role of the empire in taking the fight forward and the importance of the US in delivering ultimate victory:

> ... even if, which I do not for a moment believe, this island or a large part of it were subjugated and starving, then our Empire beyond the seas, armed and guarded by the British Fleet, would carry on the struggle, until, in God's good time, the new world, with all its power and might, steps forth to the rescue and the liberation of the old.[1]

The Dutch Caribbean provided a model of how defeated European nations might continue to operate vicariously through their colonies. And the British Caribbean was an important prize in luring the US further into a war in which, during June 1940, it was still a neutral party. Given these facts, one would have thought that the armed forces would have welcomed support from Britain's Caribbean colonies. But this was not the case. West Indian men and women seeking to join the armed forces and serve in Europe, or other theatres of combat, were turned away. When colonial authorities were informed, in October 1939, of the suspension of the military colour bar, it was made clear that this was just a formality. Governors were told: '... it is not desired that non-European British subjects should come here to enlist. How you handle this we leave to your discretion'.[2] This presented a baffling contradiction to many observers within the UK and in its colonies – Britain was in desperate need of support yet was turning away volunteers.

The Colonial Office realised that this contradiction was also dangerous. It risked alienating patriotic support within the colonies. It might also galvanise those who were more ambivalent about colonialism and encourage them to join political forces that were campaigning for independence. For these reasons, the Colonial Office would push the case for the creation of a West Indian combat unit. Within Whitehall, this would be a very difficult argument to win. The War Office continued to reject the Colonial Office's case, even when these requests were supported by the Prime Minister. To block Caribbean recruitment, West Indians were described as men of poor fighting quality – despite the history of the West India Regiment (WIR) as an effective, and at times brutal, fighting force. The Caribbean labour revolts, combined with racist stereotyping of the region, led to concerns that this was an 'unruly' population; the role of the British army in suppressing these uprisings was used as an argument against incorporating Caribbean people into the military (although the history of the WIR showed that this had not been a problem for past colonial authorities). On top of these objections were piled a plethora of others, ranging from logistical difficulties with recruitment and transportation to multiple racist anxieties.

Despite the obstacles placed in their way, many within the West Indian establishment saw the creation of a Caribbean combat unit within the British army as the ultimate prize in demonstrating loyalty to the empire. The symbolism of such a unit during wartime was seen as much greater than that of having Black West Indians in the RAF or Royal Navy. Based on the experiences of the First World War, a West Indian regiment in the British army would involve much greater numbers and visibility than the other services could provide. And so, the demand for a combat unit would persist, on and off, throughout the war. It would take years to wear down the opponents to these proposals. Once they were overcome, the British West Indies would face a desperate rush to recruit, train and deploy such a unit.

THE FIRST ATTEMPT TO CREATE A BRITISH CARIBBEAN COMBAT UNIT (1939 TO 1940)

The first of several discussions about the raising of a Caribbean combat unit started two weeks after Britain declared war, on 18 September 1939, when the Secretary of State for Colonies Malcolm MacDonald wrote to governors asking for their views. The responses were mixed. The governors of Barbados, Leeward Islands, Windward Islands and Trinidad and Tobago supported a combat unit in some form, as did Jamaica's governor, although he argued that they should only be sent to a warm climate and not Europe. The governors of the Bahamas and British Guiana suggested recruiting a labour rather than combat unit.[3] And the British Honduran governor, Sir Alan Burns, argued against a combat unit because of the trouble they caused in the previous war, but made clear that his objections related to 'negroes such as were recruited during the last war'. For recruitment of white British Hondurans, he offered his help: 'I would pick them myself after medical examination, but the selection would have to be done very quietly to avoid a rush of black men, who, I presume, would not be wanted. I suppose there would be no objection to lightly coloured men being enlisted for British regiments'.[4]

The Ministry of Information recognised the propaganda value of a Caribbean combat unit. They also understood the negative impact of rejecting such a proposal. In their note to the Colonial Office, they warned that:

> As is well known, certain elements in the British West Indies are already disposed to resent and distrust the European, and there is some danger that opinion may grow that this is in fact an 'Imperialist' war, fought exclusively for British interests. In

order to combat such sentiments, it is clearly essential that no justification should be given to the view that people of colour are being neglected or regarded as 'not good enough' to share in the defence of the Empire.[5]

In his report to the War Cabinet in October, MacDonald described the need to recruit a West Indian combat unit as being 'of the first political importance' (see Chapter Three, p61). He believed this to be a more urgent issue for the Caribbean than other colonies. Winston Churchill, who at that point oversaw the Royal Navy as the First Lord of the Admiralty, spoke in favour of a West Indian combat unit. He suggested that they could be sent to other parts of the empire to allow British troops to be redeployed in France.[6] This would not be Churchill's last intervention on the subject.

However, the responses from West Indian governors and the War Office had indicated that whatever the benefits of such a unit, the timing was not considered to be right. For a start, the Caribbean territories would need to strengthen their own defences before they could spare recruits to serve overseas. Furthermore, the unit would need to be adequately equipped, and military authorities were insisting that this would take time. The final blow came when the War Cabinet's Oversea Defence Committee ruled against the plan on financial grounds.[7] By January 1940, MacDonald was informing the War Cabinet that a West Indian combat unit of any significant size was off the cards for the next two years. Instead, they would look at the feasibility of creating a pioneer unit.[8] The pioneer unit was the equivalent of an armed labour unit – their role was military construction work such as building roads, bridges and other structures. Unlike a pure labour unit, they were armed and trained in military combat. However, the pioneer unit proposals did not last. The War Office believed that West Indians could not cope with the French climate and turned, instead, to Palestine and Cyprus for recruits. In addition, the unemployment situation in the UK featured heavily in the War Cabinet discussion. Although the unemployment rate was falling because of conscription, in January 1940 it still stood at 9.7 per cent or 1.6 million people – but it would fall to less than half this rate by the end of that year and tumble to less than 1 per cent from 1942 until the end of the war.[9]

With its proposals for combat and pioneer units shut down, the Colonial Office spent the first half of 1940 batting off further lobbying from Caribbean governors who grew more anxious about the lack of opportunities for military service. In mid June, as civil servants were contemplating their next move, the newly appointed Prime Minister, Winston Churchill, wrote to Lord Lloyd, newly appointed as Secretary of State for Colonies, raising the question of reinstating a 'West Indies Regiment' of up to three battalions.[10] The reactionary views expressed over many decades by Churchill on race are well documented (though disputed by commentators on the right of British politics).[11] His attitude towards the enlistment of West Indians of all backgrounds appears to have been driven by a commitment to using all the resources at the disposal of the British Empire in the war. Lloyd raised the issue of a combat unit with two of his civil servants – Sir Alan Burns and Arthur Poynton.

The thirty-five-year-old Poynton was a rising star in the Colonial Office who would become its Permanent Under-Secretary (top civil servant) in the 1960s. However, it was Burns who was the more senior official in that June meeting with the Secretary of State. He had just been brought into the department on secondment as an assistant under-secretary having spent six years as Governor of British Honduras. Among the West Indian governors, the fifty-two-year-old Burns had been the most outspoken critic of the proposals for a West Indian combat unit the previous year (see p128). He appears to have been successful in influencing the Secretary of State. At the end of the meeting, Lord Lloyd was satisfied that the proposals to establish a West Indian combat unit 'had no military value', although it was felt that they could be justified in the future for political reasons. He discussed the matter with Churchill, and the proposal was put on hold.[12]

As the war continued to evolve during 1941 and 1942, and the need for military personnel grew, more unsuccessful attempts were made to secure a Caribbean combat or pioneer unit. During these years, the Colonial Office increasingly accepted War Office false-hoods about the poor quality of West Indians soldiers. The only thing that kept the Colonial Office pushing the case for recruitment was lobbying from its West Indian colonies and a recognition of the political imperative. Whilst the British West Indies was dragging its feet on West Indian recruitment (except for the RAF which we will come to in the next chapter), two other Caribbean colonial powers were giving a more prominent role to their local populations.

THE DUTCH CARIBBEAN (1942 TO 1945)

Whilst Britain continued to debate whether to recruit Caribbean volunteers into its army, the Dutch government went a step further. Conscription was introduced across the Dutch West Indies in 1942. Men over the age of eighteen were conscripted into their local armed forces, with 5000 serving in Suriname and 3000 in Curaçao. In addition, the governor of Suriname created a women's home guard with 300 recruits. These men and women served in the Caribbean – protecting this strategically important region – and in Europe where the men fought in the ranks of the Dutch army and the women were health care workers in Belgium and the Netherlands.[13]

Over 700 Dutch Caribbean soldiers were also deployed to fight the Japanese in Indonesia (Dutch East Indies) and were widely praised for their heroism. But these soldiers had reason to be sceptical about the colonial system they were supposed to be 'defending'. Many were motivated by a desire for self-rule in their colonies, including August Hermelijn who believed that 'the sooner the Netherlands was liberated, the sooner we would get some sort of internal self-rule'. The importance of self-rule was reinforced by indignities of discrimination and segregation endured in US training camps before travelling to Indonesia. After helping to defeat Japan, Dutch forces were called upon to put down Indonesian nationalists who were fighting for independence, but many of its West Indian soldiers were reluctant to do so.[14]

AMERICA'S PUERTO RICAN RECRUITMENT (1942 TO 1945)

The United States recruited 65,000 Puerto Ricans into military service. To apply its strict racial segregation, the armed forces first had to place people into racial groups. This presented an additional layer of complexity for Puerto Rico where attitudes towards racial categorisation were less clear-cut than in the continental US.[15] The US navy simply refused to recruit Puerto Ricans because it considered them to be 'natively unintelligent', illiterate, disloyal and poor leaders.[16]

Despite considerable reluctance, the US military simply could not deny Puerto Ricans the opportunity to enlist and serve. The 65th Infantry Regiment was one of a number of all-Puerto Rican units. Most were deployed to garrison other Caribbean territories (see Chapter Five, pp109-112) but many also served in North Africa and Europe (Italy, France and occupied Germany). However, they were not considered a true combat unit. Used primarily as support for other units, the regiment was often referred to dismissively with phrases such as 'palace guards'.[17] Despite their training and preparation, the regiment saw limited combat during the war, with twenty-three of its soldiers killed in action.[18]

Puerto Rican and Hispanic soldiers' experience of discrimination within the US armed forces varied considerably. Some described racism similar to that seen by African Americans, others described prejudice on a lesser scale, and some said they faced no discrimination at all. For many who did experience problems, it was a cocktail of prejudice based on race, skin colour, language and accent.[19]

WAR OFFICE TAKES CONTROL OF BRITISH WEST INDIAN DEFENCE FORCES (1941 TO 1943)

The British West Indian local defence forces had emerged out of a history of local militia created to defend against European aggressors and local revolts by the Black populations. These forces were controlled by the local governors who, in turn, answered to the government in London. By the mid nineteenth century the government department these governors reported to was the Colonial Office. The war brought home to the UK government that this arrangement was not sustainable. In the face of an enemy power as efficient as Germany, the ragbag defence arrangements of its Caribbean colonies required urgent modernisation.

The only British regular forces immediately available to its governors was a battalion based in Jamaica and Bermuda (but the force located in Jamaica had been dispatched in 1940 to garrison Curaçao and Aruba following the fall of the Netherlands and France). The West India Regiment, which had played a major role in British West Indian defence and security, had been disbanded in 1927 after 132 years of service. In 1942, the combined strength of British forces in its Caribbean colonies was 5297 (of which 4399 were local colonial forces and the rest were British regular forces).[20]

After the US joined the war and restructured its own Caribbean command, Britain carried out a review of its local colonial forces. The report the War Office received on the state of the Caribbean colonial forces was damning, with those of Dominica, Montserrat, St Lucia, St Vincent and Grenada considered so weak as to have no military value. Across Barbados, the Leeward Islands and the Windward Islands, 80 per cent of police rifles were unusable.[21] Alarmed by this report, and keen to ensure adequate coordination with its American partners, the War Office requested an urgent meeting with the Colonial Office.[22] At that meeting they agreed to place the local forces under the direction of the War Office, increase their strength by 848 men to bring them up to a total of 6812, and improve coordination with US military command.[23]

The new command structures were put in place on 1 October 1942. By early 1943, Colonial Office officials were secretly hopeful that War Office confidence in the Caribbean's colonial forces would be improved by having direct control over them and responsibility for their development. They might be more likely to agree to the creation of a Caribbean combat unit if the proposal came from their own local military commanders. At an internal Colonial Office meeting on 12 April 1943, civil servants decided to give it six months for this plan to work, and then raise the issue once more.[24] Rather than six months, it took eight days for this plan to look as if it would bear fruit.

THE FINAL ATTEMPT TO CREATE A BRITISH CARIBBEAN COMBAT UNIT (1943 TO 1944)

On 20 April 1943 the War Office wrote to the Colonial Office to say it was considering, once more, the possibility of using a

West Indian combat unit in an active theatre of war. It suggested Madagascar, Ceylon or Burma as possible locations, but stressed that there were still numerous logistical and operational issues to be overcome before a final decision could be made.[25]

The Colonial Office welcomed with enthusiasm the War Office proposals, pointing out that West Indians had been recruited into the RAF (as air and ground crew) for several years, and were being recruited into skilled trades in the army. The lack of an overseas combat role in the army was therefore starker – particularly since other parts of the empire had been permitted to serve in such units. But the location proposed by the War Office was not considered 'active' enough and, instead, the Colonial Office proposed North Africa as closer to enemy action. After a few months, the War Office tried to back away from the idea, yet again, because of continued pressure on shipping.[26] The shipping shortage was, undoubtedly, a real problem in the Caribbean. The previous year, in June 1942, the Minister for War Transport Philip Noel-Baker was reluctantly informing the Colonial Office that he could not support plans for a West Indian pioneer unit because 'the West Indies is now the most dangerous place in the whole world for a ship to go to at the present time. In consequence, the Admiralty would have to send a specially [sic] strong escort to convoy the small number of ships required to carry out your plan'.[27]

In addition to the obstacles of logistics and War Office racism, the Colonial Office was also facing pressures from another quarter. Much to its embarrassment, whilst Britain was failing to recruit a combat or pioneer unit, many dozens of British West Indians of all ethnicities had been travelling to Canada to join the Canadian army. A number of these recruits were subsequently deployed in Britain.[28]

Therefore, by the spring of 1943 a broad range of issues made it more difficult than ever to justify the lack of a West Indian combat unit: governors were more supportive and impatient for progress; the Prime Minister had given his backing to these proposals on a number of occasions; the deployment of Puerto Ricans to garrison Caribbean territories had further exposed the absence of such a role for British West Indians; senior British commanders of the Caribbean colonial forces (now under direct War Office control) favoured a combat unit and were promoting the idea to their Whitehall masters; and West Indians were serving in the Canadian forces with some stationed in England. Despite growing scepticism within the Colonial Office about the military case for a Caribbean combat unit, the political case was now seen as both imperative and urgent. They would not take a further War Office rejection lying down.

Whilst battling with the War Office over the recruitment of West Indian men into overseas combat roles, the Colonial Office had also been pushing for the recruitment of Black West Indian women into the Auxiliary Territorial Service (ATS) to serve both in the Caribbean and in the UK. The ATS was the women's branch of the British army. In May 1943 the Colonial Office had secured War Office agreement to a Caribbean ATS recruitment scheme. This involved roles for white West Indian women in Washington DC, and for West Indians of all backgrounds to serve in the Caribbean and British ATS (see Chapter Nine on the role of women).

Oliver Stanley had been Secretary of State for Colonies for nine months when, on 9 August 1943, he wrote to James Grigg (now Secretary of State for War) reiterating the urgent need for a West Indian combat unit and urging the War Office to change its mind. In particular, Stanley stressed the embarrassment caused by Puerto Rican troops being deployed overseas when Black West Indians were not given a similar opportunity. He would subsequently conclude that it was this argument that had a greater impact on Grigg than any of the other points raised.[29] Through the contorted prism of racism with which Whitehall viewed the world, Stanley noted that:

These Puerto Ricans however white they may be in their own estimation, will not be accepted as such by the West Indians and, unless a West Indian contingent is sent overseas to a war theatre, they will inevitably feel that, not only are they thought incapable of overseas service, but considered so inferior that coloured troops of a foreign nation must be brought in to garrison their own Islands for them.[30]

Responding on 23 September, Grigg accepted that there were strong political grounds for creating such a unit but insisted there was no military justification, despite the fact that his own Caribbean commanders were saying differently and arguing against almost every objection raised in his letter.[31] Grigg was an unusual cabinet minister. He was the top civil servant (permanent under-secretary) at the War Office before Churchill made him secretary of state. This meant he had to secure a seat in Parliament, which he did by winning the Cardiff East by-election in April 1942. His civil service background meant he had been deeply involved, at the War Office, in scuppering every previous attempt to raise a Caribbean combat unit. In search of additional arguments against the combat unit, Grigg threw into the mix that Britain was facing enough racial problems with the arrival of large numbers of African American troops as part of the build-up of US forces for D-Day. In his view, Black West Indians would make an already difficult situation even worse. This was a particularly bizarre point since the combat unit proposals did not involve stationing West Indian troops in Britain, but in North Africa or another overseas theatre. With his arguments running thin, and no signs that the political pressure behind these proposals would go away, Grigg reluctantly accepted the inevitable. In a meeting with Stanley on 12 November, Grigg agreed to withdraw his objections. A month later he set out the War Office's suggestions on how to put the unit in place, whilst ungraciously still insisting that although he would go along with the scheme, 'I do not like it a bit'.[32]

On 6 January 1944, the War Cabinet endorsed the proposals for a West Indian combat unit of around 1000 men.[33] It would be called the Caribbean Regiment. The course of the war had already turned in favour of the Allies, and even greater advances would be made during the year. Having taken over four years discussing the role that West Indians should play in the war, the UK government would now embark upon a race against the clock to recruit and deploy the Caribbean Regiment before hostilities came to an end.

THE RACE TO DEPLOY THE CARIBBEAN REGIMENT (1944 TO 1945)

Early in 1944, discussions were taking place across Whitehall about what the new Caribbean Regiment would look like. During these discussions Ernest Sabben-Clare, a civil servant in the Colonial Office, came across official historical accounts of the role played by West Indian soldiers in the First World War, and they contradicted the myths that had been peddled by the War Office. Far from poor fighters, they had acquitted themselves well when given the opportunity. It was not that they had been poor fighters, but that they had been inadequately supported and, too often, poorly led. In a minute sent to a colleague on 9 February 1944, Sabben-Clare pointed out the misrepresentation:

> Incidentally, like everybody else, I had assumed that the War Office criticisms of the West Indian troops in the last war were correct, but on reading the section about the West Indies in Sir Charles Lucas' Official History of the Empire at War I am very doubtful whether they can be substantiated. The West Indian record seems an honourable one. Many of the difficulties there seem to have been were not the fault of the troops, viz. a large number of West Indians were sent, en route to Europe, to Halifax in cold weather without any warm clothing and many died. Again, later, there were grumbles owing to increases in British Army pay not being given to the West Indian personnel who were serving side by side with the British units. I think the truth of the matter is that problems presented by large numbers of coloured troops serving with British units was a bit too much for the authorities at the time.[34]

Recruitment for the 1st Battalion of the Caribbean Regiment would start early in 1944. Mindful of the sensitivities around race, Oliver Stanley wrote to the Caribbean governors on 4 March insisting that there must be no discrimination in the recruitment of officers and asked them to keep a close eye on local military recruiters to ensure that this was the case.[35] In reality, racism played a major role in the selection of officers. Most of the senior officers in the Caribbean Regiment were white, and most of the junior ones were mixed-heritage.[36] The rank and file was mostly Black, along with people of Chinese origin and mixed-heritage – but no white personnel.[37] Its fifty-six officers were described as a mix of 'white, black, and half-caste', but only two were Black (or 'pure negro') one of whom was a major.[38] The regiment was established on 1 April.

The following month they transferred to Fort Eustace, in the US state of Virginia, for training. Whilst in the US, the Caribbean Regiment paraded with much pomp on 8 June – the King's official birthday – and were described both as the first British army unit to parade on the monarch's birthday, and the first to train on US soil since the American War of Independence. The efforts to get media coverage for the parade (with all the propaganda benefits in highlighting military contributions from across the British Empire) produced minimal results. This was not surprising given the much bigger event that had taken place two days earlier with the D-Day landings that signalled the final stages of the war.[39]

Race would continue to dominate decisions about its formation, deployment, and actions on and off-duty. Before their arrival in the US, instructions were given to the regiment about the need to respect the colour bar they would find in southern US states. They were told that as 'guests of the people of the Southern States' they should be 'most careful not to bring discredit on themselves or the Battalion by disregarding local customs'.[40] However, Black Barbadian recruit Elvey Watson recalls being given much greater leeway and courtesy by white Americans than African Americans would have received. On a trip out in Newport News, Virginia, whilst on leave with two friends from the regiment, they took a wrong turn and were stopped by an American guard: 'He knew we were not accustomed to racial discrimination, so he allowed us to pass through the "white people's town". The coloured Americans would not have been granted this permission. Indeed, they would have had the club or gun'.[41]

It was not just American racism that was inflicted upon the regiment. British racism was constantly there, though much better hidden to avoid sparking a backlash within the ranks. The War

Office had made clear that no white soldier below the rank of lance sergeant could serve in the regiment to avoid having white soldiers billeted with Black West Indians.[42] Separately, in preparation for the regiment's move from the US to Italy in mid July, there were discussions within British military authorities on providing local catering for the West Indian troops. Although white prisoners of war could be used for a range of menial tasks for white soldiers, cooking for Black people was considered to be below them. The British military mission in Washington informed the War Office and Allied Forces HQ for Algiers that it was 'not (repeat not) desirable for European PW [to] perform menial tasks for coloured personnel nor coloured personnel share Italian messes'.[43] There was, in this, an echo of the racism meted out to soldiers of the BWIR in the First World War, who were told to clean the latrines of Italian labourers.

Whilst subjected, often unknowingly, to a range of racist decisions from the military hierarchy, the regiment also suffered from a lack of proper training. By 1944, Britain had ample experience of fighting the Germans, understood the strengths and professionalism of its enemy and had adapted in response. As a result, the British armed forces had strengthened their military tactics and training. In contrast, the Caribbean Regiment's war diaries are full of references, from July through to September, to the lack of proper equipment, facilities, training and officers with battle experience.[44] Under these circumstances, it was not a surprise that they struggled to reach the required standard of readiness for combat. At the end of July, whilst the regiment was without the training and equipment that it needed, General Henry Wilson (Supreme Allied Commander for the Mediterranean force) issued a stark report on the state of the unit to his boss in London (Field Marshall Sir Alan Brooke). Wilson reported that its officers and men required at least six months of 'intensive training before they can be considered in any way fit to take part in operations'.[45] Intensive training was started at the end of August, but the regiment's commanding officer (Lieutenant Colonel Wilkin) continued to report a lack of equipment, requested that he be replaced (as was planned) by a senior officer with modern military experience, and asked for the appointment of a training officer and team.[46]

Caribbean Regiment in Egypt (a Bren gunner and rifleman)
© Imperial War Museum, E 31193

Caribbean Regiment in Egypt during Second World War
© Imperial War Museum, E 31198

For the regiment, the final months of the war were spent moving between different theatres, with one senior commander after another refusing to take responsibility for them. One Colonial Office civil servant reported a conversation with the commander of British troops in Egypt, Lieutenant General Charles Allfrey, who spoke disparagingly of the training provided to the Caribbean Regiment. Allfrey also complained about its troublesome soldiers because 'although nearly all of them are coloured they wish to be treated exactly as white troops', prompting another civil servant to comment on the army's bigotry, noting: 'In other words the Army are colour-bar minded'.[47] By now, the War Office was showing real keenness to deploy the regiment in an active theatre but was facing constant resistance from its commanders on the ground. The War Office even looked at deploying men from the Caribbean's local defence forces to help garrison recaptured British territories in the Pacific. However, New Zealand's prime minister objected to using Black West Indian troops to defend the region on 'ethnological grounds' and, when pushed, stuck to his objections because of 'the racial intermixture that was bound to result'.[48]

British West Indian governors, along with Harold Moody of the League of Coloured Peoples, expressed increasing alarm at the prospect of the regiment not seeing combat before the war's end.[49] But despite reported improvements in the preparedness of the Caribbean Regiment as the right training and support was put in place, time had run out and they were not deployed in combat. Whilst the aspirations of many in the British West Indies for an army combat unit serving overseas was not realised, men from the Caribbean did see combat. Individuals of all ethnicities travelled to Britain, often at their own expense, and enlisted in UK army regiments. Many West Indians served in the Canadian forces, with some being stationed in Britain. And many thousands of British West Indians were recruited by the Royal Air Force as ground staff and aircrew.

NOTES

1 UK Parliament, House of Commons, Hansard, 4 June 1940, https://api.parliament.uk/historic-hansard/commons/1940/jun/04/war-situation#column_796.

2   Marika Sherwood, *Many Struggles: West Indian Workers and Service Personnel in Britain (1939-45)*, Karia Press, 1985, p27.

3   CO 323/1672/3, National Archives, UK, see telegram from Secretary of State for Colonies to West Indian governors dated 18 September 1939, and responses from governors of British Honduras (19 September 1939), Windward Islands (20 and 25 September 1939), Bahamas (21 September 1939), Leeward Islands (21 September 1939), Trinidad (24 and 25 September 1939), Jamaica (25 September 1939), British Guiana (26 September 1939), Barbados (29 September 1939).

4   Ibid, letters from governor of British Honduras dated 14 and 15 September 1939.

5   Ibid, letter from Ministry of Information (with attachment) to Colonial Office on 21 September 1939.

6   CO 323/1673/4, National Archives, UK, see extract from minutes of War Cabinet held on Thursday 19 October 1939 and letter from Churchill to MacDonald on 11 November 1939.

7   CO 323/1672/3, op cit, letter from Colonial Office to War Office on 15 December 1939.

8   CO 323/1673/4, op cit, see paragraph 55 of War Cabinet paper entitled 'Utilisation of the Man-power Resources of the Colonial Empire' dated January 1940.

9   CO 323/1801/3, National Archives, UK, see minute from Mr Poynton dated 13 February 1940 setting out War Office and War Cabinet positions. See James Denman and Paul McDonald, 'Unemployment statistics from 1881 to the present day', published in *Labour Market Trends*, by the Government Statistical Service, January 1996, p7, p11. In minutes of the War Cabinet held on Thursday 25 January 1940 (CAB 65/5, National Archives, UK, p174) Churchill opposes the proposals for a Caribbean Pioneer unit because it is 'politically dangerous at a time when over a million people were unemployed in this country'.

10 PREM 3/99/2, National Archives, UK, letter from Churchill to secretary of state for colonies on 16 June 1940.

11 Churchill's position on race has been discussed by many academics and commentators, including seminars on the subject at Churchill College, Cambridge (named after him). Some summaries on the matter can be found in the following articles: Priyamvada Gopal, 'Why can't Britain handle the truth about Winston Churchill?, *The Guardian*, 17 March 2021, www.theguardian.com/commentisfree/2021/mar/17/why-cant-britain-handle-the-truth-about-winston-churchill; Richard M Langworth, 'Was Winston Churchill a racist? A look at the evidence', *The Spectator*, 29 December 2022, www.spectator.co.uk/article/was-winston-churchill-a-racist-a-look-at-the-evidence; Benjamin T Jones,

'Deconstructing the cult of Winston Churchill: racism, deification and nostalgia for empire', *The Conversation*, 20 July 2022, https://theconversation.com/deconstructing-the-cult-of-winston-churchill-racism-deification-and-nostalgia-for-empire-185589.

12 CO 323/1787/74, National Archives, UK, minute dated 2 July 1940 and addressed to the Secretary of State from Sir Cosmo Parkinson, the permanent under-secretary at the Colonial Office; also CO 968/38/1, National Archives, UK, minute from Poynton dated 21 February 1941 referring to Churchill's intervention in June 1940.

13 Esther Captain and Guno Jones, 'Inversing Dependence: The Dutch Antilles, Suriname and the Desperate Netherlands during World War II', in Karen Eccles and Debbie McCollin (eds), *World War II and the Caribbean*, University of the West Indies Press, 2017, Kindle version, paragraph 15.

14 Ibid, paragraphs 16 and 19.

15 Dannelle Gutarra, 'Body Politics of Puerto Rican Participation in the US Military During World War II', in Eccles and McCollin (eds), op cit, paragraphs 13-4.

16 Ligia T Domenech, *Imprisoned in the Caribbean: The 1942 German U-Boat Blockade*, iUniverse 2014, Google Books version, p64.

17 Silvia Alvarez Curbelo, 'A Meditation on the 65th Infantry', in *Diálogo*, Vol 4, No 1, Article 4, DePaul University: USA, 2000.

18 The figure of twenty-three soldiers killed in action comes from the US Department of Defense website in article by Shannon Collins, 'Puerto Ricans Represented Throughout US Military History', www.defense.gov/News/News-Stories/Article/Article/974518/puerto-ricans-represented-throughout-us-military-history.

19 Gutarra, op cit, paragraphs 26 to 29.

20 WO 32/10092, National Archives, UK, see table entitled 'Atlantic Islands and West Indies Strengths' dated 6 August 1942.

21 Ibid, telegram dated 13 December 1941 from Officer Commanding Troops, Trinidad to the War Office.

22 WO 216/143, National Archives, UK, letter from War Office to Colonial Office on 19 December 1941 including Annex A on state of defence in British West Indies. In Annex A, section 6 refers to a report that the War Office received on 13 December about the state of defences.

23 WO 32/10092, op cit, telegram from secretary of state for colonies to governors dated 21 July 1942; also see table entitled 'Atlantic Islands and West Indies Strengths' dated 6 August 1942.

24 CO 968/74/18, National Archives, UK, note of internal Colonial Office meeting held on 12 April 1943.

25 CO 968/17/5, National Achieves, UK, letter from P H W Brind at the War Office to Major J.A. Holt at Colonial Office dated 20 April 1943.

26 Ibid, letter and attached memorandum from Major J A Holt at Colonial Office to Major P H W Brind at War Office dated 6 May 1943; letter from Major P H W Brind to Lieutenant Colonel W Rolleston at the Colonial Office dated 18 July 1943.

27 CO 968/74/18, op cit, letter from Noel-Baker to Macmillan dated 17 June 1942.

28 See short file CO 968/38/5 in the National Archives, UK, and referring to dozens of West Indians (of all ethnicities) travelling to Canada and enlisting in the Canadian army between September and October 1941.

29 CO 968/17/4, op cit, highly secret telegram, sent at 21.30hrs on 17 November 1943, from secretary of state for colonies to governor of Jamaica saying that James Grigg recognised that the US decision to send Puerto Rican troops to British West Indian territories made the political case for a West Indian contingent even greater.

30 CO 968/17/5, op cit, letter from Oliver Stanley to James Grigg dated 9 August 1943.

31 Ibid, letter from Grigg to Stanley dated 23 September 1943. Also see file WO 106/2854, National Archives, UK, containing a note from the Area Commander for North Caribbean Area dated May 1943 attached as Appendix C to a paper on 'Employment of West Indians in the Army' which went to the Executive Committee of the Army Council on 24 August 1943.

32 Ibid, letter from Grigg to Stanley dated 17 December 1943.

33 CAB 65/41/2, National Archives, UK, pp11-2, conclusions of 6 January 1944 War Cabinet discussions on using a West Indian contingent in a theatre of war. Also see CO 968/17/5, op cit, copy of the paper discussed at the 6 January War Cabinet (the paper is dated 3 January 1943 and titled 'War Cabinet: Employment of a British West Indian Contingent in a Theatre of War').

34 CO 968/102/4, op cit, minute from E E Sabben-Clare to Mr Rogers dated 9 February 1944.

35 Ibid, telegram from secretary of state for colonies to British West Indian governors on 4 March 1944.

36 Michael S Healy, 'Colour, Climate and Combat: The Caribbean Regiment in the Second World War', in *International History Review*, Vol 22, No 1, 2000, p80.

37 WO 204/6672, National Archives, UK, note from HQ Allied Armies in Italy tilted 'West Indian Troops' and dated 15 July 1944, see section 4 of attachment which describes 'Racial Origin' of the regiment.

38 Ibid, 'Note for File' dated 11 July 1944.

39 CO 968/102/5, National Archives, UK, see handout for the press issued on 8 June 1944, and minute dated 12 June 1944 from Ambler Thomas.

40 WO 176/41, National Archives, UK, Annex A is a note from Officer Commanding to All Ranks dated 8 May 1944 and is found at the end of the diary entries for May.

41 Elvey Watson, *The Carib Regiment of World War II*, Vintage Press: New York, 1964, p31.

42 WO 106/2854, op cit, telegram from British Army Staff in Washington to War Office dated 3 March 1944 (paragraph 12), telegram from War Office to British Army Staff Washington and Allied Forces HQ in Algiers on 21 March 1944 (third point), British Army Staff Washington reply on 28 March 1944.

43 Ibid, telegram from BAS Washington to War Office dated 9 April 1944.

44 See WO 170/1370, National Archives, UK, entries for 24 July and 1 September 1944; and WO 169/16276, National Archive, UK, see opening comment for October 1944 which refers to inadequate G1098 Stores (this is the stores of military equipment held by the unit), and then not until December 1944 does it say 'G1089 Stores are being issued'.

45 CO 968/102/5, op cit, telegram from AFHQ (General Wilson) to War Office (for Sir Alan Brooke, GICS) dated 25 July 1944.

46 WO 204/6672, op cit, letter from Lt Colonel H Wilkin dated 30 August 1944 complaining about lack of adequate support and training for the regiment.

47 CO 537/1266, National Archives, UK, see Ernest Sabben-Clare's minute of 11 April 1945 with comment scribbled in the margin by another civil servant (Mr Beckett) about the army being 'colour-bar minded'.

48 WO 106/2851, National Archives, UK, see telegrams between Dominions Office and British High Commission in New Zealand dated 12 July 1944, 27 July 1944, 19 October 1944, and 30 October 1944; CO 968/102/5, op cit, minutes from Ernest Sabben-Clare dated 15 August 1944 and 2 November 1944.

49 Healy, op cit, p84 refers to letter from Harold Moody to secretary of state for colonies in March 1945; see WO 106/2854, op cit, note from War Office civil servant Major Archie Black, dated 20 May 1945, which includes extract from letter from Commander South Caribbean Area on 7 May describing the concerns of governors at prospect of the Caribbean Regiment not having the opportunity to be tested in combat.

7

Among the few: Role of West Indians in the RAF

Although the colour bar was lifted for all three branches of the military at the start of the war, it would be the RAF that responded most positively. That is not to say the British air force was free from racism, but as the newest arm of the military it was less bound by tradition and, in many ways, swifter to embrace new ways of working necessitated by modern warfare. The RAF required highly skilled men and would willingly source these skills from different corners of the globe. As a result, the Colonial Office found the Air Ministry (the government department that oversaw the RAF) to be a more willing partner in the effort to engage West Indians in frontline warfare.

ENDING THE COLOUR BAR AND STARTING ACTIVE RECRUITMENT OF RAF AIRCREW (1939 TO 1942)

Before the outbreak of war, the RAF had put in place plans for a global network of training centres that would prepare a group of reservists. These were to be in Trinidad and Tobago, Bermuda, Malta, West Africa, Kenya, Southern Rhodesia (Zimbabwe), Straits Settlements in Southeast Asia (territories within modern Malaysia), Ceylon (Sri Lanka) and Burma. Most of these training centres would be open only to the local white population, the exceptions were the Straits Settlements (where aircrew training was restricted to white people and ground crew positions were open to people of colour) and Trinidad and Tobago where the whole scheme was open to all ethnicities. When the colour bar was formally lifted in October 1939, restrictions were removed from all schemes.[1] In spite of this, Black recruits were regularly turned away in the early months of the war.

Billy Strachan, an eighteen-year-old Jamaican, travelled to Britain in March 1940 at his own expense and made his way to the Air Ministry in Adastral House in London to volunteer to join the RAF. The corporal at the front entrance took one look at Strachan and simply said 'piss off'. Undeterred, the young Strachan insisted that he wished to enlist and, with the intervention of a friendly RAF officer who happened to be walking by, he was pointed in the right direction and was enrolled as a trainee wireless operator.[2] By mid 1940, because of the urgent need for more men, the RAF was working with colonial authorities to identify potential recruits to bring to the UK at the British government's expense.[3]

Passing-out parade of group of West Indian RAF volunteers in Britain, attended by Oliver Stanley (front right) © Imperial War Museum, CH 13850

The important role of the Caribbean as a source of recruits can be seen when comparing the numbers from across the British Empire. Unsurprisingly, it was India, with its large population, which dominated. According to the Air Ministry's official history of colonial contributions to the war, there were 25,000 Indian people serving in the Royal Indian Air Force at its peak. Many would also travel to the UK and serve in the RAF. In the West Indies, the service recruited around 6000 (5500 groundcrew and around 450 aircrew). One Colonial Office official described West Indians in the RAF as being '… by far the most numerous of the Colonial airmen'. West Africa accounted for 5000 recruits, the Middle East was 3000 and the Aden Protectorate (part of modern Yemen) accounted for 2000. Although recruitment did not include the Women's Auxiliary Air Force (WAAF), it is estimated that eighty women from the West Indies travelled to the UK to enlist.[4]

The crews that these West Indians joined were often very multinational. Unlike their American counterparts (or, indeed, their fellow West Indians who would join the Caribbean Regiment), these recruits were fully integrated. Black and white crew members flew in the same aircrafts, ate, socialised and were billeted together – they lived and died together. At the end of his RAF training in the UK, Cy Grant (from British Guiana) described how his white Canadian pilot, along with other pilots, picked a crew from among a long line of fresh trainees. Grant would be navigator within a crew that, under its French-Canadian pilot, also consisted of English wireless operator, flight engineer, bomb aimer and air gunner, along with a Canadian air gunner.[5] Although far more progressive than the other services, there was racial bias in RAF recruitment and promotion. The historian Mark Johnson suggests that a significant proportion of West Indian airmen were white, and uses the group photo of the second Barbadian contingent as an example – half of those in the photo were Black or mixed-heritage and the remainder were white.[6] Although white West Indians were over-represented, it is difficult to put an accurate figure to this, and that group photo was unlikely to reflect the overall contingent of West Indian aircrew.

In response to the demand for RAF pilots, the government of Trinidad and Tobago set up a pilot training scheme at its Piarco airfield in 1940. With two aircrafts, it was planned that each year the scheme would provide fifty hours of flying instructions to fifty local volunteers, preparing them to apply to join the RAF. The cost of their training would be met by the colonial government.[7] By now, there was a desperate need for aircrew. The Air Ministry informed the Colonial Office in November that Black West Indians would be accepted so long as they were highly skilled and considered to be 'suitable to associate with British airmen' – a phrase that indicated the class that these men, Black or white, should be drawn from.[8] Early reports on the calibre of these West Indian trainees were very impressive. For the first batch of six recruits, who graduated in November 1940, five were shown to be 'above average' and one 'average' in the flying assessment, and their mental alertness was rated as 'above the average pupil'. After reviewing the assessments in January 1941, Squadron Leader P N Shone (an Air Ministry official) wrote: 'The 6 lads were a grand lot and should by now have walked through our [Aviation Candidate Selection Board] though I haven't yet heard the results. I read the report with great interest and it excites me that while these pupils have still a lot to learn, they have certainly been started off in the right direction'.[9]

Shone would be proved right. In the UK, the Aviation Candidate Selection Board (ACSB) was delighted and recognised that even with limited training the raw talent of many of these recruits was obvious. During their training with the RAF, their chief flying instructor (Squadron Leader Hooper) gave a glowing report on the progress of the first six: 'They were exceedingly keen, their general bearing good, and they appeared to have a mental alertness above that of the average pupil'.[10] By time the UK had received the third batch of Trinidadian candidates, so impressed was the ACSB that it started to look again at some of those who had failed their training in Trinidad. In the third batch of trainees, the local Trinidad board had failed four of the ten pilots. But all ten, including the four who Trinidad had rejected, were accepted by the ACSB.[11]

The Trinidad training scheme had proved its success and plans were developed to extend it. Initially, it was intended to increase the number of aircrafts to twelve with a capability of training 150 pilots each year. This was followed by proposals for Trinidad to provide training for other British West Indian territories. The RAF responded positively and committed scarce training personnel to support the proposed extension. However, the arrival of US forces, and their intensive use of the Piarco airfield, meant the Trinidad training scheme would be dropped in May 1942.[12]

Many of the RAF's Caribbean aircrew were trained in Canada, and West Indian governors were asked to provide 240 suitable trainees a year. More than half of these trainees came from Jamaica (eighty) and Trinidad (seventy).[13]

At the end of the war, an Air Ministry report found that West Indian aircrew in the RAF performed just as well as their British comrades (as, indeed, did people of colour recruited from across the empire).[14] But this was not reflected in their advancement within the service. The RAF was reluctant to promote Black West Indians, or any person of colour, to become pilots and lead the crew on an aircraft. The Air Ministry noted that:

> In spite of the satisfactory standard of the technical and other abilities possessed by coloured officers and airmen who have qualified as members of aircrew, experience has shown that the appointment of any of this class of personnel as a Captain of Aircraft has not met with success. However good the individual may be the mere fact that he is coloured may induce a feeling of lack of confidence in the members of the crew. It is a matter entirely beyond the Captain's control and though the feeling may be only subconscious, it will tend to lower the efficiency of the crew as a whole.[15]

The RAF encouraged Black aircrew to take on other roles such as navigator, wireless operator or gunner, or if they became pilots they were assigned to smaller aircrafts (single-seat or single-engine planes) where they would not have teams of men to lead. As a result, the director of flying training wrote to HQ in July 1941 saying that 'all aircrew trainees being men of colour, should be trained on single engine types, in view of the difficulties with regard to crewing up'.[16] Cy Grant was caught up in the middle of this. He was being trained as an RAF pilot in 1941 but was switched (half-way through training) to be a navigator. He learned later, from a friend, that white aircrew had objected to serving under Black pilots.[17] However, some Black pilots continued to the deployed on larger aircrafts. Three years later, in May 1944, the Air Ministry received reports that a crew in Bomber Command had objected to flying with a Black West Indian pilot called Flight Sergeant Sylvestre. Among the white crew, Sylvestre had earned a reputation for being 'super sensitive' on race (which likely meant he was not willing to put up with the discriminatory attitudes and language that were common at the time). The case was used to reinforce the belief among senior officers that people of colour should not pilot larger aircrafts.[18]

Julian Marryshow, a Black Grenadian, was among the high performing graduates from the Trinidad pilot training scheme. He was one of six who had passed in the third batch. When an Air Ministry official checked whether Marryshow and his West Indian comrades could be assigned to larger twin-engine aircrafts, he was told: 'I think it would be better for them to be trained on single-engined types. We have already had some trouble with Indian pilots & other Dominion crews in bomber units'.[19] Despite such prejudice, Black West Indians became RAF officers (and bomber pilots) and performed with distinction. Marryshow was made a fighter pilot and his many flying missions included air support during the D-Day landings, in 1944, where he was credited with destroying several trains and rocket launcher sites. Later in the war, he was shot down but managed to evade capture and was rescued by Allied forces.[20]

The RAF was particularly concerned about the deployment of Black and brown aircrew in overseas postings (other than their own countries), or in roles that would bring them into regular contact with US and Dominion forces. It was decided that only white RAF staff would receive overseas postings away from their home territories, or serve in Transport Command which was required to fly newly built aircrafts from factories in the US and Canada to Britain and other locations.[21]

COMBAT EXPERIENCE OF WEST INDIAN AIRCREW

Few combat roles were more dangerous than RAF aircrew. The bomber command had a casualty rate of 80 per cent, including 44 per cent fatalities. The dangers faced by crew were numerous. In addition to being shot down by enemy fire (from the ground or air) they were also at risk from mid-air collisions with other RAF aircraft flying in tight formation, the bombs they were carrying prematurely exploding inflight, a direct hit from a bomb dropped by a friendly bomber above, mechanical failures and human error.[22] Billy Strachan gave an example of the intense air battles that his crew faced flying bombing missions over German controlled territory:

> As wireless operator, I sat with the navigator and pilot while the two gunners sat in their turrets at the front and rear of the plane ... We had several narrow escapes. Once, when the navigator, who was also the bomb-aimer, was ... looking down the aimer, a bullet flew over his head, under the pilot's backside and up the side of my leg – I still have the scar to prove it.[23]

Having served thirty missions, the young Jamaican was entitled to a ground-based position but decided to retrain as a pilot and become an officer. At the RAF training school for officers in Cranwell, Lincolnshire, he was given a personal servant or 'batman'. Strachan described how, in their first meeting, he automatically addressed this 'Jeeves' character as 'sir' only to be corrected by his batman who explained, 'no sir, it's I who call you sir'.[24] Strachan became a bomber pilot with 101 Squadron, gaining two promotions to become flying officer and then flying lieutenant. His flying career came to an end after his fifteenth trip as a pilot in 1942. Whilst taking off from his Lincolnshire base in foggy conditions and carrying a 12,000lb bomb on a mission targeting German shipping, Strachan's plane just missed the tower of Lincoln Cathedral, which he had not seen. It was pure luck that he had not hit the tower and crashed to earth, in this city of 14,000 people, with his 12,000lb bomb. He was so shaken by the near miss that he was unable to fly again.[25]

Flight Sergeant Colin Joseph from Trinidad (right) and Pilot Officer
Arthur O'Brien Weeks from Barbados (left). Spitfire pilots in Britain
in 1944 © Imperial War Museum, CH 11976

On bombing missions, the risk of being shot down in enemy territory was very real. For Cy Grant, this nightmare unfolded when his
aircraft was shot down on a mission over German-occupied Holland
in 1943. Grant ended up as a prisoner of war in the Stalag Luft
III camp in Poland. He was one of the camp's few Black inmates.
The prospects for a Black POW in German-occupied territory did
not seem good. The Gestapo categorised Grant as 'a member of
the Royal Air Force of indeterminate race'.[26] But incredibly, Grant
experienced very little racism as he served out the remaining two
years of war as a prisoner. He may well have been helped by the

surprisingly cordial introduction with the commander of the camp. When he informed the commander (Colonel von Lindeiner) that he was from British Guiana, the delighted commander revealed that he had visited the country. Grant said he experienced no racism from his German guards or most of his fellow prisoners – the only exception was an American airman, also held at the camp, who insisted on referring to Grant as a 'nigger'.[27]

John Blair, a Jamaican officer and flight navigator, reflected on the very special attitude that it took to be part of an RAF aircrew: 'There were people who went up for their operational first flight and then decided that they weren't ready for this at all, that they were not going back in the air. I have to admit that I believe what we did was something most people would not be able to do in the same circumstances'.[28]

The key to the success of bombing missions was the accuracy in targeting. This was not a straightforward process. From 20,000 feet in the air, a range of factors including slight shifts in wind conditions meant the bomb could land thousands of feet off target. Anything from 10 to 50 per cent of bombs landing on target was considered acceptable. To improve targeting, the best bombing crews led the way on missions, dropping their incendiary bombs and flares to light up the target for the main bombers following behind them. They were called pathfinders. A navigator in one such pathfinder crew within 139 Squadron of the RAF, was Ulric Cross (a suave Trinidadian who would serve as his country's high commissioner to the UK during the early 1990s). The squadron was known as the Jamaican squadron because of the funds the island had raised to buy aircraft for the unit. Cross recalled his most dangerous mission: '... one of the engines of our Mosquito fighter-bomber was shot up over Germany and we came down to 7000 feet from 35,000 feet. We struggled back to England and crash landed in a quarry. It was a narrow escape but we made it out alive'.[29]

After serving his full aircrew assignment, Cross went on to become a welfare officer towards the end of the war, working with the Colonial Office and Air Ministry to look after West Indians serving in the RAF. He was recommended for the role by Ivor Cummings, a Colonial Office civil servant.[30] Cummings was one of a very small number of Black civil servants in 1940s Britain and

Flight Sergeant James J Hyde, from Trinidad, a Spitfire pilot in
Britain in 1944 © Imperial War Museum, CH 11979

had been refused a commission in the army in 1939 because of
racism. He was also gay at a time when homosexual acts were still
a crime. He played an important role in many key moments in
this period of Black British history. Regular reports of discrimination had made it necessary to create a welfare officer role for West
Indians. It was a white Jamaican, wing commander J C M Gibb,
who first proposed the role. Gibb pointed out that he was already
performing this role informally, giving as an example the help he
had given to a Black West Indian pilot who was told by fellow
pilots that they did not want to sleep in the same accommodation as him. Whilst Gibb and another white Jamaican (flight
lieutenant Coke-Kerr) described such discrimination as 'not
uncommon', Colonial Office officials privately dismissed these
incidents as rare and not serious. Instead, these officials suggested
it was a form of prejudice that should be ignored because it could
never be removed.[31]

RAF GROUNDCREW

By April 1943, the RAF was around 58,000 short of the numbers of groundcrew it needed. Following its success in recruiting West Indian aircrew, the Air Ministry looked to the region again for groundcrew. The work covered a wide range of trades including electricians, instrument repairers, flight mechanics, metal workers, fitters, motor boat crew, carpenters and wireless operators.[32]

The recruitment started in the autumn, bringing in over 5500 West Indians with the first 30 men arriving in the UK in January 1944. By the end of the war, the bulk of this recruitment would come from Jamaica, which accounted for 84 per cent of the total.[33] As with other initiatives, this was a very selective process. Jamaica was rejecting two recruits for every successful applicant by November 1943, and its governor was estimating that they would receive a total of 15,000 applications.[34] Across the British West Indies, governors had estimated 1099 recruits in the first six months, but the level of interest meant that Jamaica would significantly exceed this number on its own.[35]

As well as the numbers, early recruitment got off to a good start in the quality of recruits. The first batch of 1000 were described as having 'compared very well with ordinary RAF recruits'.[36] An Air Ministry report on 14 June 1944 said:

> In general it was found that this draft as a whole showed a high level of intelligence as expressed by the psychological tests. It is considered that they were on an average better training material than would be found from a batch of 1000 airmen selected at random from amongst those coming forward at present for enlistment.[37]

Whilst the second batch of recruits were satisfactory, the third (who had arrived on 12 November) caused major concerns, and were described as 'far below the standard of the first and second contingent'. It is clear from the description of these recruits that a greater proportion had been drawn from a much poorer background, and had not had access to the same levels of education as the previous two waves. The report on the conduct of this contingent included derogatory descriptions of them such as not being 'house trained', but went on to say that early reports of the fourth contingent showed that it was of 'a much higher standard and will be nearly up to the standard of the first and second contingents'.[38]

As in so many aspects of British life, class appeared to be a big factor. Whereas West Indian aircrew were from more educated, middle-class backgrounds, the mix of trades involved in the work of groundcrew drew in many more men from working-class backgrounds. This appears to have had an impact on their experience and treatment. Although their contribution was valued, they did not receive as warm a welcome as their aircrew colleagues. One Air Ministry report suggested that racial tensions were more prevalent with West Indian groundcrew because of their 'lower' upbringing, intelligence and education.[39]

Despite many challenges, the overall experience of West Indian groundcrew was good. In their monthly summary towards the end of 1944, the censorship office in Jamaica concluded that the bulk of letters sent home from groundcrew in the UK were extremely positive. Some had complaints about their treatment and training which one Colonial Office official dismissed as an orchestrated campaign of whinging among members of Jamaica's left-leaning People's National Party.[40]

West Indian groundcrew took on essential jobs that Britain was struggling to fill. Along with West Indian aircrew, they provided vital support to the RAF and the war effort.

NOTES

1 AIR 20/1022, National Archives, UK, document entitled 'The Manpower Contribution of the Colonies to the Royal Airforce', p1.

2 Robert N Murray, *Lest We Forget: The Experiences of World War II Westindian Ex-Service Personnel*, Nottingham Westindian Combined Ex-Services Association, 1996, p55; also see Mark Johnson, *Caribbean Volunteers at War: The Forgotten Story of the RAF's 'Tuskegee Airmen'*, Pen & Sword Books, Google Books version, 2014, chapter 3 paragraphs 1-2.

3 AIR 20/1022, op cit, pp1-2.

4 Ibid, pp3-4 gives figures for recruitment from colonies. Also see CO 537/1223, National Archives, UK, minute from John Keith dated

9 March 1944 referring to West Indians being the most numerous colonial airmen.

5   Johnson, op cit, chapter 4, paragraphs 32-33.

6   Ibid, chapter 1, paragraph 9 and table 1; chapter 2, paragraphs 55-6.

7   AIR 20/1022, op cit, p9.

8   Marika Sherwood, *Many Struggles: West Indian Workers and Service Personnel in Britain (1939-45)*, Karia Press, 1985, pp29-30.

9   Ibid, p30; AIR 2/8355, National Archives, UK, P N Shone writing on 8 January 1941.

10 AIR 2/8355, op cit, memo from Officer Commanding Elementary Flying Training School at Woodley to the Air Officer Commanding at HQ in Reading, dated 17 July 1941.

11 Ibid, see document 7B which is a note by P N Shone dated 10 June 1941.

12 AIR 20/1022, op cit, pp9-9A.

13 CO 968/55/14, National Archive, UK, telegrams from secretary of state for colonies to British West Indies governors on 7 November 1942.

14 AIR 2/13437, National Archive, UK, report titled 'Coloured RAF personnel: report on progress and suitability', dated May 1945, pp1-4.

15 Ibid, 'Coloured RAF personnel: report on progress and suitability', p4.

16 AIR 2/8355, op cit, see minutes dated 21 June 1941 and 27 June 1941, and letter from the director of flying training to flying training command HQ dated 22 July 1941.

17 Stephen Bourne, *The Motherland Calls: Britain's Black Servicemen & Women 1939-45*, The History Press, Apple eBook edition, 2012, chapter 6, paragraphs 3-4.

18 AIR 2/13437, op cit, file minute dated 24 July 1944 and addressed to Mr Monk-Jones, refers to a letter from a commander in Bomber Command on 17 May referring to crew members objecting to serving under a West Indian pilot because of his race. See also Michael S Healy, *Empire, Race and War: Black Participation in British Military Efforts during the Twentieth Century*, doctoral thesis, Loyola University Chicago, 1998, p239.

19 AIR 2/8355, op cit, minute 9 dated 27 June 1941.

20 'The war heroes who walked among us', *Trinidad and Tobago Newsday*, 11 September 2022, https://newsday.co.tt/2022/09/11/the-war-heroes-who-walked-among-us.

21 See AIR 20/1022, op cit, p5; also AIR 2/13437, op cit, file minute dated 24 July 1944 to Mr Monks-Jone.

22 Johnson, op cit, chapter 10 paragraph 8 gives the 80 per cent casualty

rate figure; the description of the hazards faced by aircraft can be found in chapter 5 paragraphs 7 and 35-6.

23 Murray, op cit, p75.

24 Ibid, pp75-6.

25 Ibid, p94.

26 Gus John, 'Cy Grant obituary', *The Guardian*, 17 February 2010, www.theguardian.com/music/2010/feb/17/cy-grant-obituary.

27 Johnson, op cit, chapter 8 paragraphs 1-3.

28 Ibid, chapter 10, paragraph 8.

29 Ibid, chapter 4, paragraphs 40-51.

30 CO 537/1223, op cit, Ivor Cummings' minutes of 10 October 1944.

31 Ibid, letter from Wing Commander J.C.M. Gibb to Major Hutchinson dated 29 February 1944; also minutes from Major Hutchinson dated 16 March 1944 and from Mr Poynton dated 17 March 1944.

32 Sherwood, op cit, p38 refers to the shortage of RAF groundcrew; AIR 2/13437, op cit, see document 1A in the file headed 'Royal Air Force: Vacancies for Skilled, Semi-Skilled and Unskilled Men, and Outline of Conditions of Enlistment' dated November 1938.

33 AIR 20/1022, op cit, p12.

34 Ibid, p11; and AIR 2/8278, National Archives, UK, telegram from governor of Jamaica to Secretary of State for Colonies dated 7 October 1943.

35 CO 968/74/19, National Archives, UK, document 46 headed 'Recruitment for Tradesmen for the RAF in the West Indies' produced in May 1943. It summarises responses from British West Indian governors on the questions of potential numbers of groundcrew recruits within the first six months.

36 AIR 2/8278, op cit, third paragraph of memo from RAF station at Hunmanby Moor to HQ on 25 January 1945.

37 Ibid, letter from Central Trade Test Board of the RAF to the under-secretary of state at the Air Ministry on 14 June 1944.

38 Ibid, ninth paragraph of memo from RAF station at Hunmanby Moor to HQ on 25 January 1945.

39 AIR 2/13437, op cit, report titled 'Recruitment of personnel from Colonies into post-war Air Force' dated 21 May 1945, paragraph 4(iii).

40 CO 968/132/2, National Archives, UK, see fifth paragraph of file note headed 'Notes on Defence Matters' by Arthur Poynton, it is document number 177 attached on 9 December 1944.

8

The struggle at sea:
Royal and merchant navies

Of all the British armed forces, the Royal Navy's attitude towards Caribbean recruitment was the most condescending and racist. They believed that West Indians could not meet the standards required of such a prestigious service. As the civilian head of the Admiralty in the early months of the war, Winston Churchill's position on the colour bar was ambivalent. In an internal minute, Churchill wrote: 'There must be no discrimination on grounds of race or colour ... I cannot see any objection to Indians serving on H.M. Ships where they are qualified and needed, or if their virtues so deserve rising to be Admirals of the Fleet. But not too many of them, please'.[1]

Although a small number did serve in the Royal Navy, most West Indians with maritime skills served in the merchant navy or the local voluntary naval reserve.

After lying about his age, a sixteen-year-old Allan Wilmot enlisted in the Royal Navy in 1941 and joined the minesweeper *HMS Hauken* escorting convoys of merchant ships through the Caribbean. He described himself as coming from a middle-class background and being relatively well off compared to his compatriots.[2] Wilmot was one of a dozen Jamaicans aboard the ship and found no racial tensions onboard: 'On a small ship you become a family. You depend on each other – you're all brothers. There's no room for discrimination – in three minutes you could be at the bottom of the sea. Being the youngest one, I was more or less a mascot'.[3]

In addition to the relatively small number of Black sailors, there was at least one Black West Indian (a Jamaican) who became a Royal Navy officer during the war. Towards the end of 1942, the Admiralty were planning to publicise his appointment as the 'first Negro to be commissioned' in the Royal Navy.[4] Whilst such an appointment was highly unusual, it appears that they were unaware that another Black Jamaican (John Perkins, also known as Jack Punch) had received a commission in the Royal Navy some 163 years earlier (see p37).

IMPERIAL OVERREACH

The Royal Navy was arguably the strongest global maritime force during the interwar years, but this took its toll on resources. In the decades leading up to the Second World War, Britain had reached a point of imperial overreach, and by 1939 it was struggling to maintain a naval fleet sufficient for its imperial needs (see pp105-6). Indeed, some academics argue that when war broke out, no corner of the empire was adequately defended. The Admiralty had faced an increasing struggle to balance the demands placed upon it globally against the resources that were available. When it could not persuade the colonies to pay for the additional naval protection that was needed, the proposal was developed in 1921 to create local Royal Naval Volunteer Reserve (RNVR) units to ease some of this pressure.[5]

Of course, the empire was not just a defence 'burden' for Britain. To be a global power, the UK relied on the wealth, resources, and global network of its empire. The UK was dependent on this network for food, fuel, a range of essential commodities and the vast human resource of labour and fighting men and women before, during and after the war.

By 1937, with the emergence of new threats across the globe (Japan asserting itself in the Pacific, Italy invading Abyssinia and Germany rearming), British military commanders had to concede the limits of their power, as the Chiefs of Staff Committee did in 1937: 'We cannot foresee the time when our defence forces will be strong enough to safeguard our territory, trade and vital interests against Germany, Italy and Japan simultaneously'.[6]

Within a year of Britain entering the war, it was facing both Germany and Italy whilst coming to terms with the defeat of its French ally and the loss and damage to a significant portion of its naval fleet in the Dunkirk defeat. As a result of these setbacks, well before America would formally enter the War, the Royal Navy was in desperate need of US support to protect Atlantic and Caribbean trading routes. As we saw in Chapter Five, the destroyers for bases agreement was a product of this predicament.

THE TRINIDAD ROYAL NAVAL VOLUNTEER RESERVE (TRNVR)

At the beginning of the 1920s, discussions about creating Royal Naval Volunteer reserves were initially intended to apply only in those colonies with large white communities. It was believed that people of colour could not take on the staffing of such naval forces.[7] Despite these concerns, the reality of war and its impact on an already over-stretched Royal Navy would force the Admiralty to reconsider its racist stance on this point. Writing to the Colonial Office in May 1939, the Admiralty proposed to send nine fully equipped vessels to Trinidad for minesweeping and anti-submarine operations. They would need locally recruited and trained crew and until these vessels could be made available, Trinidad would need to convert local tugs to operate as minesweepers.[8]

The reason for the Admiralty's keenness to create a local naval force in Trinidad was obvious. Its oil production and refining were of great importance to the British navy and air force. An internal Admiralty minute of 16 June 1939 noted that: 'There is no doubt that in war the safeguarding of oil supplies from Trinidad is of the greatest importance both from the Navy and Air Force point of view, and that this is essentially an Imperial interest'.[9]

When war was declared a few months later, the director of the Admiralty's local defence division reiterated Trinidad's importance, noting that this arose from 'the need of safeguarding our oil supplies, which may be classed as an Imperial more than a local responsibility'. Whilst decisions had to be made on the total cost, and how much would be borne by the local colonial government, it was made clear that this should not delay the urgent work of establishing the naval force.[10] Accordingly, Trinidad pushed on with creating its local naval volunteer force which had a complement of nineteen officers and 141 men (or naval ratings) after the first year of war.[11] The officers were drawn from the small white population. They were former police officers and colonial officials with experience of commanding Black men, but they had little to no seafaring experience. The ratings were drawn from the Black and South Asian populations. The force would operate with a range of local vessels (two whalers that underwent a substantial refit to serve as patrol vessels, and a range of smaller vessels). The island's senior naval officer reported that their smaller crafts had been running constantly since the outbreak of war and, by August 1940, the engines on all but one were beyond repair.[12]

Despite its keenness for the force to be established, and its initial insistence not to allow arguments over cost to delay things, this did not stop the Admiralty from arguing over how to pay for this new naval unit. It was not until May 1941, once these issues were resolved, that the force was turned into the Trinidad Royal Naval Volunteer Reserve (TRNVR), charged with patrolling and defending the Caribbean. The size of the TRNVR increased during the early years of the war to just over 1200 people, making it the second largest of the sixteen RNVRs after the Malayan unit. The better wages paid to workers employed in constructing the US military bases meant the TRNVR had to draw its recruits from across the British West Indies. By the war's end, the largest number of recruits came from Trinidad and Tobago (540), followed by Barbados (349), Cayman Islands (124), Grenada (56), British Guiana (53), St Vincent (36), St Lucia (33), Antigua (13), St Kitts (3), Dominica (3) and Montserrat (1). Out of seventy-five officers, only twelve were non-white.[13] There were no recruits from mainland Jamaica (although, technically, the Cayman Islands and the Turks and Caicos were administered as part of the colony of Jamaica).

From its tiny population of 6500 people, the Cayman Islands provided the third largest number of recruits. This reflected both the strong seafaring traditions of this small group of islands and its 'racial' mix. Compared to other British West Indian territories, a greater proportion of its population was white (40 per cent) and mixed heritage (40 per cent), and a smaller proportion was Black (20 per cent), making it easier for the Royal Navy to accept Caymanians.[14] Regardless of this preference for Caymanians, and for white West Indians in general, the navy did not view them as being on a par with white British sailors. This hierarchy of naval prejudice was set out in a note from the Admiralty to its senior naval commanders some months after the end of the war:

It has been noticed that the West Indian negro, although of excellent physique, is mentally undeveloped. He is not necessarily stupid, but emotional and lacking in self-restraint and responsibility. In consequence strict but paternal discipline is necessary and the bearing of his officers is all important. Experience shows that when well led the West Indian negro can do excellent work and become a good seaman ...[15]

Thus, it was seen as the role of good white officers to turn supposedly puerile Black West Indians into decent fighting men. But white West Indians were not seen as naturally up to this task, having themselves been weakened by the Caribbean environment in which they had been raised.

With certain notable exceptions the West Indian European has made a disappointing officer. He requires considerable training in an environment other that [sic] the West Indies and should have the benefit of courses in the United Kingdom and a period in the Fleet. In consequence it would be necessary for a British West Indian Navy to be officered for some considerable time by a large proportion of the best type of Royal Naval Officer until the young West Indians could be brought forward to the necessary standard of efficiency and officer like qualities.[16]

NEAR MUTINY AT TRNVR BASE (1943)

Given the patronising and racist attitude that the Admiralty encouraged towards Black West Indians, it was no surprise that tensions and conflict arose between TRNVR ratings and officers. One manifestation of this was the disturbance at the naval base at Staubles Bay in Trinidad in May1943. It started when two ratings (Ordinary Seamen Harrington and Thomas) were arrested for disobeying orders and subsequently fought with their guards during separate escape attempts. The guards, and other ratings, were clearly reluctant to intervene in support of their officers. During some of the stand-offs with Thomas, he appeared to be able to persuade the guards to back off by appealing to them to take his side 'as coloured men'.[17] As military authority broke down, largely due to poor leadership from officers with a reputation for callousness, several other detainees also refused to comply with instructions from their guards.

One witness to the causes of the disturbance described the appalling state of morale among non-white ratings: '... in every one of their faces you can just see discontent, hatred and even fear ... they are being treated like slaves ... we are volunteer soldiers of the Admiralty – we ought to have white rights'.[18] The subsequent investigation identified multiple factors contributing to the disturbance: unpopular officers, many of whom had little contact with their men; discrimination in the disciplining of TRNVR recruits (men of colour convicted of offences were sent to the local jail, enduring much poorer conditions than their white colleagues who would be detained in barracks); the lack of marriage allowances causing real hardship for married men; inadequate recreation facilities; poor accommodation, and poor induction of the men about their pay and conditions and how to raise grievances.[19] Apart from issues relating to the marriage allowance, the report found that the men had raised no issues about their pay.

Commodore Phillips (the senior British naval officer for Trinidad) was critical of the role of senior officers at Staubles. Phillips believed that the men would have responded 'very readily to encouragement' and had previously encouraged Commander Wilkinson, the senior officer at Staubles, to provide this. However, Wilkinson had clearly not done so and had also 'not instilled this outlook in the officers at the TRNVR he has trained or in those under his immediate command at Staubles'.[20] Phillips was even more scathing of Wilkinson's boss, Captain Denison, who had shown 'a lack of initiative and failed in guidance to an officer ... whom he should have judged required correction on certain points'. He considered Denison little more than Wilkinson's mouthpiece.[21] When he received the report, Sir Alban Curteis (senior British naval officer for the Western Atlantic) was so appalled by its findings that he considered bringing Captain Denison up before a court-martial.

TRNVR IN ACTION (1942 TO 1945)

When German U-boats attacked the Caribbean in early 1942, it was the US navy and air force that shouldered the main responsibility for defeating them. The Royal Navy and TRNVR played supporting roles. Suffering from poor leadership, undertrained and under-resourced, the TRNVR's contribution was very limited.

West Indian ratings of Trinidad Royal Naval Volunteer Reserve operating a depth charge thrower – September 1944 © Imperial War Museum, K 7524

US Navy operating a depth charge off the Panama Canal during
Second World War © Imperial War Museum, NY 6121

During 1942, the TRNVR supported the US navy in carrying
out minesweeping operations in the southern entrance to the Gulf
of Paria (the semi-enclosed sea between Trinidad and Venezuela)
to clear the way for bauxite ships travelling from Suriname. The
British Admiralty were impressed by the performance of the local
force, noting that the TRNVR crew 'bore up to their duties beyond
all expectations, this being most noticeable ... when a mine was
exploded ... causing minor fractures to steam plates and hull
plating'.[22] However, the Admiralty's 'expectations' were extremely
low, and so exceeding them was not in itself a great achievement.
The force also carried out valuable search and rescue missions,
saving merchant seamen whose vessels were sunk by U-boat attacks

and aircrew forced to ditch at sea. Their rescue activities started within days of the beginning of the Battle of the Caribbean. On 21 February 1942, the 8000-ton British tanker *SS Circle Shell* was sunk by a U-boat attack 30 miles off the coast of Trinidad, leaving fifty-seven crew in lifeboats who were rescued by the TRNVR tug *Busy*.[23]

By 1943, the Allied forces in the Caribbean had established full naval superiority over the U-boats. The TRNVR had a minor role in this, but a role nonetheless. It formed part of the convoys that were essential to the safe escort of merchant vessels through the Caribbean. It also patrolled the Caribbean Sea in search of submarines. In late September, the TRNVR anti-submarine vessel, *HMS Black Bear*, used its sonar to detect a U-boat and attacked it with depth charges before calling in support from Allied sea and air defences in the area. The German vessel (U-123) escaped, but this close call was part of the turning of the tide on the U-boats.[24]

The TRNVR was established with the ability to serve not just in the Caribbean, but in other theatres of war at the discretion of the Admiralty. However, there was reluctance to use it outside of Caribbean waters because of the need to focus all resources against the U-boat campaign, but also because of the diverse ethnic backgrounds of the crew. In a note to the Royal Navy's commander in chief for North America and the West Indies (Vice-Admiral Sir Charles Kennedy-Purvis), the Captain-in-Charge at Port of Spain, Trinidad, explained the sensitivities relating to the force.

'... the Force is composed of white, coloured and black personnel, and it would be difficult to discriminate in the selection of white personnel only, for service overseas, without causing considerable discontent. It is presumed that as an alternative, coloured and black ratings could be used in tropical climates only, with forces already employing such persons'.[25]

One of the deployments away from the Caribbean was to South Africa, which was one of the most racist parts of the empire even before the introduction of its Apartheid policy after the war. Lionel Straker, (a TRNVR stoker from 1942-4) was part of this deployment and described his experience in a contribution to the BBC's *WW2 People's War* project:

We had a little problem because some of the West Indian boys in Durban, they made a mess of the place. Going into the bars – if they wouldn't serve us they would knock all the drinks off the counters ... We went into one bar, we were served with a round of drinks and when we asked for a second round the man broke the glasses at the counter in front of us, he said he didn't have any more glasses to serve us. We had a bloke by the name of John Carter, I can never forget him. So John tells the man, 'If we can't have glasses give us the bottles'. He said we couldn't do that so John, who was a very big bloke, pushed all the bottles off the shelf and broke up most of them. Then they called shore patrol and they took us back to the ships and stopped our leave for the day. But the next day it was in the South African papers that we were West Indians, we weren't Africans and we were to have European facilities. So then we spent five days there, and it was alright after that.[26]

THE MERCHANT NAVY

Many West Indians were serving on British merchant vessels before the Second World War and were part of a larger group of people of colour working as sailors (from India, China, African colonies and elsewhere). These seafarers formed visible communities in British port towns such as Cardiff, Liverpool, Glasgow and London. A few months into the war, a shortage of deck hands resulted in the Ministry of Shipping asking the Colonial Office to recruit West Indian sailors. Telegrams were sent to governors in January 1940 and they responded with an estimate of 1800 available men. But then the Ministry of Shipping got cold feet, expressing concerns that it was 'not desirable to mix coloured and white races in the same department on board ships'. It took another year for a policy to be agreed that would create a pool of West Indian sailors to crew British ships.[27] However, racism continued as a major issue for UK merchant and passenger vessels, with one official note suggesting that throughout the war, the responsible government department appeared 'to have tolerated if not encouraged racial discrimination on the grounds that white passengers, or white crew ... will not berth with or work alongside coloured persons'.[28]

One of the most important roles of the Royal Navy was protecting the merchant shipping that supplied food, vital resources and materials to Britain and its empire. Merchant sailors played a vital role in the war and paid a high personal price. It is estimated that 50,000 British merchant seamen died in action during the Second World War.[29] Such was the scale of the carnage during the height of the German U-boat campaign that Britain expressed concern to its US ally about the morale of merchant sailors. Sir Dudley Pound, the Royal Navy's First Sea Lord, wrote to Admiral King of the US Navy on 19 March 1942: '... the continued sinking of ships which are not in convoy has a serious effect on the morale of merchant seamen and there is a limit beyond which we must not push them. I am not at all certain that we are not nearly approaching that limit'.[30]

Victor Brown, a Jamaican, joined the merchant navy at sixteen and had first-hand experience of these dangers. He was serving onboard an oil tanker in the north Atlantic in 1942 when it was torpedoed by a U-boat. Thinking quickly, he used an axe to release a lifeboat to get it into the water as the ship started to list. 'If we had have left it, the ship would have eventually dragged the lifeboat down with it', he said. Another West Indian sailor, Winston Murphy, was also on the tanker and he credits Brown with saving many lives that day: 'Had he not chopped that rope we would never have got clear of that boat'.[31]

Among the crew of merchant vessels it is estimated that there were around 15,000 Black sailors. Some 5000 perished at sea – a massive fatality rate of 33 per cent. This extraordinarily high death rate may have been because these men were mainly stokers who worked in the bowels of older, slower merchant vessels where they shovelled coal into the furnaces to keep the ships moving.[32] Whilst Black merchant mariners were more likely to die at sea, the rewards they received for this higher level of risk was less than that of their white crewmates. Metzgen and Graham point out that white sailors were paid more than three times the weekly wage of their Black crewmates and were given better accommodation.[33]

As a region, the Caribbean bore its share of the suffering with more than 7000 merchant sailors dying in those waters during the war.[34] Some estimates suggest that around 20 per cent of merchant vessels in the region were lost to U-boat attacks.[35] However, these estimates are difficult to verify since records on the sinking of smaller inter-island schooners, that transported goods and people, are less reliable. What is clear is that the merchant navy suffered losses on an immense scale, yet its sailors continued to go to sea. For many of its British West Indian sailors, despite the dangers, the lack of well-paid alternative employment left them with little choice.

NOTES

1   Michael S Healy, *Empire, Race and War: Black Participation in British Military Efforts During the Twentieth Century*, doctoral thesis, Loyola University Chicago, 1998, p222, quoting minute from Churchill on 14 October 1939 in file ADM 1/10818 in National Archives, Kew, UK.

2   Interview in Caribbean Takeaway Takeover with Allan Wilmot, 3 March 2018, Essex Record Office, https://soundcloud.com/essex-record-office/allan-wilmot-3-mar-2018.

3   Simon Rogers, 'There were no parades for us', *The Guardian*, 6 November 2002, www.theguardian.com/uk/2002/nov/06/britishidentity.military.

4   CO 968/38/10, National Archives, UK, minutes between A R Thomas and Mr Haler dated 15 December 1942.

5   Daniel Spence, *Imperialism and identity in British colonial naval culture, 1930s to decolonialisation*, doctoral thesis, Sheffield Hallam University, 2012, pp24-5, 27-8, 31-3.

6   Ibid, p35.

7   Ibid, pp27-8.

8   ADM 1/10969, National Archives, UK, letter from S.H. Phillips of the Admiralty to the Under Secretary of State at the Colonial Office, file register M.03023/39, 15 May 1939.

9   Ibid, file register number M.05222/39, 16 June 1939.

10 Ibid, file register number M.08060/39, minute dated 18 September 1939 from Director of Local Defence Division (D of LD).

11 ADM 1/23215, National Archives, UK, note on Trinidad Naval Volunteer Force from Senior Naval Officer (Trinidad) to Commander-in-Chief, America and West Indies Station (Bermuda) dated 3 August 1940, paragraph 2.

12 ADM 1/23215, op cit, note dated 3 August 1940, paragraphs 5-10.

13 Spence, op cit, see table 2 on p37, table 3 on p57, and reference to the numbers of non-white officers on p58; in CO 537/1891, National

Archives, UK, see pp10 and p28 of the file which gives the peak figure for officers at 75, and 1215 men.

14 Spence, op cit, pp59, 62-3.

15 ADM 1/23215, op cit, letter from Admiralty to Commanders-in-Chiefs on 16 November 1945, paragraph 10 of the attachment entitled Appreciation of Naval Organisation in the West Indies after the War.

16 Ibid, paragraph 11.

17 CO 968/80/7, National Archive, UK, note on 'The Disturbances at TRNVR HQ May 14-15, 1943 and their Causes', dated 9 October 1943.

18 Spence, op cit, p107.

19 CO 968/80/7, op cit.

20 ADM 178/301, National Archives, UK, memorandum from Senior British Naval Officer, Trinidad to Senior British Naval Officer, Western Atlantic dated 9 June 1943, paragraph 8.

21 Ibid, paragraph 9.

22 CO 537/1891, op cit, letter from Admiralty to Colonial Office on 16 July 1946 enclosing a short history entitled 'Trinidad Royal Naval Volunteer Reserve', p29 of file.

23 Gaylord T M Kelshall, *The U-Boat War in the Caribbean*, Paria Publishing Company Ltd: Trinidad, 1988, pp49-51.

24 Ibid, p418.

25 ADM 1/23215, op cit, report from Captain in Charge, Port of Spain, to Commander in Chief, America and West Indies Station, dated 12 February 1941 (reference 27/2359/3665), paragraph 8.

26 Lionel Straker, *A Stoker in the Trinidad Royal Naval Volunteer Reserve*, BBC, 31 January 2006, www.bbc.co.uk/history/ww2peopleswar/stories/75/a9020675.shtml.

27 Joanne Buggins, 'West Indians in Britain during the Second World War: A short history drawing on Colonial Office papers', *Imperial War Museum Review*, No 5, Imperial War Museum, 1990, p87.

28 CO 537/1224, National Archives, UK, document entitled 'Colour Discrimination in the United Kingdom', produced by the Welfare Department of the Colonial Office and dated May 1946, p5.

29 Stephen Bourne, *The Motherland Calls: Britain's Black Servicemen & Women 1939-45*, The History Press, Apple eBook edition, 2012, chapter 2, paragraph 1.

30 PREM 3/385/5, National Archives, UK, telegram from Sir Dudley Pound (First Sea Lord of the Royal Navy) to Admiral King of the US Navy, dated 19 March 1942.

31 'Soldiers of the Caribbean: Britain's forgotten war heroes', BBC, 13 May 2015, www.bbc.co.uk/news/uk-32703753.

32 Mark Johnson, *Caribbean Volunteers at War: The Forgotten Story of the RAF's 'Tuskegee Airmen'*, Pen & Sword Books, Google Books version, 2014, chapter 2, paragraph 40.

33 Humphrey Metzgen and John Graham, *Caribbean Wars Untold: A Salute to the British West Indies*, University of the West Indies, 2007, p128.

34 Ibid, p194.

35 Spence, op cit, p70.

9

The role of women

The Second World War changed the opportunities available to women as labour shortages forced governments to re-evaluate their role. This was not new – the First World War had a similar impact. Across Caribbean communities that were badly affected by poverty and inequality, women of colour were often at the sharpest end of these conditions. The limited economic opportunities available to them meant that many would jump at the jobs and potential for income created by war. Like young men, many young women were also attracted by the adventure of war work and the opportunity to serve overseas. And there was also a patriotic desire to support the metropole or 'mother country'. Whilst the motivation to engage in war work was real, women of colour had to overcome both race and gender discrimination to achieve this.

SOCIAL CONDITIONS IN THE CARIBBEAN (1930s)

In the British West Indies, not only were women earning considerably less than men (around 43 per cent less for the same work in agriculture) they also enjoyed less civic rights.[1] In the judicial system, women appeared to be debarred from serving on juries or from holding positions as magistrates. In territories where women were allowed to run for office on the same basis as men, few would meet the property or income qualification. This restriction particularly affected women of colour. In three British colonies women were not allowed to stand for elections to the local legislative councils. In Barbados, they were not allowed to vote. In Jamaica, although women were allowed to run for election to the legislative council, none had ever been elected. The Moyne inquiry was aware of only one woman ever being elected to a municipal council in any British Caribbean territory. In several colonies, the voting age for women was higher than that for men. Since they were effectively disenfranchised, politicians had little incentive to address the issues that were specific to women of colour.[2]

Women played a crucial role in agricultural production. Indeed, given the importance of food production to Caribbean authorities, the role of women in this sector helped to relieve any anxieties about the risk of military service drawing large numbers of men away from the land.[3] For those women not working the land, a major alternative source of employment was in domestic service where earnings would usually range from six shillings to twelve shillings a week. But in rural areas some were paid as little as one shilling and six pence with food provided on top of their earnings. The average weekly rent for a room was two shillings, which meant that those women on the lowest earnings were depending on male 'visitors' to help them to cope. Older women without such support could face undernourishment or starvation.[4] When war was declared, this increased the region's hardship, a situation that was only slightly eased in many of the territories with US bases as they drew in American military personnel, workers and dollars.

During this period of extreme economic and social challenges, Amy Ashwood Garvey, a prominent Pan-Africanist who was also briefly married to Marcus Garvey, demanded that West Indian women should have equal access to employment opportunities in the US and Britain, which overwhelmingly focused on men. On a trip to the US for a medical operation in March 1944, Ashwood Garvey announced a plan for a work scheme for Jamaican domestic servants, and lobbied the US consulate back in Jamaica to support her scheme. The FBI's director, J Edgar Hoover, who had long held suspicions about the Garveys, advised the US State Department to intervene and stop the scheme before it got off the ground. His concern was that the success of such a scheme would simply be 'used to advantage by the United Negro Improvement Association as a device to augment their membership and increase its influence upon the members'. The US and British authorities stepped in to ensure the plans would get nowhere.[5]

Whilst criticisms could be made of the narrowness of Amy Ashwood Garvey's scheme, focused as it was only on domestic service, few other initiatives provided support for poor West Indian women. The discussions around recruitment of Black West Indian women into the armed forces was certainly not aimed at the poor.

OBSTACLES TO RECRUITING WEST INDIAN WOMEN (1940 TO 1942)

Patriotism or a yearning for adventure encouraged hundreds of West Indian women to travel to Britain, the US and Canada to join one of the women's services. Small numbers had taken up these opportunities within the first two years of the war, long before any formal recruitment in the West Indies had begun. Since they had to cover the cost of their own travel, these were middle-class women who were able to find the money for the journey. They were also disproportionately white.

In 1941, the Colonial Office had identified a total of twenty West Indians who were in the UK working in the various women's services – six in nursing, five in the Auxiliary Territorial Service (ATS), four in the Women's Auxiliary Air Force (WAAF), two in the Women's Royal Naval Service (WRENs), two in the ambulance corps and one in the auxiliary fire service.[6] Government figures were sketchy, and the actual numbers would have been much greater than this. Although the colour bar for the armed forces had been lifted in October 1939 for the duration of the war, this decision had not been consistently applied to the auxiliary services. As a result, racist restrictions were still written into requirements to become a state registered nurse – an oversight that was not corrected until the end of 1941.[7] Thus, the whiteness of Caribbean recruits across these auxiliary services (particularly in this early wave) was the consequence not only of the volunteers having to fund their own passage, but also the inconsistency with which the colour bar was lifted.

There was an established flow of male recruits of all ethnicities from the West Indies into the RAF since the beginning of 1941, but the Air Ministry baulked at the prospect of accepting sixteen Bahamian women into the WAAF in late 1942. Initially, the British authorities mistakenly thought these women were Black. This error was pointed out to London by the RAF office in Washington DC. They assured the Air Ministry that the applications were 'from white women of excellent type' and they did not 'consider the acceptance of white volunteers would in any way encourage coloured applications'. This was reinforced by a message from the Duke of Windsor who had abdicated the British throne and been ensconced as governor of the Bahamas two years earlier. The Duke informed London that 'volunteers, who are all European, are arranging through British Volunteer Movement in United States to proceed to England early next month'. However, although the Air Ministry had thought they were Black, the fact that they were white would not have prevented their rejection. On the recruitment of women, the Air Ministry appeared to be as keen as the War Office to keep Black people out and was happy to reject white West Indians (thus avoiding the accusation of racial prejudice) to achieve this. In their response on 31 December, they explained this, but deference to the former King appears to have swayed the Ministry. They agreed to treat these candidates as an exception and not object to them traveling to London in view of the Duke's telegram.[8] Whilst the Bahamian candidates had benefited from the intervention of the Duke, a year earlier Eva Wright (a twenty-six-year-old 'coloured lady in Sierra Leone' who also wanted to join the WAAF in Britain) was not so lucky.

Wright was willing and able to pay her own passage to the UK, the problem she had was in getting space on a passenger ship to carry her. It appears that the objection of her father (a prominent figure and member of the local legislative council) may have added to her difficulties. She was able to secure the support of the Black Colonial Office civil servant, Ivor Cummings, who was a friend. Cummings was born in west Hartlepool in the northeast of England to a father who was a doctor from Sierra Leone and a mother who was an English nurse. He took up Wright's case with his Colonial Office colleagues, convinced that her qualifications would make her an ideal candidate for the WAAF. However, when they took up this case with the Air Ministry, Cummings' Colonial Office colleagues were not as enthusiastic. They guided the Ministry on the best options available to them and suggested that 'there may be a few Colonies where it would be possible to obtain white volunteers only without raising delicate colour questions'. However, if the Ministry were in no great need for colonial recruits 'it would be undesirable to encourage Miss Wright or any other colonial volunteers to come to this country in the hope of acceptance for service with the WAAF'. The Ministry took the hint, made it clear that they were not in favour of a general appeal for women volunteers from the colonies, and left it for Wright to sort out her own travel difficulties.[9]

Over the first three and a half years of the war, several proposals for a recruitment campaign aimed at West Indian women were considered and dismissed. In early 1942, after the proposal for a combat unit had been rejected again, the Colonial Office turned its attention to other options for utilising West Indian manpower and womanpower. In a two-page memorandum to the Overseas Manpower Committee, the Colonial Office noted that:

> There has also been some demand on the part of women in the West Indian Colonies, including coloured women, for opportunities of war service. These cannot perhaps be recruited in units, but use may well be made of their services for certain of the more skilled occupations, and it is suggested that these possibilities should be explored between the Colonial Office and the Ministry of Labour.[10]

Nothing of substance was to come of this proposal. Meanwhile, the War Office was busy drafting and redrafting its policy on recruitment from the colonies into the ATS. As more questions were raised about each version of the policy, it would take the War Office several attempts to clarify its position. It became clear that it would have to discourage all West Indian recruitment in order to keep Black, brown and mixed-heritage West Indians at bay.[11]

THE CANADIAN WOMEN'S ARMY CORPS

In the latter half of 1941, the UK government had become aware of the scale of West Indian recruitment into the Canadian army and instructed its governors to pause this flow of young men whilst it considered the position regarding a British Caribbean combat force (see Chapter Six). Just as this pause was being lifted in the spring of 1942, the Colonial Office received a message from Sir Henry Bushe about whether fifty young Barbadian women (described as 'well educated girls, coloured and white, of good social standing') could join the Canadian women's auxiliary service. However, Canada was not keen on the idea and informed the Canadian-West Indian League in Montreal, which was coordinating West Indian recruitment, that 'for the time being at least' it did not want these women to travel to Canada.[12]

Eventually, this opportunity was opened up. Beverly Marsh, a middle-class Jamaican, would join the Canadian Women's Army Corps (its equivalent of the British ATS). Her motivation was to get a good education and improve her prospects:

> I decided I wanted to be a social worker. But you never had a university in those days and as the second of seven (children), there were all these others to look after. There was a friend of mine ... she saw this article about joining up in the Canadian Army, and that would help you to go on and when you were discharged, you could go on and do studies. I joined the Canadian Women's Army Corps, the CWACs. The thing in the back of my mind was to get studies afterwards.[13]

It was the desire to get a good education that motivated many other young men and women who joined the British forces. Odessa Gittens, a thirty-two-year-old Black Barbadian, was one of them. She would join the British ATS because she wanted to do postgraduate studies. The opportunity for her and hundreds of fellow West Indian women to join the ATS would come about because of the demands placed on Britain's military mission in Washington DC by a massive procurement programme.

AUXILIARY TERRITORIAL SERVICE IN WASHINGTON (1940 TO 1943)

Britain's Auxiliary Territorial Service had been formed a year before the war, in September 1938. Early in the war, five ATS personnel worked within the UK's military mission in Washington DC.[14] These numbers expanded rapidly as the mission grew. After Lend-Lease legislation was passed by the US Congress in 1941 (see pp98-9 and 107) the Washington mission was kept busy liaising with its American counterparts and administering the UK side of this arrangement. The War Office estimated that during 1942 the cost of military equipment purchased for the British Empire under Lend-Lease was $4 billion.[15] By the end of the war, the UK had spent $31 billion (or £7.6 billion at the prevailing exchange rate).[16] Given the scale of this procurement and the burgeoning size of the British military mission that oversaw it (more than 8000 staff by the end of 1942), the UK chancellor was determined to get the best value from this expenditure. He sent one of his Treasury ministers (Harry Crookshank) to Washington to identify substantial cost savings among the ever-growing British administrative staff. Crookshank found that far from simplifying what was an already difficult procurement process, the new Lend-Lease legislation added even greater complexity. In his report to the chancellor, delivered at the end of January 1943, he explained that a new and more laborious web of procedures had replaced a reliance on contract law.

> Under Lend-Lease, you have to put in a requisition for an article or to bid for it (instead of asking for tenders). After it is assigned to you, you cannot sit back and trust that a benevolent United States authority will just deliver it on to your ship. Experience shows that not only do you have to argue and win your case for requisition or assignment at the relevant committee, but you have to follow the article's career from its birth at the factory all down the line until it is safely packed on board ship. You have no legal rights in the way you had in contract days; it is all "grace and favour", and worse yet, if you do not ship your article within forty-five days of its leaving the factory, it may be legally taken back by the United States authorities.[17]

He concluded that these processes ate up 'a great deal of the staff' and that this 'cannot be helped'. Therefore, 'no spectacular staff reductions, on a percentage basis such as you had in mind, could safely be made'.[18] Quite something coming from a Treasury man who had been sent out to drastically cut staff numbers! Instead, Crookshank proposed relatively minor reductions in staffing amounting to around 5 per cent, but only if the present volume of work did not increase (which few believed would be the case). Another of his recommendations was about administrative support. There were already a few British ATS recruits providing some support, but the bulk of the mission's staff (around 80 per cent) came from local civilian recruits. The mission was struggling to attract and retain American secretaries who could find better employment elsewhere. Crookshank concluded that recruiting ATS clerks from the West Indies would provide better, more reliable and less costly support. After receiving the full report, the Chancellor of the Exchequer (Sir Kingsley Wood) wrote to the secretary of state for war encouraging him to implement its recommendations including the recruitment of ATS personnel from the West Indies.[19]

The War Office was, therefore, actively considering the recruitment of West Indian women when the Colonial Office wrote to them in February 1943 asking for an update on the policy on colonial recruitment into the British ATS. A year and a half earlier (in October 1941) the War Office policy was to encourage subjects from around the empire to enlist in local women's services. Those local services were to be administered and funded by the colony. Women from across the empire who wished to join the British ATS would need to travel to the UK at their own expense and be prepared to meet the cost of their return passage.[20] However, the urgent need of Britain's military mission in Washington was about to change this.

THE ARGUMENTS OVER ATS RECRUITMENT (1943)

By the beginning of 1943, the Washington mission included 145 members of Britain's various women's services including the ATS.[21] In order to confirm the viability of West Indian recruitment, Colonel Knapton of the War Office and Controller Falkner of the ATS visited the Bahamas, Barbados, Trinidad and Tobago,

British Guiana, St Lucia, Grenada and Jamaica. All the visits took place during January and were highly sensitive because the intension was to apply a rigid colour bar for this recruitment. Knapton was able to submit his report on 24 February. He informed the War Office that it had been a successful visit and they had been able to identify around 150 possible white recruits. He noted that some islands had been very sensitive about the racial problems that could be triggered by this initiative and, for those reasons, advised against doing anything in Trinidad and Tobago and to tread with care in Jamaica. Barbados, on the other hand, would pose no problems on this front and could 'produce 60 white girls with no difficulty'.[22]

Before Knapton had even completed his Caribbean visits, and weeks before he had drafted his report, the colonial governors were alarmed by rumours of the racist recruitment policy. The governor of Barbados (the island Knapton considered the most amenable to this policy) was the first to express his concerns to the Colonial Office. Writing on 22 January, Sir Henry Grattan Bushe warned the secretary of state for colonies that 'recruitment on this basis will cause resentment and I think it would be helpful to us all if the War Office could find it possible to reconsider the policy'.[23] The Colonial Office immediately raised concerns with the War Office, warning of the risk of stirring racial resentment in the region if these plans were pursued, and insisting that if the colour bar was applied to Washington recruitment, alternative overseas ATS recruitment had to be found for Black West Indians.

It did not take much to persuade the Colonial Office of the need to impose a colour bar on recruitment of West Indians to serve in Washington. They had long been willing to adjust Britain's formal approach on race to reflect perceptions of the prevailing attitudes of a particular region – whether that was the US, South Asia or some of the white Dominion territories of the empire. However, the Colonial Office would remain adamant that the cost of bending to American racism was that Caribbean women of colour must have the opportunity to serve in the ATS in Britain. It would take some pushing, but the War Office eventually backed down and agreed this compromise in May 1943.[24] Seven months before it would agree to the creation of a West Indian combat unit for men, the

War Office had agreed to the direct recruitment of West Indian women into its ranks (white West Indian women for the ATS in Washington, and women of all backgrounds for the Caribbean and British ATS).

WEST INDIANS IN THE ATS (1943 TO 1945)

At its full strength, the ATS in Washington stood at 438, which included 200 West Indians.[25] They were part of a 1300-strong administrative team that was vital to the running of the mission.[26] The West Indian women were highly regarded. Lieutenant General Gordon Macready, head of the British Army mission in Washington, told the Colonial Office in June 1944: 'The ATS girls from the West Indies have been a great success. In fact, I don't know how we could have carried on without them'.[27]

Auxiliary Territorial Service in Jamaica – 1944
© Imperial War Museum, K 5926

Those serving in the Caribbean and in Britain were also well regarded. In total, 300 would serve in the Caribbean and 100 in the British ATS.[28] The British contingent would cross the Atlantic in waves, with the first thirty arriving in the UK in October 1943 and others arriving throughout 1944. After the successful D-Day landings in June, Churchill and Roosevelt met in Quebec at the Octagon Conference in mid September where they discussed progress of the invasion of mainland Europe and future plans. After the conference, Churchill travelled back to Britain by sea, onboard the *Queen Mary*. Another passenger on that voyage was Louise Osbourne, a thirty-one-year-old Black St Lucian, who (with her fellow service personnel) enjoyed far less luxurious conditions than the prime minister:

> We landed in Scotland – we were on the *Queen Mary*. It was a troop ship at the time (it was changed into a troop ship). That was 1944, same year I joined ... We had to sleep on wire covered with canvass. Sugar bags covering wire, that was our beds! Some of them started to cry. I was always trying to make peace, telling them 'You joined it, you glad to be coming, so you must accept what you getting'. So we went across on the same ship as Mr Churchill, his secretary and others – we never saw them. When he had to come out of his cabins, we the soldiers ... and everybody had to go to their cabins.[29]

The brief given to the ATS recruiting staff in the West Indies was to identify the most highly qualified women. It had taken some persuading to get Osbourne to join:

> I was at my home one day when I was told there was a sergeant there to meet me from the ATS at Vigie. When I came down to her she told me she would like me to join the ATS in St Lucia. I asked what it was all about, and she explained to me and I told her that I was working. I had a job and was doing a lot of social work and didn't see why I should join the ATS. She told me that I would miss a lot if I didn't join, so I told her she would have to wait, I couldn't give her an answer off-

hand. I had to chat with my people and myself to see what I think. And then she gave me two or three days, and back she came begging me not to say no, and so I gave in.[30]

By now, the West India Committee was estimating that 323 West Indian women were enlisted as service personnel in the UK – twenty-six in the WREN, 212 in the Army (or ATS) and eighty-five in the WAAF.[31] This included those who would have made their own way to the UK to enlist rather than being part of a co-ordinated recruitment campaign.

West Indians in ATS in Britain – 1944 © Imperial War Museum, HU 55517

The highly selective recruitment process in the West Indies placed a heavy reliance on recommendations from the colonial authorities. References to 'the right sort' or 'excellent type' would often refer to the ethnicity or skin colour of the candidate, but it would also refer to their class background and education. This was not unique to the women's services – for example, RAF aircrew were drawn from a fairly narrow strata of West Indian society.

However, the clash of class was often starker in the ATS because of the nature of the British ATS. After conscription was introduced in Britain at the end of 1941 for all unmarried or widowed women between the ages of twenty to thirty, the ATS would peak at over 200,000 personnel. These recruits were drawn from all socio-economic backgrounds and the service had a large working-class contingent. The Caribbean recruits, on the other hand, were all volunteers from the middle and upper-middle classes. When the Jamaican historian Dalea Bean interviewed a number of women who served in the forces during the war, most said that pay was not a major concern for them (neither to support themselves nor to send home to support their families). Indeed, Beverly Marsh literally laughed at the idea: 'No, I hadn't even thought about that'.[32] In Washington, where all ATS recruits were white, those who came from richer backgrounds (whether British-born or white West Indians) and behaved in what was seen as a snobbish manner, had early run-ins with the 'far tougher and more professional ATS from Britain'. It took time for relationships to build.[33]

During her ATS service in Britain, Louise Osbourne did not recall class distinction being a factor: 'We didn't think of class at the time, I didn't think so. But in the ATS, or any of them, you could act as you wanted. After 5 o'clock it was your business to act as you want, or just feel that we are ladies'.[34]

Connie Mark was a Black Jamaican who worked as a medical secretary in the ATS in Jamaica. She reflected upon her time in the ATS with fond memories, as did the other veterans I interviewed more than thirty years ago with my late friend, Ben Bousquet (co-author of *West Indian Women at War*). In common with many of her fellow volunteers – men and women – Mark was a strong character who would make her feelings clear. This could produce tensions. Military authorities sometimes expressed their frustration about West Indians being too rigid on matters to do with their service or employment contracts, or perceived infringements of their rights. For example, many West Indian RAF groundcrew recruits expressed great disappointment when they were brought to the UK for training in trades that were not then offered to them. Given their history, West Indians had good reason to be sensitive about any perceived infringement of their rights. Some ATS leaders felt that 'the West Indians were acutely sensitive to differences in status not only between them and the European-born but among themselves as, for instance, between cooks and clerks'.[35] Mark had clear views about this and how it may have played into perceptions of class snobbishness:

> All the ATS in the army [in Jamaica] only did one thing – we worked as secretaries: that's all they asked us to do. What they may be implying is that when they came there they may have wanted us to come to their houses and clean it – because this happened to me ... Of course we have a class thing in the West Indies, and I'm not going to apologise for it. If we were white they could have handled it, but because we were black they couldn't understand these black people saying we didn't want to come to your house and clean it.[36]

In Britain, the ATS was a broad military service whose personnel carried out a vast range of duties – almost anything other than firing guns or artillery, or serving in active combat zones. They drove and maintained military vehicles, made maps in the ordinance corps, provided a range of administrative support, operated telephone switchboards, and much more. But the single biggest role was on anti-aircraft guns with over 50,000 women (more than a quarter of the ATS) placed on gun stations where they would spot, track and calculate the height and speed of enemy aircraft, enabling male gunners to target and shoot them down. Whilst this presented a wide range of choices to the West Indian recruits, ultimately they did the jobs they were assigned to. Camille Duboulay-Devaux, a white St Lucian who was among the 100 West Indians serving in Britain, would quickly find this out:

> When they were asking what we wanted to do, I wanted to go on the big guns. And they said 'too bad, the big guns are silent now because they're not used for the Doodle Bugs' ... So I said I want to be a driver and they said 'too bad, you're only five feet' and a driver had to be five feet two inches, so they decided the best place for me was as a clerk in the War Office.[37]

A full story of the West Indian contribution to the wartime military services could not be told without describing the role played by Caribbean women. Their role was important – both in the substance of what they contributed and in the symbolism of taking part. This truth was not lost on the Colonial Office and Caribbean governments that were so desperate to engage the people of the region in the war effort. But the West Indian contribution extended beyond the military services. We will see this in the next chapter, which looks at the many other aspects of war work in which the people of the Caribbean played a role.

NOTES

1   Moyne Commission, *The Moyne Report: Report of the West India Royal Commission*, Ian Randle Publishers: Jamaica, 2011, chapter 10, paragraph 12 gives details of daily rates of pay for men and women in agriculture. I have used these figures to give a rough calculation that women earned around 43 per cent less than men for the same work.
2   Ibid, chapter 11, paragraphs 10-11.
3   CO 323/1673/3, National Archives, UK, see telegram from governor of Windward Islands to secretary of state for colonies on 20 September 1939, assuring him that expansion of local food production would not be affected by military recruitment because 'women play a large part' in farming.
4   Moyne Commission, op cit, chapter 11, paragraphs 15-6.
5   Fitzroy André Baptiste, 'Amy Ashwood Garvey and Afro-West Indian Labor in the United States Emergency Farm and War Industries' Programs of World War II, 1943-1945', published in *Ìrìnkèrindò: A Journal of African Migration*, 2003, africamigration.com, pp110-2.
6   CO 968/37/10, National Archives, UK, document titled 'West Indians serving in the Forces', dictated by Mr Carstairs on 10 September 1941.
7   CO 968/38/11, National Archives, UK.
8   CO 968/81/4, National Archives, UK, RAFDEL Washington to Air Ministry Whitehall, 29 December 1942; HRH Duke of Windsor to secretary of state for colonies, 29 December 1942; and Air Ministry to RAFDEL on 31 December 1942.
9   CO 323/1828/51, National Archives, UK, see letter from Eva Wright to Ivor Cummings on 30 October 1941, minutes from Mr Bigg of 26 November 1942 and Mr Calder of 27 November 1941, letters between Mr Bigg and Squadron Leader P N Shone on 2 December and 10 December 1941.

10   CO 968/74/18, National Archives UK, Memorandum for Overseas Manpower Committee by Colonial Office, at the front of this 1942 file.

11   Ben Bousquet and Colin Douglas, *West Indian Women at War: British Racism in World War II*, Lawrence Wishart, 1991, pp84-7.

12   CO 968/74/15, National Archives, UK, telegram from Sir Henry G Bushe (Governor of Barbados) to secretary of state for colonies on 25 May 1942; telegram from UK's High Commission in Canada to the Dominions Office in London on 19 June 1942.

13   Dalea Bean, *Jamaican Women and the World Wars: On the Front Lines of Change*, Palgrave Macmillan, 2018, p203.

14   Shelford Bidwell, *The Women's Royal Army Corps*, Leo Cooper Ltd: London, 1977, p111.

15   WO 32/10688, National Archives, UK, 'Report on British Missions in the United States', dated 30 January 1943, p3.

16   Bank of England Archives, *Bank of England 1939-1945*, Unpublished War History, 1956, see Part III, Appendix I, p1108.

17   WO 32/10688, op cit, 30 January 1943 report, pp3-4.

18   Ibid, 30 January 1943 report, pp4, 6.

19   Ibid, letter from Chancellor to secretary of state for war on 27 February 1943.

20   WO 32/10653, National Archives, UK, letter from War Office to Colonial Office and Dominions Office on 4 October 1941.

21   WO 32/10688, op cit, 30 January 1943 report, p2.

22   Ibid, pp1-2 of 'Report by Colonel W G D Knapton on his visit to the British Army Staff, Washington, and to the North and South Caribbean Areas', dated 24 February 1943.

23   CO 968/81/4, op cit, telegraph from Sir G Bushe (governor of Barbados) to secretary of state for colonies, 22 January 1943.

24   Bousquet and Douglas, op cit, pp50-3, 94-105.

25   Shelford Bidwell, *The Women's Royal Army Corps*, Leo Cooper Ltd: London, 1977, the figure of 438 refers to fifteen officers and 423 other ranks mentioned on p112.

26   WO 32/12178, National Archives, UK, see p14 of 'Report on the British Army Staff (Washington) by Lieutenant-General Sir Gordon N. McReady, Period June 1942 to December 1945'.

27   CO 968/102/5, National Archives, UK, letter from Lt General Macready to A H Poynton at the Colonial Office on 21 June 1944.

28   Bousquet and Douglas, op cit, p2, 107; and Bidwell, op cit, p112.

29   Interview with Louise Osbourne in Castries, St Lucia, on 18 February 1989 by Ben Bousquet.

30   Bousquet and Douglas, op cit, p117.

31   CO 968/74/14, National Archives, UK, letter from The West India

Committee to Colonial Office on 20 October 1945 enclosing a copy of 'The West India Committee Circular' with details about numbers of West Indians serving in the UK on p222.

32 Bean, op cit, 198.
33 Bidwell, op cit, p111.
34 Interview with Louise Osbourne, op cit.
35 Bidwell, op cit, p111.
36 Interview with Connie Mark in London on 7 December 1988 by Ben Bousquet and Colin Douglas.
37 Interview with Camille Duboulay-Devaux in St Lucia, on 18 February 1989 by Ben Bousquet.

10

Beyond the military:
The essential jobs of war

Supporting the Allied war effort required great commitment across many fronts – not just the millions of men and women in the armed forces, but the millions more in munitions, manufacturing, agriculture, mining and transportation. More British workers were employed as these industries expanded and labour was also required to fill the gaps created by young men and women drafted into military service. As a result, women were recruited into agricultural and industrial work in unprecedented numbers. But this was not enough – schoolchildren on vacation were used to supplement the industrial and agricultural workforce, as were large numbers of prisoners of war.[1] With the wartime economy at full employment and drawing larger numbers of the resident population into work, Britain had to look overseas for help. West Indian skilled and semi-skilled labour would be recruited in their tens of thousands despite the reluctance (driven by racism) of many employers.[2]

FOOD PRODUCTION

The most immediate labour issue to resolve was in agriculture. Before enlisting Caribbean people in military services and war industries, the region's governments had to assure themselves that food production would not be neglected. When the secretary of state for colonies wrote to British West Indian governors on 18 September 1939 to test the support for a Caribbean combat unit, he made clear that: 'I consider it of the first importance that steps should be taken to expand local production of food in the West Indies during war, so as to reduce dependence on imported supplies'.[3] The recruitment of a combat unit could not detract from this key priority. All the responses indicated that it would not.

It was to be expected that agriculture should be the first consideration since the needs of the regional economy and the survival of the population depended on it. The Moyne report into the uprisings of the 1930s had highlighted that the bulk of employment in the British West Indies was in agriculture, but much better wages could be found in most other sectors.[4] Pulling more agrarian workers off the land into other employment posed a risk to the already fragile efforts to achieve food self-sufficiency across the region. Beyond the British West Indies, other Caribbean islands were also struggling with the challenges of their agricultural sectors and were highly dependent on imports. The decision of Admiral Robert to direct 350 of his soldiers to support food production in Martinique during the Allied blockade, and governor Tugwell's description of the plight of the people of Puerto Rico as American food imports were cut (see pp91-2), demonstrated the regional scale of this challenge.

When the Anglo-American Caribbean Commission was established in March 1942, the reinvigorating of Caribbean agriculture was among its priorities. At its meeting in Trinidad the following month it focused on food supplies and recommended that three months' stock should be kept instead of the forty days advised by the War Office. The cost of achieving this would be £1.5 million for Jamaica, Trinidad and British Guiana alone.[5] As the Battle of the Caribbean raged for much of the year, the urgency of the self-sufficiency drive became more obvious. West Indian governments introduced incentives to encourage farmers to switch away from planting cash crops to food crops. Cuba, Barbados, Jamaica and Trinidad placed obligations upon farmers to plant food crops on at least a portion of their land.[6]

As well as being encouraged to work their own land to achieve food self-sufficiency, West Indians were also invited to help on American farms, which were in desperate need of labour. Up to 64,000 West Indians were recruited to work in US agriculture (see Chapter Five, p114). A leaflet produced by the Anglo-American

Caribbean Commission to welcome Caribbean farmworkers to the US highlighted the importance of their work: 'You are here on a war job; be as proud of it as if you were in the fighting services. Food is as necessary as ammunition ...' The leaflet went on to describe differences in customs and behaviour in the US, particularly around race: '... social customs vary in different parts of the United States ... Remember that in the United States the word "Negro" is not used to offend but is used and accepted in the same way as the word "coloured" in Jamaica'.[7]

But Ivoran Fairweather, from Jamaica, remembered a mixed reception in America where 'Negro' was not the only N-word that was used. Like many other West Indians, he pushed back at segregation laws.

> I go to Charleston, South Carolina, when I was in farm work and I have ridden on buses ... We sit anywhere, and then they stop the bus. And under President Roosevelt – he brought us and said 'These West Indians are here as war workers' – soldiers and the policemen protect us ... I have been to West Palm Beach when the driver of a bus was a racist from down South, from Georgia, and a couple of we sit besides whites and he stop the bus ... We Jamaicans, we West Indians – not just Jamaicans, all West Indians – we didn't take no for an answer. We stood there for about three quarter of an hour until the driver refused to move the coach and the police get another driver and take us right in town.[8]

Recruitment would continue throughout the war and into 1946. Whilst Jamaicans made up most of this Caribbean workforce, recruits were also drawn from other territories including the Bahamas, Barbados and British Honduras.[9] Contrasting American wealth and opportunities with the lack of jobs in the West Indies, and enduring the indignities of the crudest elements of Jim Crowism, undoubtedly helped to harden beliefs among these West Indians in the causes of Caribbean self-determination and Black consciousness.

Britain was also desperate for farm labour. In early 1940, the Ministry of Agriculture approached the Colonial Office requesting that West Indians be recruited to augment Britain's agricultural workforce. However, the Colonial Office advised against and suggested that differences in agricultural techniques, as well as considerations of the 'health and morals' of West Indian workers, made this a bad idea. Instead of using West Indians, they suggested bringing in more prisoners of war from South Africa and India. The matter was dropped until questions were raised in Parliament in March 1942 and again in July 1943. Struggling to justify why tens of thousands of West Indians could support American agriculture but not British, the Colonial Secretary Oliver Stanley retreated to the old answer of lack of shipping.[10] This was ironic given the Colonial Office's frustration when this justification was being used against it by the War Office.

Although they were not recruited to work on its farms, West Indians would be employed in British forestry.

BRITISH HONDURAS FORESTRY WORKERS

The main industry of British Honduras (now known as Belize) was timber and particularly mahogany. This had been the case since Spain and Britain jostled for control of the territory during the eighteenth and nineteenth centuries until it finally became a British colony in 1862. By the end of the 1930s, the territory's economic woes were exacerbated by a decline in global demand and lack of proper management of the mahogany industry. The work involved in cutting and transporting this hardwood was seasonal and backbreakingly tough. Workers spent several months of the year in remote camps where they were entirely dependent on their employer for food, accommodation and other necessities. With a rising population, the vast forests of British Honduras were no longer able to provide the employment it needed.[11]

In Britain, meanwhile, there was a demand for forestry workers. The high demand for timber during the First World War had further exhausted British forests and woodlands. As a result, the Forestry Commission was established to replenish and manage this vital natural resource. By the 1940s, the saplings planted immediately after the First World War had grown into mature trees and were ready to be cut. The Second World War would see a huge increase in demand for timber and a loss of overseas sources of supply. Britain was heavily dependent on its recently revitalised forests to meet home demands. The scale of this home dependency would be shown in a postwar assessment that showed 11 per cent of all British woodlands had been felled.[12] Early in the war, the workforce recruited to carry out this work in Scotland included civilian lumberjacks from Newfoundland and Ireland, military forestry units from Canada, Australia and New Zealand, and Italian prisoners of war.

On 22 August 1941, 100 British Honduran lumberjacks (part of a contingent of 500 recruited in the colony) arrived in Scotland and were added to this international force.[13] They sailed across the Atlantic via Halifax in Canada. Their arrival in Scotland was reminiscent of the British West Indies Regiment, which had also travelled via Halifax twenty-five years earlier (see pp49-50). These Caribbean forestry workers were not provided with the cold-weather clothing that had been promised to them. Instead, they would endure the demands of tree felling during a Scottish autumn dressed in light clothing and footwear and often without gloves. To add to their misery, they worked the toughest sections of forest which earlier waves of foreign workers had turned down.[14] The camp provided for this first group (in East Linton) had not been completed, and men had to spend their early stay in tents. The groups that followed them were sent to Scottish camps in Duns and Kirkpatrick Fleming where they also encountered problems with their accommodation.[15]

When recruitment started, well over a thousand men applied – 857 were rejected on medical grounds and 541 were accepted. The response had been greater than the authorities in Britain had dared hope for. This owed more to the lack of options available to British Honduran workers. Work had dried up in other Central American territories and unemployment in the colony was described as 'developing into a dangerous situation'.[16] Until the scheme was brought to an end in 1943, a total of 900 workers would travel to Britain from British Honduras to join the forestry unit. But relations between these workers and the authorities in Britain would get off to a bad start before they had even set off for Scotland. The chairman of the Forestry Commission (Mr Robinson) and one of the major owners of lands on which the foresters would work (the

Duke of Buccleuch) objected to the plans to bring over 'coloured labour', and a senior civil servant in the department responsible for managing the scheme (the Ministry of Supply) warned against placing these men 'on private estates close to ... estate employees'.[17] Having expressed such concerns, the authorities would spend the following years justifying their initial racism.

Unused to the bitter cold and the local environment, the British Hondurans took time to adjust. Instead of supporting this adjustment, the authorities allocated eighty of the men to work that some described as 'skivvies' for the Australian unit. Amos Ford, one of the British Honduran foresters, wrote:

> The British Honduras Units were made up primarily of mahogany cutters, men accustomed to felling trees immeasurably larger than anything that could be found in either Australia or Canada. They were a contingent in their own proven right, not the skivvies for the other forestry contingents. Much frustration was felt on this score, by the men who thought that the Ministry was using them as lackies for the white forestry companies. Besides this, the Australians did not treat the British Hondurans as equals. The result was that while they got on well with the New Zealanders they were very unhappy with their position at the Australian's camp.[18]

The combination of sickness (as the West Indians acclimatised to the Scottish weather) and many dozens being reallocated to other units, affected the productivity of their unit. The authorities were quick to make negative comparisons between the other units and the British Hondurans, describing the latter as lazy and unproductive. They were also criticised for their behaviour towards the local community – particularly regarding women, with many officials objecting to Black men and white women forming close relationships (whether sexual or platonic). The double-standards with which these descriptions were applied have been pointed out by several historians and were highlighted by Colonial Office officials at the time.

Marika Sherwood points out that the first wave of Newfoundland loggers had very similar complaints to their British Honduran colleagues about poor treatment and lack of facilities. A third of the 2000 recruits returned home after six months rather than extend their contract. The authorities responded by recruiting more Newfoundlanders on improved contracts. But in February 1942 they were found to be in an 'almost mutinous condition'. Four months later, the Ministry of Supply had been forced into reporting to Clem Attlee (the deputy prime minister) on working conditions for the Newfoundlanders. They concluded that 'the Unit, having got a bad name at the beginning of its career, has been treated [by the department] with annoyance and suspicion ... they have been given timber to cut which was situated on very difficult ground and which had been refused by other Units'.[19] Had they investigated the conditions for the British Hondurans, they would have found a similar or worse state of affairs.

The Australian, Canadian and New Zealand units were companies of military engineers, with a combined force of 6160 by July 1942. They brought with them their own modern machinery. They also had access to amenities and entertainment available to military personnel. By contract, the West Indians were poorly equipped, left in remote locations to find their own entertainment, driven out of facilities they tried to use in Edinburgh, and criticised for their behaviour.[20] The hypocrisy of the situation was not lost on Colonial Office civil servant, John Keith, who criticised the lack of leadership and support for the Caribbean men, and noted that 'there is no real evidence that the Unit behaves in a worse way than the Newfoundlanders and the other "foreigners" in Scotland, but they are coloured men, and their immoralities get more publicity and are more shocking'.[21] The Ministry of Supply decided in September 1943 to end the scheme and most of the British Hondurans were repatriated. With the unemployment situation remaining desperate, the colony's governor pleaded with the British government to find work in the UK for as many of the men as possible.[22]

Despite the many hardships, the story of the Caribbean foresters in Scotland was not all bad. Many friendships and close relationships were formed between the West Indians and local communities, and some stayed to find work in Scotland or elsewhere in the UK. Theo Lambey, one of the foresters, recalled his time in Scotland with fondness: 'The people were grand; the village was like our own.

The people friendly and accommodating. In the public houses, we were treated like special guests. They were really good to us'.[23]

As well as the forests of Britain, West Indians worked in its factories producing essential materials for war.

MUNITIONS WORKERS AND TECHNICIANS

A modern, mechanised war required mechanics and skilled workers to keep its engines working. For Britain, among other things, this meant the production and maintenance of 27,896 tanks, 550,943 trucks and light military vehicles, and 124,877 pieces of artillery.[24] In June 1940, the top civil servant in the Colonial Office (Sir Cosmo Parkinson) expressed concerns about recruiting West Indians to carry out civilian work in the UK because of the 'complications in bringing coloured men in any numbers to this country'.[25] However, labour market pressures were at work on either side of the Atlantic that would force the hands of British authorities who were reluctant to recruit Black colonial labour.

West Indians working on a tank engine in Britain (l-r, Tom Martin, Fred Thomas, Ben Anderson and Arthur Jones from Jamaica, and Tom Prescodd from Trinidad) © Imperial War Museum, D 6203

First, there was the increasing pressure from the West Indies where its governors were expressing concern about the region's unemployment. The American bases construction programme would ease some of this pressure, but not for long. The Colonial Office recognised the West Indies as facing greater challenges of unemployment and underemployment than other colonies.[26] The second source of pressure came from within Britain and its insatiable demand for labour (see p191). A change in policy was inevitable. In June 1940, the governor of Jamaica informed the Colonial Office that the island could offer 2000 men for the British motor and mechanical industries and that their travel to the UK (and their return passage after the war) would be funded by the Jamaican Banana Producers Steamship Company. The correspondence this triggered, between Kingston and the Colonial Office and Ministry of Labour in London, would eventually result in a plan to send Jamaican skilled mechanics to the UK to work in the munitions industry. The first 117 arrived in the UK in February 1941 and were employed in munitions factories in the northwest.[27] More would follow as the scheme was extended to include recruits from

James Byfield, Jamaican electrician, working in tank factory in north of England © Imperial War Museum, D 6206

other British West Indian territories, and by the end of 1942 around 330 West Indian technicians were employed in munitions and other industries. Metzgen and Graham estimate that over 500 West Indians were employed in munitions work during the war. Over time, they were employed across a wide range of job types and industries including motor mechanics repairing military vehicles, oxy-acetylene welders working on aircraft assembly, electricians, and a range of other trades.[28]

Like the West Indian men and women who enlisted in the armed forces, these civilian workers had a variety of motivations – a desire to better themselves with decent jobs and a stable income, the appeal of overseas adventure, and the patriotic call to help the 'mother country'. One such recruit, a young Barbadian unnamed in the account, recalled a recruitment drive on the island where he and friends were called to attend a meeting at the Labour Office in Bridgetown. They were addressed by a local official:

> The gist of what he said was as follows: The Mother Country was at war, and that there was a dire need to defeat the Nazis' forces … We were not being asked to go as soldiers, there were enough of them already, but soldiers needed the tools of war with which to fight; things like guns and planes and tanks. What was needed was engineers to make these instruments of war.[29]

The West Indians were welcomed. In late 1941, Ernest Bevin, Britain's Minister of Labour, explained that since he needed 'all the men I can get to be trained for munitions work I shall be very glad to have these young men from the West Indies'.[30] In the summer of the following year, Harold Macmillan was enthusing about the quality of West Indian engineers during a BBC broadcast:

> When I was at the Ministry of Supply I used to go round a good many factories, and I used to see some of the skilled technicians from the West Indies hard at work making munitions. They were very good tradesmen, artisans, and engineers. One man in particular, I remember, who solved a technical problem in a workshop which had baffled many

British engineers of considerable skill and experience. That shows you the kind of quality they are.[31]

These skilled workers made a valuable contribution to the war effort, and many of them did this in the face of persistent racism. Although it was diluted during the war, this racism was still very real and it was experienced across the empire – in the 'mother country' and the colonies. The UK government's response to the colour bar was pragmatic, at best, and more often confused and deceitful. The attitudes of other Allied forces (the US or the white Dominion nations) were frequently used as an excuse for Britain's own shortcomings on this issue.

NOTES

1   Marika Sherwood, *Many Struggles: West Indian Workers and Service Personnel in Britain (1939-45)*, Karia Press, 1985, p55; see also Richard Moore-Coyler, 'Kids in the Corn: School Harvest Camps and farm labour supply in England, 1940-1950', in *The Agricultural History Review*, Vol 52, Part 2, 2004, pp183-206.

2   Ron Ramdin, *The Making of the Black Working Class in Britain*, Wildwood House: UK, 1987, pp86-8; James Denman and Paul McDonald, 'Unemployment Statistics from 1881 to the present day', in Labour Market Trends, Government Statistical Service, January 1996, pp7, 11.

3   CO 323/1672/3, National Archives, UK, telegram from secretary of state for colonies to governors of West Indian territories and Bermuda on 18 September 1939.

4   Moyne Commission, *The Moyne Report: Report of the West India Royal Commission*, Ian Randle Publishers,: Jamaica, 2011, chapter 2, paragraphs 11-13, and chapter 10 paragraph 12.

5   CAB 68/9/26, National Archives, UK, section 79 on p11.

6   Ligia T Domenech, *Imprisoned in the Caribbean: The 1942 German U-Boat Blockade*, iUniverse, 2014, Google Books version, pp43-4.

7   Oliver Marshall, *The Caribbean at War: 'British West Indians' in World War II*, The North Kensington Archive: London, 1992, p27.

8   Ibid.

9   Domenech, op cit, p58.

10 Sherwood, op cit, pp55-6.

11 Moyne Commission, op cit, chapter 16, paragraph 46, chapter 24, paragraphs 24-9.

12 'History of Britain's forests and woodlands: 100 years of the Forestry Commission', *BBC Countryfile Magazine*, 19 September 2019, https://www.countryfile.com/wildlife/trees-plants/history-of-britains-forests-and-woodlands-celebrating-100-years-of-the-forestry-commission.

13 CAB 68/8/58, National Archives, UK, section 28 on p12.

14 Humphrey Metzgen and John Graham, *Caribbean Wars Untold: A Salute to the British West Indies*, University of the West Indies, 2007, pp134-5.

15 Amos A Ford, *Telling the Truth: The life and times of the British Honduran Forestry Unit in Scotland (1941-44)*, Karia Press: London, 1985, p21. See also Sherwood, op cit, p103.

16 Sherwood, op cit, p99-100.

17 Ibid, p101.

18 Ford, op cit, p99.

19 Sherwood, op cit, pp101-2.

20 Ibid. See also CO 876/14, National Archives, UK, minute from John Keith on 5 August 1942 refers to US troops 'ousting' British Honduran foresters from Rest House for Servicemen in Edinburgh, and response from Sir George Gater on 11 August asking for the matter to be investigated.

21 Joanne Buggins, 'West Indians in Britain during the Second World War: A short history drawing on Colonial Office papers', in *Imperial War Museum Review*, No 5, Imperial War Museum, 1990), p88; Sherwood, op cit, pp118-9.

22 CAB 66/42/45, National Archives, UK, section 133-4 on p15.

23 Ford, op cit, p58.

24 Jean Lopez et al, *World War II: Infographics*, Thames & Hudson: London, 2019, p28 provides production figures for the period 1939 to 1945.

25 Buggins, op cit, p88.

26 There are many references within Colonial Office papers indicating their concern that the West Indies had a greater unemployment problem than other parts of the Empire. A few examples are: Sherwood, op cit, pp57-8 refers to a note for Cabinet on colonial man-power on 19 December 1940 where the Colonial Office refer to the West Indies as 'the main colonial source, so far hardly touched'; also in file CO 968/37/8, National Archives, UK, a minute from Arthur Poynton on 5 August 1941 says: 'In about every other place [except the West Indies] we know that local requirements are such as to make it virtually impossible to spare men from the territory itself', later in the same file another minute from Poynton, dated 26 September 1941,

says: '... in practice it may be that the West Indies are the only big potential sources of labour yet untapped'.

27 Sherwood, op cit, pp56-8; CAB 68/8/21, National Archives, UK, section 33.

28 Sherwood, op cit, pp60-1; Buggins, op cit, p89; Metzgen and Graham, op cit, p130.

29 Megzgen and Graham, op cit, p130.

30 Sherwood, op cit, p61 quoting from a letter from Ernest Bevin to the secretary of state for colonies, Lord Moyne.

31 Imperial War Museum, *TOGETHER!*, 1995, pp2-3 of insert 'F' which is titled 'The Colonial Effort', a broadcast from Harold Macmillan MP on 28 July 1942.

11

Britain's wartime colour bar

The UK government decisions on the deployment of British West Indian troops, and its attitude towards the arrival of African American GIs on British soil, were driven by racism. Indeed, during the final years of the war, War Office officials briefly toyed with redefining the colour bar to restrict military recruitment even further, by excluding men from southern or eastern parts of Europe (for more on the construction of whiteness, see the opening section of Chapter Two).[1] In this chapter, we will look at how wartime racism specifically affected the experience of West Indians in the Caribbean and the UK.

JIM CROW IN BRITAIN (1942 TO 1944)

Between 1942 and 1944 the United Kingdom became more ethnically diverse than it had ever been. Around 1.5 million US servicemen and women arrived in preparation for the D-Day landings, and among them were 150,000 African Americans. Britain would have to get used to dealing with Black people in numbers that it had never encountered before, and its West Indian visitors would be affected by this experience.

What made this encounter particularly difficult was that the US armed forces that had been transported to the UK were fully segregated. Although not all white American military personnel approved of the policy, the vast majority did. A US army survey conducted in 1943 found 90 per cent of white respondents in favour of segregated units and services compared to 40 per cent of Black soldiers who agreed.[2] The imposition of such segregation on British soil, along with the accompanying Jim Crow attitudes, proved to be a test of the public's patience. It placed the British government in the embarrassing position of choosing between its relations with its American ally, and its relations with its Black empire and alignment to British public sentiment. It chose American relations. In a War Cabinet meeting in July 1942, Foreign Secretary Anthony Eden expressed concern that increasing tensions would emerge because of 'certain sections of our people showing more effusiveness to the coloured troops than the Americans would readily understand'. Eden was right, but this 'effusiveness' was probably made easier because these Black soldiers were temporary visitors who were not competing for British jobs or housing.[3]

Not only were the African Americans welcomed, but when forced to pick a side, the British public would more often choose them over white American soldiers. In southwest England, where large numbers of American troops were stationed, many incidents were reported of clashes between white Americans and the British public. In one incident, African American soldiers were approached by US military police and admonished about their uniforms, bystanders questioned the authority of the military police and were said to have encouraged the Black Americans to a state of 'near mutiny'. In another, a crowd gathered during a dispute between white American officers and their Black driver. The crowd took the side of the Black man to the point of 'laying hands on the American officers to get them away from the driver'. On another occasion when American military police were arresting an African American soldier, a crowd gathered making comments such as 'they don't like the blacks' and 'why don't they leave them alone' until the local police eventually moved the crowds on.[4]

White Americans regularly made clear their displeasure at drinking alongside their Black countrymen, but landlords and landladies would often not respond as they expected. When complaints were made by white GIs about her willingness to serve Black customers, a landlady answered, 'their money is as good as yours, and we prefer their company'. A pub in Bristol displayed a sign that read 'only blacks served here'.[5] Black West Indians were caught up in these confrontations since white GIs with racist views did not make a distinction based on nationality. In certain parts of the country, it was common for West Indians to travel only in groups to avoid attacks from white GIs. George Powe, a RAF wireless operator from Jamaica, recalled an incident when a West Indian called 'Mushett' ventured into a village near the RAF station on his own and was attacked by Americans. Powe described the response: 'So we went into town ... armed to the teeth with knuckle-dusters, daggers and the lot. The fight lasted about two hours, and we cleared the Yanks out of the village. We were there about three months and for the next three months no Yanks dared to come in the town'.[6]

The famous West Indian cricketer, Learie Constantine, was working as a welfare officer with the Ministry of Labour during the war and looked into racial tensions in Merseyside between West Indian RAF groundcrew and white US soldiers. He reported back to Whitehall that Americans were damaging race relations and gave several cases of West Indians being attacked. In one case, in Birkenhead, an RAF technician queuing to enter a cinema was attacked by GIs who told him he had no right to be there – locals came to his rescue. As West Indians travelled in groups and armed themselves for protection, it was reported that razors, knives and other weapons were used on both sides.[7]

The ferocity of these fights, with deadly weapons being used, resulted in fatalities. Gerald Beard, a Jamaican who joined the RAF in 1943, witnessed an incident where a white American was killed by the West Indian he was racially abusing: '... these white Americans started to pick a fight straight away with these chaps ... Well, one of them was calling him nigger and thing ... I am not saying it's right, and I am not saying it's wrong, he just held his head and pulled him outside where the white American met his fate!' On another occasion, the table was turned. In a restaurant in London's Soho, a fight broke out between a white American and Black West Indian in which 'the West Indian dished out a terrible beating to the Yank who dashed out of the restaurant, returning shortly afterwards with a revolver, stood at the door, gunned the West Indian down without pity or compunction and departed, leaving everyone stunned'.[8] When Americans picked on Black RAF personnel, the retaliation did not only involve Black people. A Colonial Office civil servant reported to colleagues '... a case of a coloured member of the RAF being slung out of a pub by American troops and returning there the next night with white comrades from his RAF station and proceeding to beat up the Americans'.[9]

Rising tensions between white US troops and the public created a headache for the British government. They had tried to persuade the US not to deploy African American troops in Britain because, to Whitehall, it was the Black GIs who were the problem and not their white tormentors. An indication of the keenness of the UK military establishment to accommodate the attitudes of white American soldiers was shown in guidance produced by a senior British officer. Major General Arthur Dowler, in charge of administration for the army in the southwest of England, produced his infamous 'Notes on Relations with Coloured Troops' on 7 August 1942. It described 'the generality' of Black men as being 'of a simple mental outlook' and lacking 'the white man's ability to think and act to a plan'. He argued the 'necessity for us to conform to the American attitude' and justified this by explaining that allowing 'too wide associations with white men tend to make [black men] lose their heads'.[10] Although intended only for circulation to a select group of army officers in the southwest, for them to brief the men and women under their command, the note quickly leaked out and created a stir. It was brought to the attention of the Colonial Office who were appalled by the language. The resulting discussions within the War Cabinet about the need for official advice on relations with Black American troops concluded with a toned-down version of Dowler's note. Whilst the government would not co-operate with America's approach to segregating its forces, it would not stand in the way and would encourage a greater understanding of the US army's approach to race. The War Cabinet 'generally agreed that it was desirable that the people of this country should avoid becoming too friendly with coloured American troops'.[11] Regardless of these sentiments within the War Cabinet, the British people continued to largely show hospitality and friendship toward African American troops.

Although many of the African American soldiers were accustomed to segregation and Jim Crow attitudes at home, this did not mean that they would readily accept it in Britain. In the Lancashire town of Bamber Bridge, Black GIs were involved in a deadly five-hour standoff against US military police on the night of 24 June 1943. It started after last orders at the local pub (the Olde Hob Inn) when the military police confronted a group of Black GIs from the Eighth Army Quartermaster Truck Company and tried to arrest Private Eugene Nunn for not wearing proper uniform. As in so many similar incidents, a white British soldier challenged them asking: 'Why do you want to arrest them? They're not doing anything or bothering anybody'. As the confrontation grew more heated, the military police were beaten into a retreat. When they returned with reinforcements, shots were fired and Private William Crossland, another Black GI, was hit in the back and killed. As word got back to camp, the situation deteriorated into an armed standoff. The military police brought in a machine gun-equipped vehicle, resulting in the Black soldiers (convinced that they were about to be killed) drawing rifles from their stores. A shooting battle took place on the streets of the town which, for locals, must have looked like a scene from a Wild West movie. By the morning, in addition to the death of Private Crossland, four African American soldiers were injured. This was not an isolated incident – forty-four clashes would be recorded in the four-month period from November 1943 to February 1944.[12]

Beyond these violent clashes, usually resulting from provocation, the lack of evidence of bad behaviour among Black GIs was a source of frustration for British critics who looked for an excuse to force the US authorities to redeploy them.

In October 1943, Churchill asked his Secretary of State for War, James Grigg, to investigate allegations of widespread criminality among African American soldiers. Despite his poor view of these soldiers, Grigg had to concede that although many Members of Parliament had complained, the evidence was lacking: 'the police reports have, in a great number of cases, failed to confirm the reports'. Also strongly opposed to the presence of Black GIs was the Duke of Marlborough, a second cousin of Winston Churchill and one of Britain's liaison officers working with the American forces. Marlborough tried to persuade the prime minister that the Black Americans were at the centre of a crime-wave that would grow worse, and suggested that Churchill may need to intervene with the US authorities. But when he presented the evidence to Churchill on 21 October, the Duke had to concede that 'these figures are liable to belittle the arguments I tried to produce yesterday'. This did not stop him from insisting that 'although for the most part coloured troops are fairly well behaved and disciplined, there is a serious subversive element about them which I feel can do much to bring about a great deal of unpleasantness in the relationship between our two countries'. Despite the lack of substance to his cousin's concerns, Churchill passed the details to Grigg the following day and informed him: 'I consider the matter is serious and wish to have the War Office view upon it'. As much as he would have liked to corroborate Marlborough's accusations, Grigg could not and concluded that 'we should take no further action with the American authorities for the time being'.[13]

HOME-GROWN RACISM

Although Britain could, with some justice, blame America for exporting its racial tensions along with its multi-ethnic fighting force, Jim Crow attitudes could not take the blame for all domestic conflicts around race. There were two other factors driving these conflicts. The first was a tendency among some Britons to embrace US racist attitudes and even, at times, wrongly anticipate what these influential American visitors would expect. Dowler and his note on race relations was an example of this. He could give full expression to his racism and excuse his actions by saying that he was simply responding to the 'cultural' needs of the American ally. Another example involved the Imperial Hotel in Russell Square, London. In the summer of 1943, Learie Constantine was in London to play in a cricket match and brought his family to stay with him. They had booked into the Imperial Hotel but, on arrival, were told by the manager that they could not stay there because it would create problems with their American guests.[14] The incident stirred public interest, with media coverage and questions being asked in Parliament. Constantine successfully sued the hotel for breach of contract.

The second factor behind racial conflicts was an entirely home-made set of racist rules and regulations found across many different walks of life in wartime Britain. In October 1939, a government minister, Alan Lennox-Boyd, justified discrimination in employment in the air raid services because 'for certain services it is an advantage to choose persons who are in no sense strangers'.[15] The ambiguous phrase 'in no sense strangers' packed a racist punch, and would continue to be used during the war to exclude people of colour from employment in a range of services. In spring 1941, a year and a half after Lennox-Boyd's statement, a Trinidadian called Mr Penny, who was living in London, applied for work as an assistant in a London County Council (LCC) rest centre. He was rejected because he was Black. These centres, which were part of the civil defence network, provided temporary accommodation and support for people who had been bombed out of their homes. When Penny's representative raised his case with the Colonial Office, a Colonial Office minister (George Hall) wrote to the LCC for an explanation. But Hall's letter virtually coached the LCC to provide an answer that would get them and the Government off the hook. Referring to Lennox-Boyd's statement in the Commons, Hall suggested: 'It is quite possible that ... your Council ... may feel that coloured persons, as "strangers" are not always suitable for employment ...' The LCC confirmed that for jobs in rest centres 'coloured persons, as "strangers" – to use your term, are not regarded as suitable for employment, for reasons which you will readily understand'.[16] This was all the Colonial Office needed to hear, and they fed back to Mr Penny's representatives that this was not a case of race discrimination.

A colour bar operated across many professions in wartime Britain. Despite a shortage of doctors during the early years of the war, it was difficult for a person of colour to get such a role in a hospital in most parts of the country. Only when the shortage became acute later in the war did the position change and doctors from the West Indies, and other parts of the empire, found it easier to find employment. Non-white lawyers were less fortunate and continued to struggle to find work or to get the pupillage required to practice as a barrister.[17]

When seeking accommodation (rental, leased or hotel), racism was legal and blatant. Basil Rodgers, a Black Briton of West Indian origin, reported to the Colonial Office that leasing and letting agreements often refused tenancies to 'coloured people'. People of colour, whatever their means, were often forced to rent properties in the most run-down parts of London because they were turned away in more 'respectable' locations. Indeed, a Colonial Office file note in June 1941 that looked at Rodgers' case also found similar issues in finding hotel accommodation. It was common knowledge that 'the most respectable people from the Colonies' could get rooms in only the best London hotels (Claridges, Berkeley, etc) or the 'most sordid' ones.[18] In the same month, Sir Hari Singh Gour, a prominent Indian lawyer and social reformer who was visiting the UK, fell foul of this colour bar and was refused a hotel room as a result. In the House of Commons, the Home Secretary, Herbert Morrison, was asked what he would do about cases like this. In response Morrison condemned the hotel's actions but made clear: 'The matter is not one in which I have any power to intervene ...'[19]

Public attitude towards the colonies, and the people living there, could often be patronising and condescending. This was usually blamed on ignorance. The remedy commonly suggested was public education about the empire, its contribution to the war effort, and the richness of its diverse cultures. The BBC was the obvious vessel through which to conduct this public education. However, in one exchange within Whitehall about such a plan, it was pointed out that 'the BBC could do with a little educating' itself before using it to educate the public. The Colonial Office had received complaints from Sierra Leone about a BBC programme that 'persistently referred to Africans as "niggers"'. It was noted that this was 'not the first offence ... We have taken the matter up but I don't suppose the result will be satisfactory as I don't think the BBC people understand why we object so much'.[20]

Britain's problems with racism were a mix of home-made and imported. The need for the empire's full support highlighted the national harm that could be caused by conflicts around race. It would provoke serious soul-searching within government about what legislative actions, if any, could be taken to appear to be addressing these issues.

RACISM AND DISCRIMINATION WITHIN THE
WEST INDIES (1930s TO 1945)

During the turbulent 1930s, racial antagonism in the West Indies was at boiling point. Witnesses appearing before Lord Moyne's Royal Commission of Inquiry consistently painted a picture of growing racial tensions as the Black majority population experienced increasing poverty.[21] The emerging political parties and labour movements were linking racial and economic injustice in their demands for change. Each territory had its own context that had fanned the flames of unrest in slightly different ways. With the arrival of war, the tensions of the previous decade had calmed but were still evident. Of all the British West Indian territories, the Bahamas and Barbados were reputed to be the most racist. The Bahamas was said to display similarities with the Jim Crow attitudes found in southern states of the US. A plan, in October 1943, to use Nassau as an assembly point and training centre for West Indian groundcrew recruits was halted when it was pointed out that there was a 'strict colour bar in Bahamas'.[22]

The Bahamas was more heavily shaped by American attitudes than most other islands. The historian, Ashley Jackson, described its racist policies: 'Keeping the black masses poor and uneducated was an unspoken policy, and governors intent on visiting upon the island the more enlightened policies gaining currency in the Colonial Office were not at all welcome ... It was an island of idle rich, native poor, American tourists and cosmopolitan tax-evaders'. An official report on strikes and riots during 1942 'lifted the lid on the island's poisonous racial relations and condemned the local white establishment and its attitudes ...'[23]

If the Bahamas and Barbados were the most racist of the British West Indian islands, the least racist was supposed to be Jamaica. Its reputation for political unrest had meant that this was the Caribbean territory that London treated with greatest care and caution. In an article in the *New Statesman and Nation* in November 1944, Fernando Henriques (a twenty-eight-year-old Black Jamaican who had studied at Oxford and been president of the Oxford Union earlier that year) explained the changing shape of racism in Jamaica. He described how, on New Year's Eve 1937, the hotels that flaunted their racism by excluding Blacks 'were invaded by coloured Jamaicans who demanded to be admitted to the festivities'. As a result of the upheavals of the 1930s, these forms of segregation were ended in Jamaica. When American troops arrived in the early 1940s and tried to reimpose such restrictions, they were quickly taught that Jamaica was not the US. A job advert placed in a Jamaican paper for a junior role on a US military base said that 'white applicants would be preferred'. It produced an outcry that forced a swift apology from the American military who insisted that the advert had been placed without their approval.[24]

Although racism was less blatant in Jamaica, it would be foolish to suggest (as many colonial leaders did) that it was non-existent. Across the British West Indies, racism was a constant fact of life. Wealth and poverty were determined by race, as was access to the best jobs and education. All the main businesses, the armed forces, and the most senior ranks of political and civil administration, were in the hands of white people. The only difference between Jamaica and most of the other territories was that the rules of racism usually went unwritten and unstated, but they were widely understood, nonetheless. Henriques described the warped attitude towards race in Jamaica and across the Caribbean.

> In every community which has been dominated or controlled by Europeans there arises an evitable bias toward the white because that is the colour of the dominant race. The mulatto will consider himself superior to the black, and will feel more in common with the European than the Negro ... The parents of brown children will encourage them to marry fairer people as it means a definite step up in the hidden social scale.[25]

The 'colourism' that Henriques alluded to was a powerful force. It infected social attitudes and was woven into the racism around employment decisions. A wide range of jobs and facilities were open only to white people, with occasional exceptions made for people of colour with the lightest shade of skin. The senior ranks of British West Indian colonial service and the banking system were prime exemplars for this form of discrimination. On a visit to the UK in November 1941, as part of a delegation of Caribbean editors,

Garnet Gordon (from St Lucia) drew attention to this fact. On their way to London, the delegation had stopped off in Bermuda and had been booked into a local hotel. The hotel had been informed in advance that the delegation included 'coloured gentlemen', but the proprietor refused to accommodate them when he saw 'how black they were'.[26] Thus, these issues were fresh in Gordon's mind when he met with the Colonial Office's Permanent Under-Secretary (Sir Cosmo Parkinson). Gordon explained that the West Indian banks would not employ 'coloured men' except for a few cases where they employed men who were 'very lightly coloured'. But they absolutely would not 'employ men of really dark colour'. He also told Parkinson that there was a colour bar in recruitment to inspectors of police. The Colonial Office investigated and a search through the files of all its West Indian police inspectors revealed 'only one coloured Inspector of Police – Mr Crosswell of Jamaica – and he is but slightly coloured'. Incredibly, they concluded that this discrepancy had nothing to do with racism, even though they acknowledged that governors did, occasionally, specify that they wanted people of 'pure' European descent for specific roles. As for the banks, a civil servant confirmed Gordon's observations, noting that '... from what little I saw of bank staff in Jamaica ... there is a good deal in it as far as the senior staff are concerned'.[27] The Colonial Office decided to take no action about the appointments of inspectors of police and would probably have done nothing about racism in banking if its hand had not been forced.

In June 1943, a year and a half after Garnet Gordon alerted the Colonial Office to the colour bar in banking, David Adams MP raised the issue through a question in Parliament. He asked the secretary of state for colonies 'whether he is aware that there exists a colour bar in the staffing of a banking institution, of which he has been advised, in the West Indies; and whether he will make representations to the directors of this concern ...'[28] This triggered a flurry of activity, beginning with discussions with the London offices of Barclays' overseas division. It became apparent that Harold Moody (and his League of Coloured Peoples) had been corresponding with them about their practices in the West Indies and had probably briefed Adams to ask the parliamentary question. Despite coming under considerable pressure, the bank's director responsible for the

Caribbean refused to budge on the issue, using as their defence the racial divisions that were in place across the region:

> The great majority of white children in the West Indies are educated in the same schools with coloured children. They sit together in school and play games together and no serious racial difficulties arise between them. Beyond this however, there is very little social contact; coloured children do not, generally speaking, go to the homes of the white children and vice versa, and once school age is passed the social cleavage widens. In the larger islands there are a few (but very few) coloured people who are generally accepted such as one or two judges, a leading lawyer or two and so on, but in Barbados even this would not apply. In the smaller islands, there is perhaps rather more social contact though even there it is not really extensive.[29]

The racism found in Barclays was common practice across the wider British West Indian banking sector. Discussions with Barclays, the Royal Bank of Canada, the Canadian Bank of Commerce, and the Bank of Nova Scotia would drag on throughout the following year. The banks rebuffed every Colonial Office effort to squeeze even the smallest and most tokenistic concession from them.

RESOLVING THE BRITISH POLICY ON RACE

The colour bar in all its forms aggravated tensions across an empire where citizens were growing more assertive in combating racism. Aware of this, the Colonial Office felt compelled to act. As is often the case with civil servants, action meant writing a policy statement. But there was great confusion about how and where to start in developing such a statement. After some head scratching, it was decided that the best place to start was to conduct a quick study into racist laws across the colonial empire. The suggestion was that once these discriminatory laws had been identified, Britain could proceed to scrap them as part of an announcement of its vision for racial equality.

In October 1941, the civil servant Charles Jeffries (Assistant Under-Secretary of State at the Colonial Office) suggested that before the end of the war, there was only one credible position that the government could adopt: 'Nothing short of absolute equality of all men before the law will serve, either to satisfy the aspirations of the majority of inhabitants of the Colonial empire or to justify our existence as a Colonial power'. The department's top civil servant, Sir Cosmo Parkinson, agreed and sought the approval of the secretary of state. It was not until August 1942, ten months later, that approval was given to commence the work. But whilst approving for the research phase of the work to begin, the Secretary of State (Lord Cranborne) insisted that the time was not right to make a public statement along the lines that Jeffries had suggested in case it offended Americans: 'A public declaration, at the present juncture, by [the government] that they are opposed to any form of colour bar is likely to be interpreted by white American troops in this country as a direct rebuke, indeed, insult to them, and can only have the result of exacerbating an already sufficiently difficult situation'.[30]

Outside of the military and government services, race discrimination was seen as beyond the domain of legislation and direct government action. Housing landlords, private sector employers, hotel and restaurant owners were common culprits. It was, for example, in the hotel sector where both Learie Constantine and Sir Hari Singh Gour had brushes with the colour bar. The government considered these to be private matters caused by 'bad manners' among a class of business owners who chose to discriminate in this way. It was not seen as an infringement on the civil rights of those who were the victims of this discrimination. Given this view, it is difficult to understand what the Colonial Office's policy statement would have achieved in Britain or in the empire. But there was no rush to complete this work, and so it plodded along. Sir Mervyn Tew, a former Chief Justice of Sierra Leone, was commissioned to quietly carry out the review, under the guidance of Colonial Office officials including Dr Audrey Richards, one of few prominent women civil servants.

The review was completed in late 1943 and focused mainly on African colonies (particularly in east and southern Africa). Little in the way of discriminatory legislation was found in the West Indies. Tew's work did not provide the definitive picture that had been hoped for. He had made clear that more work would be needed to look beyond the statute books in the colonies and to take account of actual custom and practice.[31] The Colonial Office sat on it, not knowing what to do. This was not only because of the many gaps in the review. In truth, the Colonial Office did not have the appetite to tackle this issue and take the steps toward the principle of 'absolute equality of all men before the law' that Jeffries had set out two years earlier. And so, at the end of 1944, a review that had already lacked any urgency was simply kicked further into the long grass and would not re-emerge until after the war.

The Second World War provided Britain with its first experience of a Black population well over 100,000 strong – although the vast majority were African Americans. It was the slightest glimpse at what a multi-ethnic Britain might feel like, and Whitehall disliked what it saw. By the end of the war, the government was glad for the support received from across the empire and from multi-ethnic forces of its allies, but it would now have to strike a balance. On the one hand, Britain had to show a greater respect towards the 500 million people, mainly Black and brown, who made up the empire. These were increasingly self-confident peoples with aspirations of self-government. On the other hand, postwar governments wished to discourage the creation of large Black communities in Britain. This would create constant policy tensions. Hesitatingly, and most often reluctantly, governments would oversee the growth of a multi-ethnic country that has taken decades to become more at ease with this fact, and where the history of those communities' relationship to the UK through empire has often been obscured.

NOTES

1 WO 32/10592, National Archives, UK, enclosure 18A entitled 'Memorandum of the present situation concerning the commissioning of alien and/or colonial officers'; also see minutes 18 (13 January 1943), 19 (10 February 1943), 20 (17 February 1943), 21 (23 February 1943), 22 (7 March 1943).
2 Joseph Connor, 'Leveling the Playing Field', in *World War II*, HISTORYNET: Arlington, VA, USA, August 2021, p40.

3   David Olusoga, *Black and British: A Forgotten History*, Pan Books, Apple eBooks version, 2017, chapter 13, paragraph 6 the quote from Eden and paragraph 9 refers to the reasons for African American soldiers being welcomed.

4   PREM 4/26/9, National Archives, UK, paragraph 5 of letter from James Grigg (secretary of state for war) to Winston Churchill on 21 October 1943.

5   Olusoga, op cit, chapter 13, paragraph 11.

6   Robert N Murray, *Lest We Forget: The Experiences of World War II Westindian Ex-Service Personnel*, Nottingham Westindian Combined Ex-Services Association, 1996, pp112-3.

7   CO 876/15, National Archives, UK, see document headed 'Relations between American white soldiers and British coloured civilians in Liverpool', 11 January 1943.

8   Murray, op cit, p114.

9   CO 537/1223, op cit, minute from Arthur Poynton dated 17 March 1944.

10 Ben Bousquet and Colin Douglas, *West Indian Women at War: British Racism in World War II*, Lawrence & Wishart, 1991, pp72-3, 162-5.

11 Ibid, pp73-6; CO 876/14, National Archives, UK, extract from conclusions of the War Cabinet meetings on 13 October 1942 and 20 October 1942.

12 Professor Alan Rice, 'Black troops were welcome in Britain, but Jim Crow wasn't: the race riot of one night in June 1943', *The Conversation*, 22 June 2018, https://theconversation.com/black-troops-were-welcome-in-britain-but-jim-crow-wasnt-the-race-riot-of-one-night-in-june-1943-98120.

13 PREM 4/26/9, op cit, letter from Grigg to Churchill dated 21 October 1943 in an attachment headed, 'Report on Coloured Troops in Great Britain'; letter from Duke of Marlborough to Churchill dated 21 October 1943; note from Churchill to Grigg on 22 October 1943; response from Grigg to Churchill, 2 December 1943.

14 CO 859/80/8, National Archives, UK, minute from John Keith dated 6 August 1943.

15 UK Parliament, House of Commons, Hansard, 11 October 1939, https://api.parliament.uk/historic-hansard/written-answers/1939/oct/11/air-raid-precautions-service.

16 CO 859/80/9, National Archives, UK, letter from George Hall MP (under-secretary of state for colonies) to CG Amon MP (chairman of London County Council) on 31 March 1941, and response from Amon on 17 April 1941.

17 CO 537/1224, National Archives, UK, see p2 of document titled 'Colour Discrimination in the United Kingdom', dated May 1946.

18 CO 859/80/7, National Archives, UK, file note from John Keith dated 20 June 1941.

19 UK Parliament, House of Commons, Hansard, 19 June 1941, https://hansard.parliament.uk/Commons/1941-06-19/debates/9351bf2d-daa0-41ed-a04e-6f429804874f/CommonsChamber#contribution-7d2e1d57-ec89-458a-baac-bc2aebea2760/.

20 CO 859/40/4, National Archives, UK, John Keith's memorandum of 7 November 1940, and minutes from Mr Keith on 26 November 1940, Mr Williams on 19 March 1941 and Sir Alan Burns on 20 March 1941.

21 The Moyne Commission, *The Moyne Report: Report of the West India Royal Commission*, Ian Randle Publishers: Jamaica, 2011, chapter 5, paragraphs 12-18.

22 CO 968/74/19, National Archives, UK, telegram from secretary of state for colonies to Jamaica on 16 October 1943 for forwarding on to Bahamas and RAF mission in Washington.

23 Ashley Jackson, *The British Empire and the Second World War*, Hambledon Continuum: London, 2006, pp87, 92.

24 CO 859/126/6, National Archives, UK, cutting from [New] Statesman and Nation, dated 17 November 1944 titled 'The Colour Bar in the West Indies'.

25 Ibid.

26 CO 859/80/16, National Archives, UK, minute from Mr Downie of 5 November 1941.

27 Ibid, Sir Cosmo Parkinson's note of his meeting with Garnet Gordon dated 6 November 1941; minute from an official dated 3 December 1941; and minute from Mr Rogers of 12 November 1941.

28 UK Parliament, House of Commons, Hansard, 9 June 1943, https://api.parliament.uk/historic-hansard/commons/1943/jun/09/colour-bar.

29 CO 859/80/16, op cit, see p2 of letter from Mr A T Dudley of 10 June 1943 (attached to letter from Mr E H Holden of 1 July 1943).

30 CO 859/80/13, National Archives, UK, minute from Charles Jeffries on 8 October 1941, and minute from Lord Cranborne on 27 August 1942.

31 Ibid, see 'Discrimination in Colonial Legislation between Europeans and non-Europeans' followed by 'Memorandum' both dated 14 October 1944 on the file.

IV

Aftermath: Postwar Changes

12

Postwar Caribbean: Unfinished business

During the war, many British people gave a warm welcome to their West Indian guests, recognising the valuable contributions they were making to the war effort. Indeed, police and newspaper reports were full of stories of white Britons standing on the side of Black West Indians and Americans in the face of racism. But the experience of the tens of thousands of West Indians who travelled to Britain during the Second World War was not one of undiluted British kindness. Large numbers experienced racism in forms that were seldom seen in the Caribbean, whether at the hands of white GIs who abused and attacked them on British streets, or in the racism of British landlords and landladies who refused to rent to them, or business owners in the hospitality sector who refused to serve them in pubs, restaurants and hotels. One Second World War veteran, Robert Murray, said: 'I never heard of racism until I got to Britain'. His Guyanese compatriot, Cy Grant, had a mixed Scottish, African and South Asian heritage, and 'discovered his blackness when he arrived in England' and faced blatant racism.[1] Living and working in a majority-white country gave them a new perspective on racial inequality. Tens of thousands of West Indians also spent time working on farms and in factories in the US, often experiencing the bluntness (and brutality) of American racism.

The experience of the Black veterans and workers of this war was not the same as their parents and grandparents who had served in the First World War. That war had radicalised a generation of young West Indian men, who would return home to advocate for

Black consciousness and self-determination. Compared to this, the impact of the Second World War was less dramatic – partly because the political consequences of the First World War, and the 1930s uprisings that came after it, were still playing out through the political and labour movements of the region. However, the experience of West Indians overseas in the 1940s helped to accelerate the pace of change in the Caribbean. They returned home, often with a diminished sense of the grandeur of the so-called mother country, and varying degrees of resentment about the treatment they had received.

The vast majority of West Indians had seen out the war at home and endured a period of greater economic hardship. Jobs, food and provisions had been difficult to come by. A common theme was that life could and should be better, and that it was they (and not their colonial masters) who would make it so.

For much of the Caribbean, decolonisation was the unfinished business. There would be no single template for decolonisation. Instead, a multitude of arrangements were put in place, with the most extreme constitutional change occurring within the British West Indies. Like the rest of the world, the Caribbean had to recognise a change in context. There had been two big shifts in global power. First, the rise of the US as a dominant force was accelerated by the war. Although not able to control all the changes that were taking place across the Caribbean, the US would take extraordinary steps to prevent any change that conflicted with its ideological and economic interests. The second shift was the emergence of the Soviet Union as a new superpower. The USSR would be a counterbalance to US power among the independent states that emerged in the decades after the war.

THE US, PUERTO RICO AND THE INDEPENDENT CARIBBEAN STATES

For the independent states (Cuba, the Dominican Republic and Haiti) the issue was not decolonisation, but a continued struggle in a neo-colonial relationship, particularly with the US. It was Cuba where the most dramatic political realignment was to take place.

The domination of Cuban politics by the pro-American Batista regime would produce an anti-American backlash that helped to propel Fidel Castro to power in his 1959 revolution. Its political and economic survival was helped by the Soviet Union. This reality served to harden America's anti-communist paranoia and determination to limit Soviet influence in its backyard. That paranoia would be tested across the region, including the Dominican Republic. The war had entrenched the brutal Dominican dictatorship of Rafael Trujillo who had seized power in 1930 and would rule until his assassination in 1961. To the consternation of the Organisation of American States, the US would intervene in 1965 as it sent in troops to prevent the emergence of another left-leaning government – at its peak the US deployed 22,000 troops in the Dominican Republic.[2]

Haiti saw a change of government in 1946 as its military seized power from President Élie Lescot following a wave of strikes and violent demonstrations from workers and students. Elections held under military supervision gave power to the populist reformer Dumarsais Estimé only for the military to resume control in 1950. Several presidents followed in an increasingly unstable political environment until François Duvalier ('Papa Doc') was elected in 1957. His promise to end the reign of a 'mulatto' elite and empower the Black masses did not last, and his regime descended into a brutal, authoritarian police state as he created the Tonton Macoutes as his personal paramilitary. On his death in 1971, control was handed to his son Jean-Claude Duvalier ('Baby Doc'). Haiti would not manage to rid itself of the Duvaliers until 1986 when Jean-Claude was forced to flee into exile in France.

Whilst Cuba was at the extreme end of postwar change, Puerto Rico was at the minimalist end. The earlier wave of nationalism had calmed during the war. But before this wave had completely stilled, Muñoz Marín led his Popular Democratic Party to victory in the 1940 elections to the island's senate under the slogan 'land, bread, liberty'.[3] But demands for independence would fade, with the US granting only limited concessions to Puerto Rican self-determination, including an elected governorship in 1947. In 1952 the US granted the island commonwealth (or associated free state) status. Calls for independence diminished and were increasingly replaced by calls for statehood within the US.

INDEPENDENCE IN THE BRITISH CARIBBEAN
(1940s TO 1960s)

In the British Caribbean, important steps were taken towards independence with decisions to extend the franchise before the war ended. But Britain did not view this as a precursor to separation, instead seeing this as a way to strengthen colonial ties by responding to demands for reform. Following the recommendations of the Moyne Commission, the franchise was extended in Barbados in December 1943, Trinidad and Tobago in June 1944 and British Guiana in September 1944 (though racial and religious tensions in British Guiana would cause discussions to drag on beyond the war). But these reforms were limited. It was Jamaica where change was most dramatic with full adult suffrage granted in October 1944. After the war, others followed – Trinidad and Tobago in 1946 and the rest of the British Caribbean during the next two decades.

Whilst the gradual extension in voting rights was taking place, there was also a focus on greater cooperation across the region. One example of regional cooperation was the creation of the welfare and development organisation (led by Sir Frank Stockdale) to address the economic and welfare deficiencies identified by the Moyne Commission. Another example was the wartime coordination of transport and agriculture under the Anglo-American Caribbean Commission in response to the U-boat attacks. Britain had long toyed with the idea of unifying its Caribbean territories as a more efficient way to administer them – but nothing of any practical substance had ever come of this.[4] However, as the prospects of greater autonomy loomed, the impetus behind creating a federation grew stronger.

At a conference in Montego Bay in September 1947, there was consensus between Britain and all its Caribbean colonies that the most secure route to self-government, and ultimately independence, was through the creation of the West Indies Federation. It would take another ten years of negotiations and wrangling over the constitutional and administrative details before the federation came to fruition in January 1958. It was made up of ten islands (British Guiana and British Honduras had withdrawn from the scheme) with a total population of 3,100,000 across a landmass of

8,000 square miles. Two countries dominated this arrangement. Jamaica accounted for more than half the federation in population and landmass (1,600,000 people across 4,400 square miles). Trinidad and Tobago was the other great force, covering 1,980 square miles with a population of 826,000. In economic terms, the oil producing economy of Trinidad and Tobago surpassed that of Jamaica. The other eight territories were Barbados with 232,000 people, the Windward Islands (Dominica, Grenada, St Lucia and St Vincent) with 314,000 people and the Leeward Islands (Antigua and Barbuda, Montserrat, and St Kitts-Nevis-Anguilla) with 123,000.[5] But the federation was not independent – Britain controlled external affairs, defence and had ultimate control over its purse strings.

After more than ten years in gestation, the federation was launched in 1958 and lasted only four years before falling apart in 1962. Although it was the Barbadian premier, Grantley Adams, who became the first and only federal prime minister, it was two other West Indian premiers who would seal its fate. Both Dr Eric Williams of Trinidad and Tobago, and Jamaica's Norman Manley, were strong advocates of the federation early on in its conception. Whilst Williams held true to his convictions on the matter, Manley found himself exposed as Jamaicans increasingly expressed concerns at proposals for the federation to assume greater powers at the expense of the constituent countries. In the end, it was undone by dissatisfaction about its colonial status and limited powers, disagreements between the dominant political figures in the region about how strong the federal centre should be, and concerns among the larger islands that they were getting little in return for this union. These differences were compounded by an unbridgeable distance (geographic and cultural) between Jamaicans who made up the majority of its population and the other nine territories that sat 1,000 miles to its east. As its weaknesses grew starker, Bustamante declared the opposition Jamaican Labour Party unequivocally against the continuation of the federation. Manley felt obliged to put the matter to the Jamaican people in a referendum which he lost by 48 per cent to 52 per cent in September 1961. Jamaica left the federation and achieved independence the following year under the leadership of Bustamante as its first prime minister (he had beaten Manley in the general election that followed the refer-endum). Efforts to save what was left of the federation were short lived. The people of Trinidad and Tobago voted to leave in January 1962 and the West Indies Federation was dissolved in May 1962 by an act of the British Parliament. Over the course of the next two decades most of Britain's Caribbean territories achieved independ-ence, leaving Anguilla, British Virgin Islands, Cayman Islands, Montserrat, and the Turks and Caicos Islands to remain as British Overseas Territories.

Among the most difficult routes to independence was in British Guiana. There, the Marxist firebrand, Dr Cheddi Jagan, fell foul of America's anti-communist paranoia. His People's Progressive Party (PPP) built a mass following, winning elections in 1953, 1957 and 1961. But as British Guiana prepared for independence, the prospect of a Communist-led government displeased Washington. With encouragement from the US, Britain suspended the constitu-tion and amended the electoral system to a form of proportional representation rather than the first past the post system that applied in the rest of its Caribbean colonies. In the 1964 elections, Forbes Burnham led his Peoples National Congress to victory in a centrist coalition with the United Force and went on to lead the country to independence as Guyana in 1966.[6]

THE DUTCH AND FRENCH CARIBBEAN

As with the British Caribbean, the Dutch territories came out of the war with a much-diminished sense of the majesty and mystique of their colonial ruler. After the fall of the Netherlands, its Caribbean territories sent aid and raised funds for the war effort. With the liberation of the south of the country from German occupation in September 1944, the Dutch government in exile sent a request to the West Indies for urgent relief aid. The Aruba Relief Fund for the Netherlands was established and collected 126,000 guilders in aid (the equivalent of around €1.3 million in 2009 prices). The people of Suriname provided generous support too, raising 50,000 guil-ders for war relief within two months. Its Dutch governor recalled that after Holland's liberation in May 1945, the people of Suriname would send 'a stream of goods … to the hungry Netherlands'.[7] The weakening of the Dutch state, with this reversal of dependency, strengthened the nationalist movement. This was particularly evident in Suriname where moderate nationalists, such as Wim Bos Verschuur and Johan Wijngaarde, were also active supporters of the relief effort.[8]

The Dutch government owed the Caribbean a debt of gratitude, and this would have to be repaid by delivering on the commitment made by Queen Wilhelmina and her government, in 1942, to give autonomy within an equal partnership of the Dutch kingdom after the war. It would take twelve years from the commitment to autonomy and partnership being made, to its eventual delivery by the Dutch government. In 1954, the Statute of the Kingdom of the Netherlands set out this new relationship, granting its Caribbean territories the status of autonomous and equal parts of the kingdom. For Suriname, this would be a temporary measure before achieving full independence twenty-one years later in 1975.[9]

In France's Caribbean colonies, the people had enjoyed a greater degree of democratic involvement than in the British or Dutch colonies prior to the war. In 1946, Guadeloupe, Martinique and French Guiana were absorbed into France as *départments d'outre mer* (overseas departments), and the United Nations, accordingly, removed them from the list of non-self-governing territories since they were now part of France. Their status would be further enhanced in 1982 when they became *régions d'outre mer* (overseas regions). Although there have been many small parties within the French Caribbean that have agitated (some violently) for independence from the old colonial master, none have acquired significant popular appeal.[10]

NOTES

1   Robert N Murray, *Lest We Forget: The Experiences of World War II Westindian Ex-Service Personnel*, Nottingham Westindian Combined Ex-Services Association, 1996, p180; and Mark Johnson, *Caribbean Volunteers at War: The Forgotten Story of the RAF's 'Tuskegee Airmen'*, Pen & Sword Books, Google Books version 2014, Chapter 1, paragraphs 3-5.

2   Eric Williams, *From Columbus to Castro: The History of the Caribbean 1492-1969*, André Deutsch, 1983, p466.

3   Ibid, pp468-9.

4   Hugh W Springer, 'Federation in the Caribbean: An attempt that failed', in *International Organization*, Vol 16, No 4, Autumn 1962, University of Wisconsin Press, p758.

5   Ibid, pp758-9.

6   James Millette, 'Decolonization, Populist Movements and the Formation of New Nations, 1945-70', in Bridget Brereton (ed), *General History of the Caribbean, Volume V: The Caribbean in the Twentieth Century*, UNESCO, 2003, pp207-213.

7   Esther Captain and Guno Jones, 'The Dutch Antilles, Suriname and the Desperate Netherlands during World War II', in Karen Eccles and Debbie McCollin (eds), *World War II and the Caribbean*, University of the West Indies Press, 2017 Kindle version, paragraphs 22-6.

8   Ibid, paragraph 27.

9   Ibid, paragraph 28.

10 Anne S Macpherson, 'Toward Decolonization: Impulses, Processes, and Consequences since the 1930s' in Stephan Palmié and Francisco A Scarano (eds), *The Caribbean: A History of the Region and Its Peoples*, University of Chicago Press, 2011, pp478-9. Also see James Millette, chapter 5, in Brereton, op cit, pp181, 221-3.

13

Postwar Britain: Rebuilding begins

With the war at an end, Britain turned its attention to rebuilding. There was the physical infrastructure, damaged by years of German bombing, that needed to be rebuilt for a modern era. There was a new social infrastructure to deliver the vision of the Attlee government for universal healthcare and welfare domestically (though not for the empire). And there were new international relations to be built across a world dramatically altered by the war – America was even more dominant than before, the Soviet Union was now a great global power, new relationships would need to be developed in preparation for a postcolonial world, Europe would need rebuilding from the destruction of war, and new global institutions (such as the United Nations) had to be put in place. All these issues had an impact upon the Caribbean – some more directly and significantly than others.

ADDRESSING THE COLOUR BAR IN THE ARMED FORCES AND COLONIES (1942 TO 1948)

In addition to building peacetime structures, wartime structures had to be dismantled. As it put the armed forces back onto a peacetime footing, the UK government had to decide whether to reintroduce the colour bar that had been suspended during the war. These discussions had started midway through the war as the War Office prepared to appoint officers on permanent commissions who would serve in the postwar regular British army. This raised the question of whether these appointments would be available to people of colour. And if they were not to be, recruitment into the ordinary ranks of the permanent army would also need to exclude people of colour because it would have been problematic to have Black recruits who could not climb beyond the ranks of non-commissioned officers.

From 1942 throughout the remaining years of the war, the arguments between the Colonial Office and War Office would drag on. The Admiralty, unsurprisingly, supported the War Office wish to appoint only white officers. The Air Ministry, with its substantial experience of West Indian recruits, came down on the side of the Colonial Office. In October 1944, the then Secretary of State for Air Archibald Sinclair informed senior RAF officers of his strong objections to reintroducing the colour bar after West Indians had displayed great bravery: 'to erect a colour bar against an officer who had earned a DFC [Distinguished Flying Cross] would be indefensible and barbaric'.[1]

A year later, in November 1945, the Air Ministry decided to act on its own and permanently remove the colour bar in RAF recruitment. But in a compromise with the other armed services, it agreed to do this as 'unobtrusively as possible' so as not to cause them embarrassment.[2] On the other hand, the War Office line was hardening. On the eve of the final Cabinet discussion on the matter, it was pointed out to War Office officials that the National Services Bill (which proposed continuing conscription for young men) meant all young male British subjects, living in Britain, were subject to call-up and this would include Black Britons. The War Office response was to suggest that Black British subjects should be excluded from National Service.[3] It would not get its way, and on 3 June 1947 the Cabinet decided the military colour bar should be ended permanently.

Whilst the colour bar in the UK armed forces was under consideration, the government was also considering the impact of racist laws and regulations across the empire. The review of these laws had been undertaken by Mervyn Tew (see pp216-7), but his draft report had been regularly kicked down the road since 1943. In May 1946, Colonial Office officials were about to kick it away again but Mr Seel suggested to his colleagues that they use it to prepare for the United Nation's work on racial discrimination which was part of the development of what would become the Universal Declaration on Human Rights. Seel suggested that if the UN were to get 'busy on the question of legal discrimination on colour grounds, it might be desirable to be able to say that HM Government had already taken the matter up with Colonial Governments'.[4] His colleagues agreed, and a piece of work that had been conceived for the purpose of identifying and ending discriminatory legislation across the empire was turned into a briefing note to defend the UK government against potential criticism from the new United Nations organisation. This was the current reality – a world of changed relationships where the UK would need to defend its colonial past, explain its new colonial present, and prepare for a postcolonial future.

West Indian governors were asked for their comments on Tew's report. The comments they fed back bore little relation to the reality of racism in the region. Sir Bede Clifford said of Trinidad and Tobago that it was 'singularly free from such discrimination' but made clear this did not imply a great deal of mixing between people. He criticised Black people who complained about racism as no more than '"colour-bar" mongers' who dramatised 'small incidents' of discrimination. Whilst the Barbadian governor, Sir Hilary Blood, insisted that there was no discriminatory legislation on the island, his counterpart in the Windward Islands (Sir Arthur Grimble) pointed out that 'in Barbados ... colour-hatred among the privileged classes is most rampant and vocal'. As for the Bahamas, as renowned for its racism as Barbados, its governor (Sir William Murphy) simply observed: 'There is no racially discriminatory legislation in this colony'.[5] Although lacking in substance, the report was sufficient to provide the defence Britain needed as it engaged in discussions on the drafting of the UN's Declaration on Human Rights.

Whilst looking at discrimination in the empire, the government again dismissed the idea of introducing anti-discrimination legislation in the UK. Having previously discussed and rejected the proposals with the Home Office in 1941, the Colonial Office was lobbied again in 1945 on the matter.[6] This time it was the Anti-Slavery and Aborigines Protection Society that raised it, pointing to examples of anti-discrimination legislation in France, the USSR and a number of US states. But unsure of the benefit of such legislation, and seeing no evidence of sufficient public clamour for it, the Colonial Office decided not to pursue it.[7] With that, the idea was put to bed and legislation to make discrimination illegal would not see the light of day for another twenty years. It was the emergence of a large, visible Black and brown presence in the UK fighting for their rights that would force a change of mind.

REBUILDING BRITAIN AND POSTWAR IMMIGRATION (1946 TO 1962)

Britain needed workers to rebuild. In June 1946, the government identified that an additional 940,000 workers were required – an estimate that was raised to 1,346,000 the following year. To help meet this demand, 100,000 Polish soldiers and their families were given the right to settle permanently in the UK, and 80,000 displaced Europeans living in German and Austrian camps were brought over. But at the same time, the Ministry of Labour opposed bringing in Black West Indian workers.[8] Regardless of the views of the ministry, the reality of labour shortage would dictate the future. The postwar migration of West Indians from the Caribbean (where work was hard to come by) to the UK (where there were labour shortages) would start with a trickle. First, it was an unknown number of West Indian service personnel and war workers who remained in Britain after the war. People like Baron Baker from Port Antonio, Jamaica, who had lied about his age to enlist in 1944. When the war ended, he was a twenty-year-old RAF policeman based in Britain: 'After the war most of the West Indian troops were forcibly sent back to the West Indies and demobbed. I stayed on in Britain and was demobbed in 1948'.[9]

Then small numbers of postwar migrants arrived in Britain. Many of them had returned to the Caribbean after the war and found conditions as bad as they had been a few years earlier, and in some cases worse. These ex-service personnel and war workers swelled the ranks of West Indians arriving in Liverpool in March 1947 onboard the *Ormonde*, a former troopship carrying 100 Jamaican passengers. Then on 21 December the *Almanzora*, another ex-troopship, docked at Southampton, and among its 200

Caribbean passengers was the Jamaican Second World War veteran Allan Wilmot – he had served in both the Royal Navy and RAF. In uniform during the war, West Indians could expect a mainly warm welcome from the British public and, as serving military personnel, accommodation was provided or arranged for them. But Wilmot found things very different living life as a Black civilian in postwar Britain, struggling to find accommodation: 'You would see a room to let: "no Irish, no coloureds, no dogs" and that was in print. Doors were slammed in my face'. In his first year, he made a living by taking various casual jobs, such as washing dishes at the Lyons Corner House in London's Tottenham Court Road, whilst sleeping rough in London:

> In order to survive just after my arrival in London, a friend and I had to catch the last underground train to Uxbridge, Middlesex, and sleep in the carriage until morning. Our one suitcase (or 'grip') was placed at Waterloo Station left-luggage unit. We befriended a few railwaymen, most of whom had also served in the Royal Air Force. They would lend us blankets to keep warm, as we were not prepared for the winter weather.[10]

Six months after the arrival of the *Almanzora*, the *Empire Windrush* docked at Tilbury on 22 June 1948. Because of the debate around the 1948 British Nationality Act which would protect the rights of colonial subjects to settle in Britain as citizens of the UK and colonies (it received royal assent the following month), the arrival of the Windrush attracted greater political and media attention than its predecessors. On the day of its arrival in Tilbury, the Labour MP Mr J D Murray and ten colleagues sent a joint letter to prime minister Clement Attlee expressing concerns that the Windrush would mark the beginning of an 'influx of coloured people'. They demanded controls on immigration. Attlee would later reassure them that an influx of such migrants was unlikely.[11] Unbothered by the political debate, the immediate focus for the Windrush passengers was on finding accommodation and employment. Baron Baker, who was active in the local Black community, liaised with Colonial Office officials about preparations:

I was told about the Windrush by Major John Keith and so I went to see him. I asked him what preparations the Colonial Office was going to make for those people and he said none. So I suggested he use the Clapham Common Deep Shelter.

They had used the Air Raid Shelter to house Italian and German prisoners of war, and even myself, when I came to London some times and couldn't get a bed, I had to use it. So why not open it for the people on the Windrush.[12]

Before disembarking, the passengers were greeted by the Black Colonial Office official, Ivor Cummings, who welcomed them, wished them success in achieving their objectives whilst in Britain, and briefed them on the support that would be available in their first few weeks.[13] A short piece in *The Times* the following day reported that 'of the 492 Jamaicans who arrived in Tilbury on Monday to seek work, 236 were housed last night in Clapham South deep shelter. The remainder had friends to whom they could go with prospects of work'. The numbers accommodated in the deep shelter was an indication of the challenge that many faced in finding somewhere to live. But *The Times* was wrong in its description of passenger numbers and nationalities. These were not '492 Jamaicans', but 802 West Indians out of 1027 passengers.[14] It was the lack of jobs at home that drove these migrants away from the warmth of the Caribbean. Sam King, an RAF veteran and *Empire Windrush* passenger, would go on to lead a distinguished life of public service in south London, becoming the first Black Mayor of Southwark Council in the early 1980s. King recalled the conditions in his native Jamaica when he returned in 1947 after the war: 'When we got home the economy was still suffering from a hurricane in 1944 that destroyed most of the banana, coconut and coffee crops. Many of us were unemployed and we decided to take the first ship back to England'.[15]

There was much work to be done in Britain. Less than a fortnight after the arrival of the *Windrush*, the National Health Service was born. It struggled to fill vacancies. In Tottenham, North London, more than 700 vacancies were advertised for hospital staff, but it produced only seventeen enquiries. Nursing was struggling to recruit young women who were turning, instead, to better paid work in teaching or administration with more convenient hours. By 1949, the government was turning to the colonies (particularly the West Indies) to fill NHS vacancies.[16] But the British public's tolerance was already showing cracks. Liverpool, with a Black population of around 8000 (most of whom had come to Britain during the war), experienced racist riots in 1948, with white people turning violently against their Black neighbours after the unions condemned Black people for 'taking white men's jobs'.[17] It was reminiscent of the rioting that had occurred immediately after the First World War.

Although the *Windrush* carried more West Indians than the *Ormonde* and *Almanzora* combined, it still represented less than a trickle compared to the hundreds of thousands of European immigrants entering Britain. Indeed, from the end of the war until the end of the 1940s, the total numbers of West Indians entering Britain would be less than 4000. This number started to climb from the early 1950s, with just over 2000 entering each year from 1951 to 1953. The numbers jumped to 9200 in 1954 and 24,400 the following year. By 1961, more than 50,000 a year were arriving (at this point, more than 244,000 West Indians had arrived since the end of the war).[18] For many of them, a British passport was the only one they ever had – being born British subjects and having travelled to the UK before their home colonies had achieved independence. Although the numbers of West Indians settled in Britain at the beginning of the 1960s was roughly equivalent to the number of Polish people, there were hardly any issues raised by politicians or journalists about Polish immigration.[19] But political anxieties, which had started to build even with the arrival of a few hundred West Indians during Attlee's Labour government, were now at fever pitch under Macmillan's Tories.

The public mood had turned sour. In 1958, London's Notting Hill saw rioting as white teddy boys led violent attacks on Black people.[20] The government's response to this mood was the introduction of the 1962 Commonwealth Immigrants Act, beginning a series of racist immigration legislation that has continued since. Such legislation gave rise to the 'Windrush scandal' where Black citizens, who had come to live in the UK between 1947 and 1971, were denied their rights and in some cases wrongfully deported to the West Indies. This was a continuation of the British Caribbean experience: fighting with Britain during global wars, and during times of peace fighting British authorities for justice.

NOTES

1   AIR 2/13437, National Archives, UK, 'Extract from draft conclusions of Air Council meeting 10 held on 3 October 1944', section 4 (b) (vii).

2   Ibid, letter from secretary of state for air to First Lord of the Admiralty on 19 November 1945.

3   WO 32/10592, National Archives, UK, see briefing note for secretary of state for war for the Cabinet discussion on 'The Admission of Non-European Personnel into the UK forces' for 3 June 1947; also see minute 177 dated 2 June 1947.

4   CO 859/126/5, National Archives, UK, minute by Mr Seel on 27 May 1946.

5   CO 859/130/8, National Archives, UK, Sir Bede Clifford letter on 1 February 1947; Sir Hilary Blood letter of 15 February 1947; Sir Arthur Grimble letter of 11 February 1947; Sir William Murphy letter of 26 July 1947.

6   CO 859/80/7, National Archives, UK, 'Colour Prejudice … Note of a Meeting held at the Colonial Office on Monday 14 July 1941', and also minute from Sir Cosmo Parkinson to Secretary of State for Colonies (Lord Moyne) dated 29 August 1941.

7   CO 537/1224, National Archives, UK, letter from The Anti-Slavery and Aborigines Protection Society on 6 November 1945 and 1 April 1946, and minutes from Mr Edmonds of 22 February 1947 and 'I.T.' on 24 February 1947.

8   David Olusoga, *Black and British: A Forgotten History*, Pan Books, Apple eBooks version, 2017, chapter 14, paragraphs 5-6.

9   *Forty Winters On: Memories of Britain's post war Caribbean Immigrants*, Lambeth Council: London, 1988, p17.

10 Allan Wilmot, *Now You Know: The Memoirs of Allan Charles Wilmot, WWII Serviceman and post-war Entertainer*, Liberation Publishers: London, 2015, pp32-4.

11 CO 876/88, National Archives, UK, letter from Prime Minister Clement Attlee to Mr J D Murray MP on 5 July 1948.

12 *Forty Winters On*, op cit, pp17-8.

13 LAB 26/218, National Archives, UK, Annex I in report on Empire Windrush dated 30 June 1948.

14 'The Empire Windrush and the post-war ships that came before', UK

National Archive blog, 22 June 2022, https://blog.nationalarchives.gov.
uk/the-empire-windrush-and-the-post-war-ships-that-came-before.

15 *Forty Winters On,* op cit, p7.

16 Ann Kramer, *Many Rivers to Cross: The history of the Caribbean Contribution to the NHS*, The Stationary Office and Sugar Media Limited: London, 2006, pp15-6.

17 Peter Fryer, *Staying Power: The History of Black People in Britain*, Pluto Press: London, 1985, pp367-371.

18 *Forty Winters On*, op cit, p13.

19 Ron Ramdin, *The Making of the Black Working Class in Britain*, Wildwood House: UK, 1987, p189.

20 Ben Bousquet and Colin Douglas, *West Indian Women at War: British Racism in World War II*, Lawrence & Wishart, 1991, pp142-4; Fryer, op cit, pp378-381.

14

Conclusion

The relationship between the Caribbean and the Allied war effort was a pivotal one. Without the vital materials (such as oil and bauxite) provided by the West Indies, and the support of its people in extracting those resources and supporting the wider Allied cause, the war effort would have been seriously damaged and ultimate victory delayed. And without the catalytic effect of the war, the decolonisation of the West Indies would have been much delayed. Not only did the war further embolden Caribbean colonial subjects in their demands for better treatment and political equality, it also weakened their colonial rulers and made it more difficult for them to resist these demands.

In this pivotal time for the Caribbean, the old contradictions in the relationships between its colonised peoples and their colonisers would be evident. These were relationships of loyalty and rebellion. The Caribbean swung behind the Allied war effort out of both hatred for Nazi Germany and a sense of loyalty to the metropole. But many of the region's territories continued to crave better relationships with their rulers as they pushed against the many iniquities in the existing colonial systems. This duality can be seen not only in the politics of the period, but also in the individual stories of the many tens of thousands of West Indians who volunteered and served under Allied flags. They fought for the Allied cause and, at the same time, for their own rights and dignity as people of colour. But as we reflect on these important individual contributions, we should not lose sight of class as a key factor. Since many had to fund their own passage to the UK or Canada to volunteer, and because of the educational requirements for specific roles, those who volunteered were mainly middle-class West Indians. Despite their education, many struggled to be get into the British army or royal navy, whilst the airforce (which required higher levels of education and technical skills than the other two branches of the military) was happy to accept them.

For the US, the West Indies was a key component in its long-term defence strategy – inevitably so since the Caribbean provided the only sea route into the Gulf of Mexico and the southern states of the US that border it. Even without its vital mineral resources, the region was of critical importance to US defence. For these reasons, America took an interest not only in military strategy for the region but also in its political direction – much to the annoy-ance of the colonial powers who resented US interference. The US desire for stable and friendly governments in its backyard would be intensified by the cold war politics that emerged from the Second World War.

The Caribbean is a diverse region of many languages, which was subjected to colonisation by different European powers, producing distinct local histories shaped in turn by the ethnic compositions, cultures, and vastly different political institutions of each country and territory. These differences affected the impact the war had across the region. They also shaped the varied approaches towards postwar decolonisation. But despite these differences, it is not possible to look at key points in West Indian history without taking a Caribbean-wide perspective. The Second World War is such a point in history. It highlighted the interdependencies across the region such as the vulnerability of the main trading routes that ran through the Caribbean, the cross-regional cooperation required to exploit key minerals, patterns of migration within the region during times of economic hardship, the need for a region-wide defence strategy to counter the U-boat attacks, the influence of US and global geopolitics within the region, and the importance of regional cooperation and coordination in addressing the big economic challenges.

The contribution of the Second World War to the shaping of postwar West Indian history is well appreciated. But the contri-bution of the Caribbean to the defeat of the Axis powers is still understated.

Index